RJ Pettey

The Biblical Heritage

The Biblical Heritage

In Modern Catholic Scholarship

EDITED BY

John J. Collins
John Dominic Crossan

 Michael Glazier
Wilmington, Delaware

First published in 1986 by Michael Glazier, Inc. 1935 West Fourth Street, Wilmington, Delaware 19805.

Library of Congress Catalog Card Number: 86-45347
International Standard Book Number: 0-89453-587-0
Typography by Richard Smith.
Printed in the United States of America.

*A celebration
for
Bruce Vawter, C.M.
on his
sixty-fifth birthday*

Table of Contents

PREFACE

The Second Vatican Council inaugurated an era of unprecedented change in the Roman Catholic Church. One major aspect of that change has been the rediscovery of the Bible and the acceptance of modern critical methods in studying it. The foundations for this Catholic revival had been laid with the Papal encyclical *Divino Afflante Spiritu* in 1943 and more directly by the rise of a generation of scholars trained in the modern methods in the 1950's. The occasion of this volume is to mark the 65th birthday of one of the leaders of that generation, Fr. Bruce Vawter. We are happy to number other pioneers of Catholic scholarship, including Vawter's former senior colleague, John McKenzie, among the contributors.

The core of this volume consists of eight review essays, four on the Old Testament and four on the New. Our purpose has been to summarize the state of the question on central issues of ecumenical biblical scholarship. The reviews are necessarily selective, and are guided by the major scholarly debates in the various areas. The volume describes the present consensus or spectrum of opinions. It does not attempt to discern the cutting edge or the way of the future. We have not attempted to deal with extrabiblical material, except incidentally, or with the burgeoning new methods and approaches which challenge the dominance of the historical critical method, important though these all are. The objective here is to consolidate and celebrate the scholarship which has won wide acceptance in Catholic circles, thanks to the labors of Bruce Vawter and his colleagues. The volume concludes with retrospective essays by John McKenzie and Walter Harrelson which give complementary perspectives on the progress and trials of Catholic scholarship in the last three decades.

The contributors to this volume have all been associated with Bruce Vawter for many years, especially in the forum of the Catholic Biblical Association. Dennis McCarthy, S.J. was among the first to complete a contribution and so it was substantially in hand at the time of his premature death in August, 1983. Another member of the original team, George McRae, S.J., had resigned his assignment because of ill health when he too died suddenly in September, 1985. Both men represented the best in ecumenical Catholic scholarship and their loss will long be felt in the entire scholarly community.

OLD TESTAMENT THEOLOGY

John J. Collins

University of Notre Dame

The story of biblical scholarship in the last century is predominantly the story of the triumph of historical criticism. The crucial battles between those who advocated this method and the conservatives who opposed it were fought in Europe in the nineteenth century and in America in the early decades of the twentieth. The Catholic Church came down heavily on the conservative side in the modernist crisis under Pope Pius X, but the encyclical of Pius XII in 1943 gave positive encouragement to critical research. Since Vatican II Catholic scholarship has entered the mainstream of critical biblical study, unimpeded by ecclesiastical restraints. There are of course still Christian churches which resolutely reject any critical treatment of the Bible, and the principles of historical criticism have not deeply influenced the laity of either Catholicism or mainline Protestantism, but in theological circles the "battle for the Bible" has been decided for some time.

1. The Principles of Historical Criticism
(See Bibliography numbers 18, 34)

The hesitation of the churches to accept historical criticism is not difficult to understand if we reflect on the principles of critical method. These principles received their classic expression from the great German scholar Ernst Troeltsch at the end of the last century and have been lucidly reformulated in the present generation by Van A. Harvey. First, critical scholarship requires autonomy. No authority, secular or ecclesiastical, can prescribe for the scholar conclusions which *must* be reached. The full implications of this point are not always appreciated because even when ecclesiastical authorities do not interfere scholars often feel obligated to agree with the tenets of traditional faith. Critical method however does not allow that faith as such is a source of knowledge. We believe because we have evidence or some reason to believe. A mere assertion that we believe something, unsupported by evidence or reasoning, carries no more weight in a theological discussion than it would in a court of law. The principle of autonomy, then, is accompanied by a principle of rational assessment: evidence must be weighed and evaluated. When we rely on evidence, however, we can never claim absolute certainty. Historical knowledge is a matter of relative probability, and the confident conclusions of one generation can always be overturned by new evidence in the next. Finally, Troeltsch's most controversial principle was his declaration of "the almighty power of analogy," by which he meant that we must assume that human experience in any generation is analogous to our own. If human nature, or the physical world, has changed drastically since biblical times, then we cannot hope to assess the probability of the ancient narratives at all.

Harvey has rightly pointed out that what is at issue in the debates over historical critcism is a question of morality. Traditional Christianity celebrated faith and belief as virtues and regarded doubt as sin. Critical scholarship regards unwarranted belief as naiveté and regards skepticism as the mother of true knowledge. Criticism is not motivated by impiety but by the pursuit of truth and the desire to base our beliefs on as firm a foundation as possible. It should be clear that this conflict of moralities is not confined to judgments of historical fact. It pertains equally to questions of philosophical truth and moral value. The teachings of a prophet can be subjected to critical assessment as well as the statements of a historian.

It is easy to understand why the traditional churches have hesitated to endorse these principles and indeed have done so with reservations. The Constitution on Divine Revelation from Vatican II emphasized the appreciation of "literary forms" and claimed inerrancy only for "that truth which God wanted put into the sacred writings," and thereby gave free rein to scholars to establish what that truth might be. Yet it insisted that "all of what has been said about the way of interpreting Scripture is subject finally to the judgment of the Church." In short, it retained a reservation on the question of autonomy, recognizing the potential conflict of authority to which critical method gives rise. Critical study may of course confirm traditional beliefs, but it can also undermine them. Troeltsch's "principle of analogy" has been especially controversial in this regard since it is intrinsically skeptical of miraculous and supernatural events. Theologians may protest that analogy with present experience is too limiting and that it unduly restricts our sense of what is possible. Yet the fact remains that those things which have no analogy in our experience are *only* possible and must be accorded a relatively low degree of probability.

Despite the apparent conflicts between critical method and traditional faith, the new methods have brought many benefits to the churches. Much of the impetus for historical criticism came from dissatisfaction with traditional dogma, which had become largely irrelevant to modern experience. Historical criticism offered the possibility of a fresh appropriation of the biblical material in terms more congruent with contemporary interests. The critical method also lent itself to ecumenical dialogue, since it offered a basis for discussion independent of the confessional tenets of any given church. Most of all it dispensed with the intellectual schizophrenia which has often been a burden of religious life in the modern age. The criteria of truth and value which we presuppose in everyday modern life need not be set aside when we sit down to read the Bible.

2. Biblical Theology as an Historical Discipline
(See Bibliography number 20)

The tensions between traditional faith and critical scholarship have been especially evident in the discipline of biblical theology. The emergence of biblical theology as a distinct enterprise is usually traced to the inaugural lecture of J. P. Gabler at the University of Altdorf in 1787. Gabler insisted that biblical theology be distinguished from dogmatics and be conceived as a descriptive historical discipline, whose purpose was to make clear "what the holy writers felt about divine matters." Only when the opinions of the sacred writers had been collected and clarified could their possible dogmatic use be established. In effect, Gabler demanded that the biblical witness be heard in its own right and not be filtered through later dogmatic presuppositions. This program for biblical theology was established in the following century by the triumph of the historical critical method.

Yet, two hundred years after Gabler's lecture, the goal of a truly historical biblical theology remains elusive. The difficulty of the enterprise may be seen in three areas: a) the persistence of dogmatic presuppositions which distort the historical evidence; b) the persistent attempt to impose a system on material which is characterized by diversity; and c) dissatisfaction with the distance between "what it meant" and "what it means," or the relevance of historical study.

a. Dogmatic presuppositions (See Bibliography numbers 5, 10, 11, 23, 25, 27, 35, 38, 39)

The persistence of dogmatic presuppositions in Old Testament theology can be illustrated in two areas: the problem of history and the attitude to Judaism.

Critical scholarship is, of course, sharply opposed to the Fundamentalist view that every event mentioned in the Bible, from Adam and Eve to the predicted end of the world, must be historically factual. Nonetheless, even biblical theologians who are committed to historical criticism have often felt constrained by faith to affirm the historicity of certain crucial events. An exceptionally forthright statement of this viewpoint was provided by Roland de Vaux, a French Dominican who was one of the foremost archeologists of his generation. De Vaux admitted that there is a world of difference between the history of Israel as it is reconstructed by modern historical science and the salvation history written by the authors of the Bible. He continued, however, "But salvation history depends on facts which the historian with his positive methods should be able to check." For de Vaux, this point was of basic importance: "It makes all the difference in the world, since it involves the truthfulness of God and the foundation of our faith" (see Bibliography no. 35, p. 59). Specifically, "God reveals himself in history. His choosing of the people of Israel, their salvation, the promises made to them and the punishments imposed on them are reported as facts. In the New Testament, the Incarnation is a fact, and the Resurrection is a fact. 'If Christ has not been raised to life, our faith is in vain'" (p. 57). In this approach, faith is the source of fundamental knowledge. Historical research serves only to support and illustrate. De Vaux had not broken with the traditional morality of belief and, whatever its merits, his theology was not based on historical criticism.

While de Vaux was exceptionally forthright in stating his presuppositions, his approach bears great similarity to the so-called "Biblical Theology Movement" which dominated American Protestantism in the decades after World War II. The most prominent spokesman of that movement was G. E. Wright, who was, like de Vaux, a leading archeologist. In his last book, in 1969, Wright quite properly criticized de Vaux's confessional approach and insisted that biblical theology must start from the descriptive work of the theologian, not from the tenets of faith. Yet in his earlier and most famous book Wright had written: "Now in Biblical faith everything depends on whether the central events actually occurred... To assume that it makes no difference whether they are facts or not is simply to destroy the whole basis of the faith. Or even to infer that these facts, if they are such, are irrelevant, would to the Biblical mind be a form of faithlessness and harlotry" (see Bibliog. no. 38, pp. 126-127). We may wonder whether an historian can assess the evidence critically if threats of faithlessness and harlotry hang over him, but Wright did, in any case, think that historical research could establish the historicity of the central biblical events. In fact, however, central events such as the Exodus and Conquest are matters of unending debate, because the evidence is far from clearcut. More fundamentally, while historical research might possibly establish that the Israelites left Egypt and overran Canaan, it could not possibly show that these events were acts of God. Such an interpretation involves a "projection of faith into facts" and is a matter of the perspective of the interpreter. Consequently the central biblical affirmations can never, in principle, be established by historical research. This point has been widely perceived in more recent biblical theology, and has contributed greatly to the decline of the "Biblical Theology Movement." Consequently, the category "story" or "narrative" has come to replace "history" as the focus of discussion, although these categories may pose their own problems for biblical theology.

A second area where dogmatic presuppositions have distorted historical description can be seen in portrayals of Judaism in biblical theologies. The disparagement of the law and of post-exilic Judaism in general in the classic works of Wellhausen and Schuerer is notorious. The same prejudices persist in the most influential Theologies of the Old Testament in this century — those of Eichrodt and von Rad. The case of von Rad is especially revealing, since he tried harder than most to respect the historical diversity of the Hebrew scriptures. Yet his whole vision of the development within the biblical tradition was colored by his faith that it found its fulfilment in Christ. Von Rad of course did not return to the pre-critical view that the prophets spoke directly of Christ, so that Isaiah 7 or 53 could be read primarily as predictions. He was however especially sensitive to the ways in which old traditions were taken up and given new meaning in new situations and he saw the New Testament as the fulfillment of this process. Consequently he opposed those who take "the Old Testament in abstraction as an object which can be adequately interpreted without reference to the New Testament" (see Bibliog. no. 27, vol. 2, p. 321). Von Rad's viewpoint here is not that of the critical historian but of the confessing Christian. The Christian theologian is naturally inclined to devalue those aspects of Judaism, such as the law and the cult, which were not continued in Christianity, but the theological preference can easily distort the historical description of biblical religion.

b. System and diversity (See Bibliography numbers 9, 11, 19, 22, 27, 28, 40)

Despite the avowed intention of respecting the historical particularity of biblical texts, biblical theologians have always been inclined to systematize. Even Gabler believed that the historically conditioned ideas in the Bible could be distinguished from "universal notions" or "pure notions with which divine providence wished to be characteristic of all times and places" (see Bibliog. no. 20, p. 3). The most common approach to writing a biblical theology has been to present a cross section of biblical views on basic ideas (God, election, etc.) and there have been persistent attempts to single out one such idea as "the center" of biblical theology. The most successful biblical theology of this kind has been that of Walter Eichrodt, who singled out the covenant as the central concept. Any such attempt to unify the biblical message is in tension with historical criticism, which has amply demonstrated the diversity of the different biblical viewpoints. There is still no agreement on the history of the idea of covenant in ancient Israel. In any case there are clearly areas of the Bible (e.g. Job, Ecclesiastes) where the concept of covenant is not central. Systematic theologies of the Old Testament have had great difficulty in integrating the Wisdom literature. It has recently been pointed out by Rolf Knierim that even the concept of God is not consistent, and that the God of Job cannot easily be reconciled with the God of the Deuteronomist, even though he be called by the same name. The canon of scriptures, in either Testament, is not a harmonious and systematic work of theology (even one distinct from later Church dogmatics) but a collection of writings which reflects the religious history of a community and reveals the variations and conflicts which that history entailed.

In view of the diversity of the scriptures, scholars have sometimes concluded that a biblical theology is simply impossible and that we can only write a history of the religion of Israel and of early Christianity. For a time, in the late 19th and 20th century, this was the prevailing view. The value of such a history has never been in doubt. The question is whether a specifically theological treatment is possible without doing violence to the diversity. The scholar who made the most far-reaching attempt to accomplish this was the great German scholar Gerhard von Rad. Von Rad denied that the Old Testament had any "focal point" analogous to Christ in the New Testament (see Bibliog. no. 27, vol. 2, p. 362). Even the notion of God was constantly changing. Accordingly, he sought to do justice to "the tremendous differences evinced in the specific literary units" (vol. 1, p. 106), but he claimed nonetheless that there was something which united them all. This was "a theology of history" in which certain kerygmatic events were proclaimed and then re-interpreted in the light of new situations. This unifying factor is subject to objection similar to those brought against other proposed "centers": it neglects too much of the actual biblical material. Not only must von Rad acknowledge that it is absent in Job and Ecclesiastes, but he also subordinates the legal and cultic aspects of the Hebrew Bible to the historical kerygma. Von Rad effectively made the point that the Old Testament is not a static doctrinal system but is constituted by the on-going re-shaping of traditions. Yet even he may be justifiably accused of imposing a false unity on the process.

Even after von Rad, attempts continue to locate the "center" of biblical theology. Such attempts should by now be discredited. Biblical theology will have to live with the diversity of the biblical texts.

c. The Relevance of Historical Study (See Bibliography numbers 12, 29, 32, 33)

As a descriptive enterprise, biblical theology is based on a distinction between "what it meant" and "what it means" (in the famous phraseology of Krister Stendahl) but biblical theologians have always had to struggle with the temptation to collapse the distinction in the hope of more immediate gratification. The distinction, as Stendahl insists, is designed to ensure that we hear the text in its own right. Viewed as an ancient document the Bible may sometimes lack theological relevance. "Spiritual" and political interpretations can often yield greater relevance but they may also uncritically impose the prejudices of the interpreter on the text.

Recently more serious criticisms have been advanced which question not only the desirability but also the possibility of preserving a clear distinction between "what it meant" and "what it means." No field of study is free from prejudices and presuppositions and biblical criticism cannot claim to be theologically neutral. The perspective of the historian inevitably helps shape the reconstruction of history. Von Rad's view of Israelite religion tending towards fulfilment in Christ is a clear illustration of this process, but a purely secular reconstruction is also shaped by philosophical presuppositions. The value of any reconstruction will depend on the context in which it is presented. The importance of presuppositions was emphasized by the famous German New Testament theologian Rudolf Bultmann, but a similar point has more recently been made by advocates of various approaches, from radical liberation theology to the rather conservative canonical approach.

It is indeed true that every approach to biblical theology rests on some presuppositions. A careful scholar will qualify his or her presuppositions in light of the data, but an element of circularity is inevitable. The meaning we find in a text will depend to a degree on the questions we bring to it and the context in which we discuss it. We should not conclude however that all presuppositions have equal value, or that since no one is fully objective we might as well be fundamentalists. Presuppositions can be critically compared. As we have seen, historical criticism is based on a moral vision whch is devoted to the pursuit of truth, and is based on the evaluation of public evidence, rather than on confessional faith. Those who choose the presuppositions of the critical method do so because they believe that this moral vision is more satisfying and responsible than the avowedly "spiritual" alternatives.

3. The Canónical Approach
(See Bibliography numbers 1, 2, 3, 7, 8, 24, 30, 31)

In 1970 B. S. Childs published a book under the title *Biblical Theology in Crisis*, which effectively marked the end of an era. The attempt of the so-called Biblical Theology Movement to combine historical criticism with confessional faith had run its course. The categories which had dominated biblical theology in the previous decades — history, kerygma, covenant — were by then seen as problematic or inadequate, although some biblical theologians would continue to focus on them and to pursue the mirage of a center of the Old Testament. Others before Childs, notably James Barr, had seen the limitations of these categories. Childs however used this critique as a preface to his own program which focused on the biblical canon.

Childs' proposal differs from previous biblical theology in several important respects:

a. "Canonical analysis focuses its attention on the final form of the text itself" (see Bibliog. no. 8, p. 73). In his massive *Introduction*, Childs displays great mastery of form-critical and redaction-critical research, and he grants that these methods are of some value for the historian. He denies, however, that they have any significance for the theologian. He is not concerned with the history lying behind the text or with historical act of God, but with the *word* as proclaimed in the text.

b. Canonical analysis is holistic. Childs speaks repeatedly of the canonical shape of a book. Passages are not to be pulled out of context. The significant shape, moreover, is that given the book by the final editor. So Second Isaiah (Isa 40-55) should not be distinguished from First Isaiah but should be read in the context of the whole book. The editorial comments at the end of Ecclesiastes should not be excised as glosses but taken as authoritative indications of how the book should be read.

c. It is Childs' conviction that the canonical process cuts the individual texts free from the limitations of their historical context so that they are not merely records of a response to an historical situation but can confront the reader directly as the word of God.

d. The canon as a whole provides the context for the study of any individual text. In his *Biblical Theology in Crisis*, Childs illustrated this point with a study of Psalm 8, in the light of the Epistles to the Hebrews and Romans. He does not claim that the Psalmist intended to refer to Christ, but that the psalm must now be read in light of the Christian view of man as fully expressed in Christ. The interplay between the Testaments receives little attention in the *Introduction to the Old Testament as Scripture*. It is clear however that the principle of canonical context requires that the Bible be read as a harmonious whole. Childs deplores the tendency of critics such as Paul Hanson to find a dialectic of opposing views, or even outright contradiction in the biblical text.

The biblical books have been preserved for centuries in the context of a canon. The ways in which the meaning of a text is modified by inclusion in the canon raise valid and interesting questions. Childs' insistence on the final form of the text and on meanings beyond the original context might be accepted as a salutary correction to the usual practice of historical criticism. Childs insists however that he does not merely wish to add another stage to the critical process (after source, form, and redaction criticism) but advocates an entirely new way of approaching the text, which is not a "criticism" at all. He objects to the tendency of historical criticism to assume "the determining force on every biblical text to be political, social or economic factors" (see Bibliog. no. 8, p. 41). Instead he views the scriptures "as the divine imperative and promise to a historically conditioned people of God whose legacy the Christian church confesses to share" (p. 77). In short, the issue is whether the texts are viewed as human responses to historical circumstances or as the transcendent word of God.

While Childs' view of the canon is highly original, his approach to scripture is distinctively Protestant and is especially reminiscent of Karl Barth. It differs from Fundamentalism in so far as Childs is not concerned with questions of historical fact and does not dispute the results of historical criticism on such matters as the date or authenticity of Daniel. Yet it is thoroughly anti-critical in matters of theological importance. Historical criticism has questioned not only the historical accuracy of the scriptures but also their religious truth and moral value. A critical biblical theology might question the value of Abraham's obedience in Gen 22 or dispute whether the slaughter of the

Canaanites was justified by appeal to a divine command. No such questions are permitted by Childs' approach. The issue is confused when his approach is called "post-critical" because it rejects rather than incorporates the basic principles of critical method when theological issues are at stake.

Childs' canonical approach "works" in the sense that it is quite possible to read the Old Testament in the way that he prescribes. This in itself is not a compelling reason why anyone should do so. The claim which Childs makes is theological: that the idea of scripture requires this approach. Yet, as his critics (especially James Barr) have pointed out, Christians (and Jews) of all generations have used the scriptures in various ways. The New Testament writers pulled passages out of context with no regard for the canonical shape of prophetic books. Childs explicitly rejects the allegorical method favored by the Church fathers. Even Luther was guided not by the shape of the canon but by his ideal of Christ and he could judge the canonical epistle of James quite negatively. Neither scripture itself nor Christian tradition demands a "canonical" approach. Needless to say, Childs' approach is especially problematic for Catholics, whose Old Testament has a quite different canonical "shape" because of the deutero-canonical books and who give greater theological weight to the ongoing tradition of the Church. Childs' approach represents one theological option in reading the biblical text, but it is not a necessary or obligatory one.

The canonical approach may also be advocated on grounds that are literary rather than theological. The focus on the text itself rather than on the events lying behind it accords well with a tendency in literary criticism to value sense over reference. There has been a widespread reaction in recent biblical scholarship against the excessive preoccupation with sources and origins, and a growing appreciation of the coherence of texts as literary wholes. There is also a growing realization that the meaning of a text is not exhausted by its original referent, and that it can take on new significance in a new context. This insight was fundamental to the tradition-history of von Rad and the canonical criticism of J. A. Sanders as well as to the work of Childs, but both von Rad and Sanders place their emphasis on the process of continual re-actualization rather than on the one final canonical form.

The crucial issue here is whether the theological meaning of a text can be adequately understood without taking full account of the social, political and other factors which shaped its origin. Texts may imply ideologies and express vested human interests, but these implications may only become clear if we see the text in its historical context or study its use in concrete historical situations. The issue here is, again, a moral one: can we responsibly accept a text as the word of God without critically examining the human interests it favors? Historical criticism is enriched by increased literary sensitivity and by awareness of the different contexts in which a text can be understood. It can not, however, neglect the fact that a text is also a human product. A social-historical method, so far from imprisoning the text in the past, provides indispensable analogies for the way a text functions in concrete historical situations.

4. The Sociological Approach
(See Bibliography numbers 6, 13, 14, 15, 16)

Diametrically opposed to the canonical approach of Childs is the sociological method, best illustrated in American scholarship by the work of Norman Gottwald. Gottwald's approach may be understood as anti-theological in a sense, but in fact it has clear theological implications and has important affinities with Latin American liberation theology. Gottwald views the biblical texts as ideological documents, and not all have equal value. Yahweh's distinctive identity is seen in the emergence of Israel as a distinct people, in a process which Gottwald views as a social revolution. Yahweh is seen as the "primordial power to establish and sustain social equality in the face of counter-oppression from without and against provincial and nonegalitarian tendencies from within the society" (see Bibliog. no. 13. p. 692). This definition implies a selective view of biblical revelation: Yahweh is the God of Joshua or of Amos, but scarcely the God of Solomon. Some biblical texts and episodes of biblical history must be evaluated as reactionary from this perspective. Gottwald's approach may be viewed as a re-statement of the older "God who acts" theology of G. E. Wright and others, with greater sociological sophistication. Gottwald, however, is clearer in elevating the egalitarian society as a normative ideal. He is also willing to de-mythologize Yahweh as "the symbol of a single-minded pursuit of an egalitarian tribal social system" or as "the spirit of the people" (see Bibliog. no. 14, pp. 52, 47). In short, the God of Israel is not a transcendent Being, responsible for all creation, good and bad, but a symbol for the impulse to liberation. Gottwald has much in common with Liberation theologians who single out the Exodus as the normative revelation of God, but they do not usually de-mythologize in this way.

Gottwald's approach is based on a reconstruction of history rather than on the biblical text, and his reconstruction of the origins of Israel is very controversial. The approach does not stand or fall with that reconstruction, however, and could be based more directly on the texts. The ideal of liberation and of a just society is clearly supported by the Exodus story and by many of the great prophets, and so can claim a central place in the Old Testament. Yet the normative status ascribed to these themes in Liberation theology is not simply imposed by the Bible, where Yahweh is also the creator, and the guarantor of the monarchy. The principle of selection, which defines Yahweh *only* in terms of liberation is imposed by the concerns of the interpreter. This in itself is not an objection against Gottwald's approach. We have seen that every interpreter has presuppositions, and that the choice of perspective is a moral question. There is much to be said for the moral superiority of the liberationist perspective, but we should be clear that it is perspective and not imposed by the Bible itself.

The sociological approach "works" just as well as the

canonical approach of Childs: it provides a method applicable to any part of the Bible. In many ways it seems preferable. It deals far more adequately with the human interests and motivations which shaped the biblical literature, including those which imposed the final canonical shape. This point is especially evident in the use of sociological criticism by feminist critics. (See the essays by Carol Meyers and Phyllis Bird, on the OT, and by E. S. Fiorenza on the NT in Gottwald, *The Bible and Liberation*, see Bibliog. no. 15). Moreover, feminist criticism has taught us to view the male-dominated God language of the Bible as conditioned by social and hisotrical circumstances.

The sociological approach also has its pitfalls. First, a strong ideological commitment inevitably tends to distort history. Gottwald's presentation of Israelite origins as peasant revolt rather than invasion very probably contains such an ideological distortion. The historical details, however, must be evaluated by the normal methods of historical criticism. The fact that a scholar is ideologically committed does not in itself invalidate his or her scholarship.

Second, the liberationist approach, which is based on Marxist social theory, tends to exaggerate the conflicts between different viewpoints. Walter Brueggemann's antithesis of Mosaic and Davidic trajectories is a case in point. Such schematizations have some heuristic value but they often oversimplify and miss the ambiguities of history.

Finally, there is a danger of reductionism, when God is defined in purely sociological categories. This danger is especially evident when God is identified with a single principle such as liberation; less so in the model proposed by Paul Hanson, which insists on the dialectical interaction between structure and reform, and on the transcendence of God. A critical theology, however, must also ask whether the biblical statements about God are compatible with what we can know of ultimate reality by philosophical means. Are the biblical statements adequately explained as social ideology or do they have metaphysical implications?

5. The Idea of God
(See Bibliography numbers 4, 21, 22, 26, 37)

The sociological approach to biblical study focuses primarily on ethical questions. The revelation of God is identified with the disclosure of a social idea. This ethical emphasis was also characteristic of the older Biblical Theology Movement, with its focus on history. There is, however, a quite different way of approaching the question of God, which is equally amenable to critical method. In this case the emphasis is on explaining reality, or that which is, and God is conceived as creator rather than as redeemer. (Needless to say, these alternatives are not mutually exclusive). This approach is especially characteristic of the Wisdom literature, which has often been neglected in biblical theology. All parts of the Bible, however, presume the reality of God, as the power that ultimately governs the universe, and not only as a symbol for a social or ethical ideal. If theology is properly understood as talk about God, then the central task of biblical theology is the critical study of the ways in which God is portrayed in the Bible.

Two factors bear on our understanding of biblical God-language: the notion of God which we bring to the text and the genres of the texts themselves. The interplay of these factors can be seen if we consider the example of Process Theology, which provides a rare attempt to correlate the God of the scriptures with the categories of contemporary philosophy.

Process Theology rejects the classical notion of God as the unmoved mover as both philosophically inadequate and incompatible with biblical revelation. Building on the metaphysics of A. N. Whitehead, it conceives of God as a principle of order and value, which may be metaphorically expressed in personal terms. This divine principle is immanent in the world and fully involved in the process of historical change. Such a conception of God is more compatible with biblical statements than the unmoved and unchanging God of classical theism.

The philosophical adequacy of the Process view of God involves complex questions which go far beyond the scope of this essay. The more immediate question for our purpose is whether this view of God is of any relevance for the Bible. No one would claim that the prophets of Israel consciously thought in Process categories, but then they didn't think in the categories of classical Christian theology either. A metaphysics which allows for a changing God is obviously attractive as an underpinning for much of the biblical narrative. There is a question however as to whether philosophical categories can be imposed on all biblical texts without doing them violence. What is at issue is a question of genre. Does a passage like Hosea 11, which speaks of God changing his mind so that he will not destroy Israel, give us any metaphysical information? or is it rather an expression of a human conviction that mercy is better than anger? Many prophetic texts which speak of God in anthropomorphic terms are primarily concerned with human social values rather than with metaphysics. On the other hand, passages such as Proverbs 8, or some reflections on creation, are more directly concerned with metaphysical questions and may be more appropriately correlated with philosophical categories. In short, the question of genre is the necessary preliminary step in the theological evaluation of any biblical text. When a biblical text is understood to make a metaphysical claim, it must then be evaluated in the light of our other ideas about ultimate reality. Old Testament theology, however, as practiced hitherto, has rarely attempted a critical assessment of biblical God-language at all.

6. Conclusions and Prospects

If we consider the theological positions represented by Childs, Gottwald, and Process theology, the diversity is striking and there is little prospect of consensus. Nonetheless some conclusions can be drawn regarding the basis for future proposals.

a. Some of the familiar pre-occupations of biblical theology, such as the quest for a center, or even for a unifying principle, should now be abandoned as dead ends.

b. We have become aware of the different contexts in which biblical theology is practiced. No context is neutral or value free. In the past, theologies which claimed to be objectively historical were found to rest on blatantly confessional foundations. We can no longer entertain the hope for a "pure" objective, universally acceptable biblical theology. If the aspirations of historical criticism have been somewhat chastened by this development, they have not been completely undermined. The distinction between "what it meant" and "what it means" is still crucial if we are to grant the Bible independence over against our particular confessional tradition. The methods of historical research can still provide common ground for people who approach the text with quite different faith perspectives. The appeal to public evidence and commonly accepted methods is a pre-requisite for dialogue, even if it can never remove the diversity of perspectives held by the dialogue partners.

c. Before we can evaluate a text theologically we must understand its genre, and know what kind of truth we can legitimately expect from it. We cannot expect reliable metaphysics from a piece of political propaganda. The problem of genre is in no way short-circuited by the canon since a book does not lose its literary character by inclusion in a collection. A major example of the importance of genre can be seen in the shift from "history" to "story" as a designation of the biblical narratives. It would be a great mistake however to regard "story" as simply *the* genre of the Bible and neglect the law-codes, prophecies, proverbs and other forms of expression.

d. Biblical theology has in the past been too preoccupied with questions of historicity. These are not the only critical questions which must be asked. Even if the book of Exodus is a "story" rather than history, we must still ask whether the rendering of reality is true to our experience and what is its value. Most fundamentally, biblical theology must critically assess the various portrayals of God which we find in the biblical texts.

Despite occasional claims that critical method has run its course, and that we are now in a post-critical era, there remains an unfinished agenda for critical biblical theology. In view of the vitality of the sociological approach, which is the most radical approach to biblical theology now current, the continued relevance of that agenda can not be in doubt.

BIBLIOGRAPHY

1. Barton, John. *Reading the Old Testament. Method in Biblical Study.* Philadelphia: Westminster, 1984.

2. Barr, James. *Holy Scripture. Canon, Authority, Criticism.* Philadelphia: Westminster, 1980.

3. Barr, James. *The Scope and Authority of the Bible.* Philadelphia: Westminster, 1983.

4. Beardslee, W. A. and D. J. Lull. *Old Testament Interpretation from a Process Perspective. Semeia* 24. Chico: Scholars Press, 1982.

5. Blenkinsopp, Joseph. "Old Testament Theology and the Jewish-Christian Connection." *JSOT* 28 (1984) 3-15.

6. Brueggemann, Walter. "Trajectories in Old Testament Literature and the Sociology of Ancient Israel." *JBL* 98(1979) 161-85.

7. Childs, Brevard S. *Biblical Theology in Crisis.* Philadelphia: Westminster, 1970.

8. Childs, Brevard S. *Introduction to the Old Testament as Scripture.* Philadelphia: Fortress, 1979.

9. Clements, Ronald E. *Old Testament Theology. A Fresh Approach.* Atlanta: John Knox, 1978.

10. Collins, John J. "The 'Historical' Character of the Old Testament in Recent Biblical Theology." *CBQ* 41(1979) 185-204.

11. Eichrodt, Walter. *Theology of the Old Testament.* 2 vols. Philadelphia: Westminster, 1961, 1967.`

12. Gadamer, H. G. *Truth and Method.* New York: Crossroad, 1982.

13. Gottwald, N. K. *The Tribes of Yahweh. A Sociology of the Religion of Liberated Israel, 1250-1050 B.C.E.* Maryknoll: Orbis, 1979.

14. Gottwald, N. K. "Biblical Theology or Biblical Sociology?" *Radical Religion* 2 (1975) 42-57.

15. Gottwald, N. K., ed. *The Bible and Liberation. Political and Social Hermeneutics.* Maryknoll: Orbis, 1983.

16. Hanson, Paul D. *Dynamic Transcendence: The Correlation of Confessional Heritage and Contemporary Experience in a Biblical Model of Divine Activity.* Philadelphia: Fortress, 1978.

17. Hanson, Paul D. *The Diversity of Scripture. A Theological Interpretation.* Philadelphia: Fortress, 1982.

18. Harvey, Van A. *The Historian and the Believer.* New York: Macmillan, 1969.

19. Hasel, G. F. *Old Testament Theology: Basic Issues in the Current Debate.* Revised edition. Grand Rapids: Eerdmans, 1975.

20. Hayes, J. H. and F. Prussner. *Old Testament Theology.* Atlanta: John Knox, 1984.

21. Janzen, J. G. "The Old Testament in Process Perspective: Proposal for a Way Forward in Biblical Theology." *Magnalia Dei: The Mighty Acts of God. Essays on the Bible and Archeology in Memory of G. Ernest Wright.* F. M. Cross, W. E. Lemke, and P. D. Miller, Eds. New York: Doubleday, 1976. 480-509.

22. Knierim, R. P.   "The Task of Old Testament Theology."
Horizons in Biblical Theology 6 (1984) 25-58.

23. Levenson, J. D. "The Hebrew Bible, The Old Testament
and Historical Criticism" *The Future of Biblical Studies.*
Ed. R. E. Friedman and H. G. M. Williamson (forthcoming).

24. McEvenue, Sean. "The Old Testament, Scripture or
Theology?" *Interpretation* 35 (1981) 229-42.

25. McKenzie, John L.   *A Theology of the Old Testament.*
Garden City: Doubleday, 1974.

26. Murphy, Roland E.   "Wisdom and Creation." *JBL* 104
(1985) 3-11.

27. von Rad, Gerhard.   *Old Testament Theology.* 2 vols.
New York: Harper and Row, 1965.

28. Reventlow, H. G. *Problems of Old Testament Theology
in the Twentieth Century.* Philadelphia: Fortress, 1985.

29. Ricoeur, Paul.   *Essays on Biblical Interpretation.* Ed.
Lewis S. Mudge. Philadelphia: Fortress, 1980.

30. Sanders, James A.   *Torah and Canon.* Philadelphia:
Fortress, 1972.

31. Sanders, James A. *Canon and Community.* Philadelphia:
Fortress, 1983.

32. Stendahl, Krister.   *Meanings. The Bible as Document
and as Guide.* Philadelphia: Fortress, 1984.

33. Stuhlmacher, Peter.   *Historical Criticism and Theological Interpretation of Scripture.* Philadelphia: Fortress, 1977.

34. Troeltsch, Ernst.   *Gesammelte Schriften.* Aalen: Scientia,
1962. 2.729-753. Essay first published in 1898.

35. de Vaux, Roland.   "Is it Possible to Write a Theology of
the Old Testament?" *The Bible and the Ancient Near East.*
Garden City: Doubleday, 1971. Pp. 49-62.

36. Vawter, Bruce.   *Biblical Inspiration.* Philadelphia:
Westminster, 1972.

37. Vawter, Bruce. "The God of Hebrew Scriptures." *Biblical Theology Bulletin* 12(1982) 3-7. Reprinted in *The Path of Wisdom*. Wilmington: Glazier, 1986.

38. Wright, G. E. *God Who Acts: Biblical Theology as Recital.* London: SCM, 1952.

39. Wright, G. E. *The Old Testament and Theology.* New York: Harper and Row, 1969.

40. Zimmerli, Walter. *Old Testament Theology in Outline.* Atlanta: John Knox, 1978.

TWENTY-FIVE YEARS OF PENTATEUCHAL STUDY

Dennis J. McCarthy, S.J.
Pontifical Biblical Institute, Rome

1. Tradition and History
(See Bibliography numbers 5-8, 10, 11, 13, 15-17, 22, 26,
30-35, 37, 38).

Twenty-five years ago the documentary hypothesis about the formation of the Pentateuch lived in peace, though a rather uneasy one. The Pentateuch was supposed to be a mélange of pieces from a southern document of the 10th-9th centuries (J, the Yahwist), a northern Elohist document from the 8th century (E, the Elohist), and a Priestly document reflecting Jerusalem tradition (P). Each of those told from its own point of view the early history of Israel and pre-Israel. There was also the addition of a separate whole, Deuteronomy, from c. 700 (D). In fact — and this may be a sign of changes to come — there was little research done on identifying these sources. The results of earlier work were accepted and used as the base for other activities. Interest centered on going beyond the written sources through form and tradition criticism seeking the oral antecedents of the written documents. Hère the dominant work was that of Martin Noth and Gerhard von Rad (see Bibliog. nos. 26, 35).

Martin Noth contributed the theory of a pre-monarchical amphictyony in Israel, an association of twelve tribes who gathered periodically at one of several central shrines where the Ark was kept to reaffirm their unity as worshippers of Yahweh, to hear his law proclaimed, and to settle difficult legal cases. This gave a rough picture of pre-monarchical Israel. More important for us, by drawing attention to the shrines, it encouraged the existing tendency to treat the shrines as custodians of tradition and so offered real centers which remembered and passed on oral traditions. Von Rad made an important step in this direction when he divided the Exodus tradition from the Sinai tradition and located Gilgal as the focus of the former and Shechem of the latter. He believed that J was the first to unite the two. Indeed, J organized many traditions into a brilliant theological synthesis beginning with creation and sin, running through the patriarchs and the trials of their descendants, and closing with the occupation of Palestine as the climax of a history of sin, grace, and divine promise. In other words J created the basic outline of the Hexateuch (i.e., Pentateuch and Joshua).

Let us note with regret that here we refer largely to German work. Twenty-five years ago there was dialogue if not agreement between Europe and North America on the aims and results of exegesis. Now it seems these two principal centers of OT study, despite multiplying international conferences etc., seem further apart, using different methods in the pursuit of different aims *without realizing it.* We are dealing with the results of exegesis, not its circumstances, but this divergence, if it widens, can only lead to a regrettable confusion in results and should be noted for this reason.

Noth accepted the separation of traditions proposed by von Rad but not the formative role of J. He sought to distinguish the basic traditions, and found five major and a host of minor, related ones (see Bibliog. no. 27). One major tradition was that of the patriarchs. Jacob was originally the most prominent, with two centers of different traditions, Bethel and Gilead. Abraham was associated with the holy place at Hebron. The Isaac stories are the oldest (because the most exiguous) and centered at Beersheba. Originally unconnected, these stories were organized in the father-son-grandson scheme as the different tribe fused into Israel and sought to bring their various traditions, still in oral form, into line with their unity (see Bibliog. no. 37).

Another major traditional element was the exodus. Actually, the escape from Egypt was experienced by only a few Hebrews (elements of Joseph and Benjamin?), but the tale was much expanded in the telling, e.g., the "plagues" were added to lead up to the miracle of salvation at the sea, though the old idea that Exod 1-15 was a literary construct created for the passover rite has been abandoned. The basic story was brought to Palestine by the group that also created the conquest tradition. This group actually "conquered" a corridor from the Jordan to the central highlands, that is, made their way through to the mountain country. The tradition emphasized a local Ephraimite hero, Joshua, and extended his conquest to the whole land. This tradition displaced the traditions of other tribes (see Bibliog. no. 38). The universal adoption of this and the exodus tradition is attributed to the eventual size and power of the Joseph tribes and the importance of Shechem and Gilgal, shrines controlled by these Rachel tribes.

The Sinai tradition was a kind of alternative to the exodus, telling of a meeting with God at a mountain pilgrim shrine in the desert. It was at home in Judah. The Wilderness traditions were Judean too, reflecting knowledge of semi-nomadic life in the Negeb and beyond, and probably centered at Beersheba. Judah entered the tribal federation late, and when it did, its traditions were incorporated with the others. However, the northern traditions had already taken some shape as a whole. The intrusion of the Judah traditions accounts for incoherencies still seen in our texts, but in general the whole set of traditions was given a coherent over-all form from the patriarchs and their promise through Egyptian slavery and the exodus, the wilderness wanderings, the Sinai covenant to the final conquest. This was done orally but probably was written down in a *Grundschrift* (G) which was J's basis (see Bibliog. nos. 5, 7).

Noth revolutionized the view of the Pentateuch in another way. He showed it to be a Tetrateuch, with Deuteronomy belonging not so much to it as to the following history (Jos - 2 Kgs) (see Bibliog. no. 28). This means that the original JE and P story of the conquest was dropped and the ending of Numbers reworked to round it out as a conclusion, though later redaction tried to undo this by adding some of the material to the end of Deuteronomy and interweaving Deuteronomistic (henceforth Dtr) material at the end of Numbers. Thus the story of the conquest instead of being the climax of the Pentateuch becomes the opening rather of the Dtr story of Israel in Palestine, a story which explains the loss of the land on the basis of Deuteronomic theology. A faithless people destroyed the covenant and were banished. The tragic story is told through a selection of traditional archival material arranged to show the ups and downs of Israel's history, and this with speeches and comments, Deut 31; Jos 1; 12; 23; Jgs 2; 1 Sam 12; (2 Sam 7); 1 Kgs 8; 2 Kgs 17:7-18 (21:5-16). Noth does not include 2 Sam 7 nor 2 Kgs 21, but they are key interpretive passages in Dtr's scheme (see Bibliog. nos. 22, 8).

Noth sees the history as entirely a threnody: the people of Yahweh simply are no more and cannot return. Noth's idea of the structure of the Dtr History is widely accepted; his pessimism is not. The Dtr History has hope of a true son of David who will save the people, and this is never rescinded. Further, the people *can* turn their hearts and return to God. Again, the covenant is not a contract but a personal relationship including true affectivity so that an errant partner can always seek and obtain again the favor of a generous lord. In fact, the sequence: sin, God's anger, punishment, calling on God, sending of a savior, and salvation, is an iron law for the Dtr History. God will not abandon his people if they look to him, even in exile. Thus the History is not a threnody but a call to *metanoia*.

There have been efforts to show that the Dtr History underwent thorough redactions emphasizing law (Dtr N, for Nomist)— and prophecy (Dtr P), but while they have unearthed occasional interpolations and glosses, as arguments for total redactions they do not convince. More persuasive is the idea of a double redaction, optimistic under Josiah, and pessimistic during the exile. The negative explains the exile: even the splendid Josiah could not undo the evil of Manasseh. In any event the concept of the Dtr History has withstood criticism. This cannot be said of the documentary hypothesis and the tradition history based on it.

There had long been doubts about E, and Scandinavian scholars fought the hypothesis as the product of a modern "book mentality." Others were uneasy at the fragmentation of the books the hypothesis involved. It seemed odd that the redactors were so inept, and modern study of the forms of traditional literature tended to show that at least some of the "incoherencies" found by source critics are in fact normal. Finally, Noth's theory of an Israelite amphictyony collapsed, as it was shown that early Israel had no central shrine for all Israel, that the whole group of tribes did not meet, that the number of tribes need not always be twelve. That is, Noth's central arguments could not stand, and the solid centers for tradition history he had posited disappeared (see Bibliography nos. 11 and 12). Still for some years no systematic attack on the hypothesis itself was made.

Then the questions began to arise thick and fast. Van Seters questioned the whole hypothesis. Applying discoveries of folklore scholars, he read many of the duplications and inconsistencies used to argue for distinction of documents as unitary stories in the oral mode. He has not been widely followed, but he did draw attention to the oral basis of our literature neglected by source critics, and in doing so he did justice to the evident truth that there were not so many idiot redactors. They must have found some coherence in their stories; the source critics' insistence in treating them as creators of jig-saw puzzles did them an injustice and led to some odd scholarly results. On other ground Van Seters uses the appearance of Dtr and Deutero-Isaian vocabulary to date the composition of the Pentateuchal materials late, during the exile, thus undermining any claim it had to proximity with the matter in the text (see Bibliog. no. 33). H. H. Schmid takes the same tack in dating the Pentateuch. Though he is ready to accept documentary sources, this late editing means that the place, date, and form of the documents are far different from the old J and E (see Bibliog. no. 32).

In another line, R. Rendtorff argues for taking tradition history seriously. This means applying it within the text, not, as usual, to an effort to get behind the text. That is, he tries to identify individual stories from various traditions in the text and then to identify the links oral tradition used to tie these stories into cycles. The cycles were then written down, but much later than the classic J or E. He is most successful with Jacob, perhaps because the "trickster" is a character tradition can handle easily. Theoretically, one could still hold that this is simply a later reworking of J and E traditions, but Rendtorff finds so many E and J characteristics in unified stories and cycles that the distinction seems meaningless (see Bibliog. no. 30).

One cannot declare the documentary hypothesis dead. It is still used; it is defended. Perhaps the best recent work supporting though not directly defending the hypothesis is a philological, literary, and archeological synthesis of great power which presupposes it (see Bibliog. no. 8). However it would be a bold writer who based an OT theology on it now. Perhaps it has done its work, disabusing us of the notion that the Bible is through and through literal history. Some such feeling lies behind the drive to analyze the text as literature ("rhetorical criticism"), perhaps in part historical, but still literature. That is, it is a meaningful whole with its own assertions to make about man and God and their interaction (see Bibliog. no. 1). Such analyses have been made of parts of Genesis and result in rich readings of the text, and one study even analyzes the way the whole

Pentateuch develops the promise-fulfilment theme (see Bibliog. nos. 13, 6). These studies tend to scout the problems of historicity and literary history, perhaps an inevitable reaction to the over-emphasis on these matters earlier, but still a weakness. Nonetheless, the text does come first.

It is time now to face the problems with the historicity of everything before the monarchy, which doubts about the documentary hypothesis, among other things, have caused. If J came from the 10th century, it was reasonably close to some of the events it records. If it (or its theoretical substitute) is exilic or the like it loses credibility. As for tradition history, it moves from the known text to a hypothetical antecedent, a weak base for an historical argument especially since such work tends to depend not on a single hypothesis but on an interlocking series of them. Finally, the confidence in traditions was in part based on a confident association of them with particular shrines which presumably cherished them carefully. Without the "amphictyony" this confidence is gone, and many are reluctant to push back to any historical reconstructions before our texts were written down except, perhaps, for some undateable incidents from Judges. Douglas Knight has written the history of tradition criticism. Movements tend to have their history written when they are dying (see Bibliog. no. 17).

This is one immediately Biblical problem with the historicity of the patriarchs, the exodus, and the conquest. Another is the types of stories recounting these events. They are types identifiable almost universally in folklore. They use motifs: the triumphant younger son, the trickster, the wondrous birth story, and others just as universal, but history is about particulars. Do these tales even intend to tell of facts or merely to amuse us and instruct us about national ideals? I do not see why the use of traditional motifs rules out a reference to basic fact, but the technique does make it difficult to distinguish the fact from traditional technique.

In this situation many once turned to outside evidence to confirm the tales, and twenty years ago data from archeology and philology were supposed to do this. In the United

States, at least, many believed that these sciences revealed a second millennium background for the patriarchal stories. Abraham's route from Ur to Haran to Canaan was natural then, a shorter one later. Personal names and place names show that peoples using names typical of the patriarchal type were in Ur and Mari early in the second millennium. Abraham's relatives, Terah, Sarah, and Milkah, had names related to the moon god popular at Ur and Haran, while Nahor is a place name in the Haran area. Family law from Nuzi, a fifteenth century city on the upper Tigris, seemed to parallel oddities in Genesis: adopting a slave as heir (Gen 15:2-3), a childless wife acquiring sons by giving her slave to her husband (Sarah, Rachel, Leah), and inheritance attached to possession of the family gods (teraphim: Gen 31:19, 34, 35). Abraham bought a tomb seemingly in accord with Hittite (second millennium) law. Even the name Hebrew ('ibri) parallels a class of restless people (*habiru, 'apiru*) widely mentioned in the second millennium. Finally, some sought to fit the odd story of Abraham the warrior (Gen 14) into second millennium conditions. The patriarchal stories, written in the first millennium, seemed to reflect the second and so show that Hebrew traditions preserved much from a pre-settlement past (see Bibliog. no. 10).

Now, to say the least, all this is in doubt. The laws cited have parallels in the first millennium from places closer to Israel than remote Nuzi or Hatti. The Habiru were ubiquitous with no special relation to the Hebrews; though they may have given their name to them they do not define them. To assign Gen 14 to the second millennium is to misjudge its literary character and its confused content. The special names remain, but, while unusual, the connections to ancient forms are not unique. Besides many parallels come from too early to fit the patriarchs; others were as available to the story teller in the first as in the second millennium, e.g., the names related to Haran. Most conclude that West-Semitic type names could appear at any time among West-Semites, not that they are peculiar to the patriarchs. So, between the problems raised by our text types and the lack of solid archeological support for the patriarchal stories, historians now deny any recoverable historicity to them (see Bibliog. no. 34), or reach exiguous conclusions from genealogies (see Bibliog. no. 16).

The same problems arise with the exodus. The miracle at the sea is found in four versions which do not add up to a coherent picture. Did God raise a wind to divide and close the waters? Did the Egyptian chariotry get mired? Did Moses' staff divide the waters? Did God himself fight with the water as his weapon? As we have seen, the material in Exod 1-13 is a story-teller's preamble to this great act. How are we to distinguish fact from narrative motifs? And again archeology and philology are no help. Does the introductory Joseph story show a good knowedge of Egypt? To an extent it does, but it gives Joseph duties that no known Egyptian official had. The interest in dreams is Egyptian — it even uses the Egyptian word for dream interpreters — but such interest is universal, not just Egyptian. Joseph's Egyptian name is correct, as are those of his wife and father-in-law, but all are first millennium names, as is the oath by Pharoah's life (Gen 42:25, 26). There is but a straw, the pharaoh Merneptah's thirteenth century victory stele (*ANET*, 376-378) mentioning the destruction of Israel in Canaan. At least this would put Israel there c. 1230 B.C., *if* it refers to our Israel, which is in doubt, and it does not say how Israel got there. Anyway, the stele is an insecure support: it is propaganda affirming Egypt's tenuous claim on Canaan and uses conventional lists to create its content. Merneptah, whatever his stele says, may never have seen Canaan or Israel. Once again historians wonder about the exodus.

So too with the conquest. We saw that the story in the book of Joshua is a construct based on the primacy of the Rachel tribes and their shrines which extended their traditions to all Israel, or, if the shrines are out of the picture in the new interpretation, probably the account is the work of story-tellers in the northern kingdom and very late indeed. If there was a "conquest," it took place very gradually in small skirmishes under diverse leaders defending their land, as in the individual pictures of heroes in the Book of Judges. In fact, it has long been held that the Hebrews infiltrated gradually and unopposed into unwanted mountain land, leaving the cities with their fertile valleys and great trade routes alone. Major Canaanite centers fell only to David (see Bibliog. nos. 10, 15).

This picture is confirmed by archeology. The showpieces of the conquest, Jericho and Ai, were not even inhabited, let alone conquered, at any time when the conquest could have occurred. Of the major cities named in Joshua, only Hazor was conquered in a possible conquest time-frame, but in Jgs 4 it is back in business as a Canaanite stronghold. Perhaps there was a successful raid, but need it have been by Hebrews? In any case it resulted in no lasting Hebrew occupation. The conquest as shown in the book of Joshua is a theological statement, a promise shown to have been kept, not simply history.

The problem is more severe if we accept the popular American concept of "conquest" not as invasion but as revolution. It sees no sudden attack or gradual infiltration of Palestine. Rather oppressed Canaanite peasants rose against their feudal masters, the city lords. Hence the failure to include large cities in the early federation. The federation was an organization of the rebels into artificial tribes, each largely on its own, but distinguished by their common acceptance of Yahwism. They even gathered regularly to reaffirm their allegiance, their covenant, at different holy places. This brings us back the shrines and central cult lost with Noth's amphictyony. It also explains the failure to take cities, and the twelfth century rural centers with a characteristic, ruder culture discovered by archeology. They were the rebel peasant villages disassociated from the cultured cities. However, this archeological evidence is secondary to the comparative sociological and ethnological argument. The Hebrews pictured in Joshua and Judges are said *not* to conform to the patterns of nomad or especially, semi-nomad cultures. The mixture of fixed farming and short movements of flocks within a fixed area, along with the familial-tribal defensive organization, fits into typical form of peasant organization, one found in Mediterranean lands until quite recently (see Bibliog. nos. 14, 25).

This theory has been criticized as being based on too narrow a set of anthropological assumptions. Before the fact, J. W. Rogerson had warned of the problems in using anthropological data, and Gottwald especially has not avoided some of the difficulties he raises (see Bibliog. no. 30). Further the theory rests on a rather narrow textual base, much of it late (P). Still, it must be taken seriously, and given further investigation and criticism. As it stands it restores a certain reality to the conquest idea, even if the "conquest" turns out to be a rebellion, not an invasion. This is not the OT picture, but neither is it total skepticism about the history of the era. However, it confirms doubts about the patriarchal, exodus, Sinai, and wilderness traditions. Rebellious Canaanite peasants had no semi-nomadic Aramaen fathers (Deut 26:5) nor ancestors in Egypt nor in the desert. Basically the important problem of historicity becomes more acute.

The rebellion theory of the conquest has its own theology. In it the only true Israel is the people freely covenanting with Yahweh and working out their affairs by popular consensus at all social levels. A return to kings and leading priests is a backsliding into Canaanite practice to be rejected. This leaves as theological evil much that the OT accepted, and it has not been widely followed. However, it does accentuate a problem much discussed but outside our subject: the integration of the Sinaitic and the Davidic covenants .

Let me conclude this section on historicity with a personal reflection. The old archeological supports for the factuality of the patriarchal-exodus-Sinai-wilderness-conquest stories have been undermined. Thrown back on the stories themselves we find these constructed from motifs common to folklore the world over. There is the further problem, that this could in theory be a mode of expression covering kernels of fact. In fact, if there was no wandering, no Egypt, no kind of conquest in the past, why were stories made up as though there had been. Why not "proletarian" tales of heroes fighting oppression such as the American revolutionary experience produced? (see Bibliog. no. 4). It seems that arguments against historicity in our traditions stop halfway: they claim to tell us what the stories are not. They are not reflections of historical or social memory, but they do not tell us what they are. Doing so is a major task remaining for scholarship.

2. Sinai and Covenant
(See Bibliography numbers 2, 3, 18, 19, 22, 24, 29)

But we must return to a topic just mentioned, the *covenant*, specifically the Mosaic *Covenant*. Of course, if the whole Pentatuech is non-historical, as so many think, Moses and his Sinai *covenant* become a fiction with the rest of it. However, it is still there as a literary and theological, perhaps even an historical, entity. In fact, twenty years ago this was no problem. Rather the Sinai narratives were used to authenticate the antiquity of Sinai and its attached traditions. This was done by a formal comparison with the Hittite treaty which began with an historical prologue, continued with stipulations, demanded recording, called on the gods, and ended with blessings for fidelity, curses for infidelity. Sinai was said to have an historical prologue in the opening of the decalogue: "I am Yahweh who brought you out of Egypt," stipulations in the decalogue and other laws, and the two tablets as its recording document. Of course, Israel, could not invoke a multiplicity of gods, but there is evidence for blessings and curses, the result of divine invocation. These were not necessarily sought in the book of Exodus, though 19:3-8 and 23:20-33 were invoked as possible examples, although these are intrusive in their contexts. More appeal was made to other texts like Jos 24 or Deut 27:15-26 to show that curses and blessings were integral to Israelite *covenant*. Since the Hittites and their treaties disappeared in the thirteenth century and later Israel would hardly imitate an obsolete and remote literary form, the essence of the Sinai narratives in the treaty form must be from the thirteenth century or earlier, contemporary with Moses and so almost "eye-witness" records (see Bibliog. nos. 24, 3).

Others were wary of the literary analysis and historical dating involved in this argumentation (see Bibliog. nos. 2, 22). "I am Yahweh who. . ." is not an historical prologue but a cultic introduction of the present LORD. The Decalogue as such cannot be so old. The passages from Exodus alluded to will not do as blessing and curse: one is a condition (stipulation), the other a promise with commands. I argued that there was a *covenant* at Sinai, but its central feature was a cultic affirmation of a special relationship with Yahweh, not a verbal oath as in the treaties, and that the treaty form did not appear in full until *Urdeuteronomium* in Deut 4:44-26:19 & 28:1-68. L. Perlitt also discusses this, but he does not really deal with what the *covenant* is, only when the word came into use (see Bibliog. no. 29).

This remained more or less the *status questionis* with the addition of an idea which would change the meaning of *covenant* wherever it appeared. This was the claim that *covenant* meant a one-sided promise, command or duty (see Bibliog. nos. 18, 19). That is, even if one were to find some historical value in the Sinai texts, it is questionable whether they involved *covenant* in the meaning later biblical texts and Jewish and Christian tradition assumed. More, Kutsch and others believe that Sinai was not denominated a *covenant* in any sense until a later date.

There is no doubt that *covenant* does often mean promise or duty, but even in many of these cases there is metonomy based on the relationship underlying promise or duty. There is no such thing as a promise without a promiser and a promisee nor, in biblical times, a duty without its being owed to someone. If either side scorns the other, promise or duty become meaningless. Thus *covenant* means a relationship; it is not merely a given or something imposed, it must be accepted (cf. Deut 29:17-18 where pretended acceptance is already perjury). In fact, *covenant* in its most fundamental meaning is probably an especially strong oath binding one to something because he has tied himself to it under God. Far from being separable, *covenant* and relationship are almost a tautology. In his graciousness God is ready to join with his creatures like a family or a *comitatus*. Finally, it must be noted that when the thing is clear, the absence of the word is not significant.

Thus it seems to me that the Sinai narratives, whether a description of actual experience or a theological construct, do describe covenant making, though they use *covenant* sparingly. The collection of ratifying ceremonies contained in Exod 24:1-11 are all covenant oriented. Eating before the LORD (24:10-11) is a covenant ceremony uniting chief and men attested as long ago as the eighteenth century B.C. and still practiced. The people's assent to Yahweh's word is the heart of the covenant idea: approach and response (24:7). The sharing of blood by God (altar) and people (24:6-8), a remarkable ceremony given Israelite attitudes toward blood, and early because later orthodoxy abhorred such a usage, is a sign of sharing stronger even than the sacrifices. Yahweh and the people are one through a material sign of assent more vivid than a mere verbal oath: an act speaks louder than words. Even the chastening of the people and the return to Yahweh in Exod 33 can be seen as assent to the renewed covenant in chapter 34: repentance means acceptance of what Yahweh will offer.

If we try to understand what *covenant* means, an approach to the people made by God and their free response — in Deut 26:17-19 the two enter into covenant with identical acts and words — we need not be so concerned about the words used. Sinai is a covenant presented to us through many symbols of union. The gracious acceptance of the representatives of the people is one kind of union, superior and retainers or extended family. The sharing of blood is another, a forceful symbol of a shared life "for in the blood is life." Verbal assent emphasizes free, willed union. Such diversity, probably due to memories of rites at different times and places, is not contradiction but richness of meaning through multiple, complementary symbols.

3. Creation and Fall
(See Bibliography numbers 20, 21, 36)

A review of Pentateuchal studies in a collection with theological interests like this must say something about creation and fall, indeed about Gen 1-11, even though changes of interpretation had already taken hold at the beginning of our twenty-five years. The chapters have colored the Christian imagination and affected theology too much to be ignored.

Creation, of course, comes in two stories, Gen 1:1-4a and 2:4b-24. The first is the later (P) and, though reflecting some pagan mythic features remotely (see Bibliog. no. 36), is strongly Israelite in its theology. Unlike comparable Semitic myths, here the creator has no struggle with an evil opponent to achieve order. His almighty word produces what he wants, an ordered world in which humankind exercises dominion. Recently there has been speculation that this dominion given by God has encouraged careless exploitation of nature. I know of no Christian or Jewish interpretation which takes this direction, and in the text "have dominion" refers to royal power extended to all humankind. According to ancient ideals this implies responsible and righteous direction, not exploitation: cf. Ps 72 or Ezek 34 for a description of the dominion humankind is to imitate. Besides, the paradise context — nothing kills to eat, for example — implies an idyllic order, not exploitation.

However, the idyll does not continue. The second creation story is the story of the end of paradise. It is, in fact, the opening of the "history of sin" which goes on through the tower of Babel (11:1-9). This tells of disobedience. It tells of fratricide and brutal revenge (Lamech). It tells how even the "sons of God," entities greater than men in the hierarchy of being, some of whom constituted the heavenly court, were led astray. It tells how all humankind was corrupted so that God felt compelled to destroy it. Only Noah, the good man, was saved and made a party to a covenant, a mark of grace but with no human instrument to guarantee its continuity. Creatures fell back into pride and sought to raise themselves to the divine, thus closing the "history of sin" as it opened with Adam and Eve, by means of a great tower. Only then with the genealogy which leads to Abraham and the great promise in 12:1-3 does the picture grow lighter with a sign of grace which is to shine beside sin in the centuries to come.

The "history of sin" as literature, then, builds up to a striking turning point, to a sign of salvation central in importance to OT theology. However, its weight is theological, not historical. The "history" is full of myth and folklore motifs, e.g., the dark tower, the flood (a worldwide tale; the biblical form is paralleled almost exactly in Mesopotamian literature) fraternal (and pastoral-peasant) rivalry, etc. Such motifs, if anything, cluster in the fall story: the tree of life, as old a religious symbol as is known, Adam's knowledge of the animals as a sign of wisdom (cf. the wise Solomon in 1 Kgs 5:13), the snake symbolizing fertility, wisdom, *and* chaos — a perfect figure for much said and implied in the story — the etiologies explaining the snake's mode of progress and the particular hardships of peasant society etc. Further, the story is full of Hebrew puns and the like. All this links the story, on the one hand to the timeless, placeless world of folklore and, on the other, to a time and place far from paradise.

This story of creation and fall, then, is not history. It does describe how the ordered world planned by God was broken up by human disobedience, sin. The nature of the sin is much discussed. Was it induced by the devil disguised as a snake? Hardly as the devil of later theology, though the snake is something of a misfit in a world where humankind controlled (named) *all* animals. Some have thought that maturity and sexual union are the "sinful knowledge" involved, but, apart from the real question of what would be sinful in this, the man and woman who were rulers of animals and custodians of paradise are at ease in their nakedness. This is surely the innocence of maturity, not of ignorance. It seems best to take the text as it is. Humanity aspires to become God-like by its own efforts. Instead, ironically, Adam and Eve ("man and woman"!) are expelled from paradise. In the immediate sequel their sons are at work in non-paradise conditions and one murders the other. It is hard to think that the first sin did not open the door to others. However, there is no expression of inheritance or transmission of sin. Some even have thought that the sin of Adam and Eve was just another example of man's tendency to evil. However, forbidding them paradise and the tree of life implies more than this, an interpretation confirmed by the emphasis on sin-caused murder among workers outside paradise in chapter 4. In some way the first sin opens the way for the history of sin and grace. It is for later theology to make this more precise.

However, this opens a large problem. Creation in itself can be the object of theological and philosophical study. Traditionally, philosophy has demonstrated the fact of creation, if not the details Genesis gives. But the Judaeo-Christian tradition goes beyond this. It deals not merely with philosophical truths. It affirms as a fundamental tenet that certain events, facts, are God's intervention in history or bring that intervention about. The special character of the tradition is that God acts and saves not in a "higher world" or *in illo tempore* or through an escape from the rough course of events but in history. If the fall and God's grace through Abraham are in no way historical, then basic elements of the tradition are actually outside the tradition!

Attempts have been made to deal with this crucial problem. One of the most interesting is Karl Rahner's. He argues that the inspired author, a Hebrew under the monarchy, saw sin all around him — it is easy enough to do this any time! — and yet knew that this could not come directly from his good God. Therefore he took a story, the elements of which were familiar in his society (cf. the parallel in Ezek 28:11-19) and applied it to an explanation of the anomaly. God *had* planned an ordered world, but humankind had early upset that order through disobedience and so opened the gate to sin. N. Lohfink (see Bibliog. no. 20) approves Rahner's idea, though not the terminology "etiology," and gives references to the work of Rahner and others; the condensation lacks the references (see Bibliog. no. 21). This acutely explains the why and how of the story, but for historicity Rahner must appeal to revelation. We know it happened because the inspired author says so. This works in part as an elegant *ratio congruentiae*, but it is not usable as history.

4. History and Theology

This simply emphasizes some of the larger problems the present state of Pentateuchal studies raises for theology. Historicity is a property of Judaism and Christianity: they claim that God works not just "out there" in pre-time or beyond space but here and now in human affairs. Moreover, certain events have pride of place in theology. All is in the hand of God, but in some things like the exodus and the Sinai covenant the OT claimed to see that hand at work more clearly. Hence the anxiety of an earlier generation to find confirmation for events like these in archeology and the like, though these efforts seemed often to arrive at no more than showing that the Bible was "almost correct." One cannot in any case gainsay the modern refutation of these archeological arguments. Indeed, archeology (and secular history) can never deliver evidence that *digitus Dei est hic*. More, the uncertain state of the literary analysis plus an increasing knowledge of the vagaries of oral tradition make the use of our texts a very delicate task when we are searching for history. Still, I have offered some reason for believing that a certain valid historical or social memory lies behind them. A task for literary-exegetical work is certainly to investigate the problem and, with refined instruments, to see if allusions to an ancient reality can be found in the texts.

Secondly, it is surely a task for theologians to give us an acceptable definition of the concept of God at work in history. The old "Salvation history" (*Heilsgeschichte*) will not do: it has often seemed to use "salvation" as an extra-historical defense when real historical problems were brought up and to turn to "history" when these problems go away. Nor is the appeal to miracles used in classic apologetics of much use here. Even those who might accept miracles as such can do nothing with material which may describe miraculous "events" which did not happen. What, then, does it mean to say that we have an historical religion, that God intervenes concretely in history? That is the crux, but the exegete who is properly concerned with interpreting the text cannot answer a philosophical or theological problem of which the text does not speak.

However, within the Catholic tradition, the exegete cannot be indifferent to these problems. That tradition has steadfastly, since Paul, held to the validity of natural theology and, therefore, to the ability to "give a reason (not an apodictic proof) for the faith that is in me." With the reduction of the key points of divine intervention in the OT to fables, this tradition is in serious trouble. Emphatically this fact must not influence our exegesis. That must remain honest in looking at the text as it is with all the tools modern learning offers to help understand it. At the same time, it is essential to incorporate our new insights into the basic Catholic tradition, and here an informed and sympathetic collaboration between exegete and theologian seems necessary.

Further, the exegete may have to rethink the task in view of the situation, and this strictly as an exegete. We spoke of "all tools" a moment ago, and one tool we have is holistic reading of whole texts. Modern exegesis with its almost exclusive concern for history, social or literary, *behind* the text has tended to break the biblical text into small units and ask about their meaning in their original historical context, not their literary context. Yet these texts are now part of larger wholes. The primary context for them is literary. Thus we have seen that Gen 2-3 is not simply a story on its own. It introduces the "history of sin," and this affects, even changes, the meaning of the originally separate tale.

Holistic reading attempts to take this primary literary fact into account. It is called "rhetorical criticism" because the proper English phrase, literary criticism, has been misused for source criticism. Its weakness is that it often ignores or denies any importance to the sociohistorical context, which is to abandon the valuable contributions of modern historical-critical scholarship, which help even the literary analysis of a text. We might be on the way to solving our theological problems if we can find some way to combine the insights of the different methodologies. Frankly, this is a lonely hope. Literary theory in other fields is a jungle of quarrels about method, including the relation of text to social context of author and reader. If English literature cannot solve the problem with its huge data base, how can biblical exegesis with its narrow base? And yet we must do something. I suggest for one that exegetes reflect more on the nature of meaning. In the text is it a given absolute, e.g., the author's intention, which I try to discover? Or does the text have multiple meanings, e.g., as a single story and then as a larger context, or even within itself as different approaches reveal references and symbols at work? I suspect that some North American biblical scholars, at least, because of uncritical unconscious acceptance of theories of single meaning (mostly the product of neo-Kantian thinkers) are locked into the first half of our disjunction.

At least we should make a distinction here. We can study the texts as reflections of historical eras and as sources of historical information. This has been the preoccupation of modern exegesis, and it is certainly a legitimate study. But we can also study the texts as having their own meaning. Many find this a difficult idea, but texts do have meaning in themselves. Moreover, we have seen, they acquire meaning as parts of larger wholes, as we saw for Gen 2-3. However, the whole is larger still. Oddly, since the fall story seems to impress most imaginations deeply, it lay dormant for centuries, but it did reappear in references in the Greek OT books, Tobit, Wisdom, and Sirach, and finally, of course, in Paul. Another central example is the theme of covenant. Whether there was an *historical* Sinai covenant is open to debate. Whether *textually* there is one is indisputable. The current exegetical tendency is to close the case with the historical question, but this will not do. Sinai is part of a book in which covenant is central. The Sinai covenant in Exodus does resemble Deuteronomy, *the* OT covenant expression, although the resemblance is a rough one. It is a covenant, the covenant in a book centered on covenant, and we cannot read that book properly unless we accept what it contributes to the concept of covenant and its place in the story of OT covenant. Further, it opens the theme of the "blood of the covenant" which is taken up in the Eucharistic words, the central words in the rite central to the early Church and so to the NT. For a Catholic there is continuity in the text which should not be ignored (though it may be prescinded from in doing special kinds of work) and is not to be eliminated by historical problems.

One could multiply examples but these are pertinent to our subject and clear enough by themselves. Exegetes cannot abandon historical criticism. Neither can they forget the fact that sections of the Bible are literary wholes combined into one large whole. Literary interpretation — and all interpretation of the Bible is interpretation of a literature — cannot go on in isolation. For years historical exegesis has pretty much done so, but until it rejoins the study of the whole text —rejoins, note, without suppressing the positive results of 150 years of historical study — it is bound to be a limited and limiting enterprise. Perhaps we should be grateful for the present turmoil in Pentateuchal studies. It may force us to examine the foundations of our exegetical work, not to abandon them but to strengthen them to produce a better, fuller understanding of the Bible.

BIBLIOGRAPHY

1. Alter, R. *The Art of Biblical Narrative.* New York: Basic Books, 1980.

2. Baltzer, K. *The Covenant Formulary.* Oxford: Blackwell, 1974.

3. Beyerlin, W. *Origins and History of the Oldest Sinai Traditions.* Oxford: Blackwell, 1965.

4. Bowra, C. M. *Heroic Poetry.* London: Macmillan, 1966.

5. Childs, B. *Exodus.* OT Library. Philadelphia: Westminster, 1974.

6. Clines, D. J. *The Theme of the Pentateuch.* JSOTSuppl XX. Sheffield: Sheffield University Press, 1977.

7. Coats, G. W. *The Murmuring in the Wilderness.* Nashville: Abingdon, 1968.

8. Cross, F. M. *Canaanite Myth and Hebrew Epic.* Cambridge, MA: Harvard University Press, 1973.

9. de Vaux, R. *Histoire ancienne d'Israel.* 2 vols. EBib. Paris: Gabalda, 1971-73.

10. _____. *The Early History of Israel.* Philadelphia: Westminster, 1978.

11. _____. "La Thèse de l'amphictyonie Israélite," *HTR* 64 (1971) 415-436.

12. Fohrer, G. "'Amphyktyonie' und 'Bund'?" *TLZ* 91 (1966) 801-816; 893-904.

13. Fokkelman, J. *The Narrative Art of Genesis.* Semitica Neerlandica 17. Assen: Van Gorkum, 1975.

14. Gottwald, N. K. *The Tribes of Yahweh.* Maryknoll, Maryknoll Press, 1979.

15. Hayes, J., and J. M. Miller. *The History of Israel and Judah.* OT Library. London: SCM, 1977.

16. Herrmann, S.   *A History of Israel.* London: SCM, 1981.

17. Knight, D.   *The Traditions of Israel.* SBLDS. Missoula, MT: Scholars Press, 1973.

18. Kutsch, E.   *Verheissung und Gesetz.* BZAW 131. Berlin: De Gruyter, 1973.

19. Lohfink, N.   *Die Landverheissing als Eid.* SBS 28. Stuttgart: Katholisches Bibelwerk,   1967.

20. _____.   "Genesis 2f. als'geschichtliche ätiologie". Gedenken zu einem hermeneutischen Begriff," *Scholastik* 38 (1963) 321-34.

21. _____.   "Genesis 2-3 as 'Historical Etiology.'" *TD* *13(1965) 11-17.*

22. McCarthy, D. J.   "II Samuel 7 and the Structure of the Deuteronomic History." *JBL* 89 (1965) 13-138.

23. _____.   *Treaty and Covenant* (2nd ed.; An Bib 21A; Rome: PBI, 1963).

24. Mendenhall, G.   *Law and Covenant in Israel and the Ancient Near East.* Pittsburgh: Biblical Colloquium, 1955. (*BA* 17[1954] 26-46; 50-76.)

25. _____.   "The Hebrew Conquest of Palestine." *BA* 25 (1962) 66-87.

26. Noth, M.   *Das System der zwölf Stämme Israels.* BWANT 14/1. Stuttgart: Kohlhammer, 1930.

27. _____.   *A History of Pentateuchal Traditions.* Englewood Cliffs, NJ: Prentice-Hall, 1971.

28. _____.   *The Deuteronomic History.* Sheffield: University Press, 1981.

29. Perlitt, L.   *Bundestheologie im Alten Testament.* WMANT 36. Neukirchen-Vluyn: Neukirchener Verlag, 1969.

30. Rendtorff, R.   *Das überlieferungsgeschichtliche Problem des Pentateuchs.* BZAW 147. Berlin: De Gruyter, 1977.

31. Rogerson, J. W. *Anthropology and the OT.* Burning Points in Theology. Oxford: Blackwell, 1978.

32. Schmid, H. H. *Der sogenannte Jahwist.* Zurich: Theologischer Verlag, 1976.

33. Seters J. Van. *Abraham in History and Tradition.* New Haven: Yale University Press, 1975.

34. Thompson, T. L. *The Historicity of the Patriarchal Narratives.* BZAW 133. Berlin: De Gruyter, 1974.

35. von Rad, G. "The Form-Critical Problem of the Hexateuch." *The Problem of the Hexateuch and Other Essays.* New York: McGraw-Hill, 1966. Pp. 1-78.

36. Westermann, C. *Genesis.* BKAT I/1. Neukirchen-Vluyn: Neukirchener Verlag, 1979.

37. _____. *The Promise to the Fathers.* Philadelphia: Fortress, 1980.

38. Weippert, M. *The Settlement of the Israelite Tribes in Palestine.* London: SCM, 1971.

PROPHET, WHO ARE YOU?

Carroll Stuhlmueller, C.P.
Catholic Theological Union, Chicago

Prophecy is one of the more elusive and frightening aspects of Old Testament religion: elusive because the very name for prophet evolved over the centuries just as the institution of prophecy itself, in the words of Bernhard Duhm, "has its history [and therefore] is not a timeless revelation"; frightening, because the prophet so often when present turned into a "disturber of Israel" (1 Kgs 18:17), and when absent caused people to "wander from sea to sea and rove from the north to the east in search of the word of the Lord" (Amos 8:12). Prophets seldom gained acceptance in their native place (*cf.*, Jer 26; Luke 4:24); and when they were called to look beyond their native place and to be "a prophet to the nations" (Jer 1:5) or "a light to the nations" (Isa 49:6), their words would have made little or no sense to the nations and certainly would have exerted little or no attraction for them (*cf.*, Matt 10:7; 15:24).

It is a bedeviling task to determine what and who is a prophet. If we are confused, so were the Iraelites when "the prophet Jeremiah answered the prophet Hananiah in the presence of the priests and all the people" (Jer 28:5). We can footnote this passage from the prophecy of Jeremiah by stating: "the [true] prophet Jeremiah answered the [false] prophet Hananiah," but the people at that time did not have the benefit of our commentary! The editor of Jeremiah's book made no such judgmental qualifications. Nor are we much better off in our inability to distinguish between our true and false prophets today.

Yet we must address the question, from the title of a book by L. Monloubou, *prophète qui es-tu?* — *Prophet, who are you?* The search is necessary, first because prophecy in the traditional Jewish division of the Bible occupies the largest single section of the Hebrew Bible: the early prophetical books of Joshua, Judges, 1-2 Samuel and 1-2 Kings; the latter prophetical books of the three major prophets (Isaiah, Jeremiah & Ezekiel) and the twelve minor prophets. Still another reason for pursuing the nature of prophecy lies in the synagogal service where prophecy always accompanies the sabbath reading from the Torah or five books of Moses. While the Torah constitutes the substance of Israel's religion as well as the line of continuity from Moses onward, nonetheless this line is not properly understood — perhaps we can add, it is not worthy even of survival — without prophecy.

In our search the words of Bruce Vawter, from one of his earlier books on prophecy, come to mind:

> If we are to understand correctly the prophets and what they said, ...there is no substitute for seeing them against the backdrop of the history in which they lived. We must see them for what they considered themselves to be and were, devoted Israelites, believers in the destiny of their people, looking for a regeneration of Israel that it might continue to be what Yahweh had planned for it *(The Conscience of Israel,* 7.)

This article approaches an answer to the question, *prophet, who are you?* First, by exploring the development of Israel's religion to see where prophecy fits into the pattern; second, by highlighting the major aspects contributed by Israel's religion to prophecy and by prophecy to Israel's religion; third, by investigating against this background the various titles and roles of prophet; and finally, by looking somewhat quickly into the distinction between true and false prophet.

1. The Development of Israel's Religion
(See Bibliography numbers 1, 2, 14, 16, 18, 19, 20, 21, 22, 26)

In this initial section we explore a pattern of development in Israel for appreciating the evolution and the spirit of prophecy. For this inquiry a five-stage rubric will be followed. Although prophecy does not appear till stages three and four, nonetheless, stage one offers the basis or pattern for its reaction.

(1) The first stage lays out the origins of biblical religion, and therefore of prophecy. It can be considered the pre-religion period, before the formal structures essential for religion were adequately put into place. Israel did not begin in a conspicuously religious way. A people that were to become the Israelites lived as slaves in Egypt. Under such conditions over decades of time individuals and groups among them were attempting every means possible either to leave Egypt or to lighten their burden. As to the former, the Dominican archaeologist Roland de Vaux wrote: "Just as there were several entries into Egypt, so too is it possible that there were several exoduses, some groups being expelled, others fleeing from Egypt" (*The Early History of Israel*, 375). None of these exoduses, individually or altogether, made any dent upon the economy, politics, religion and social fabric of Egypt; truly life in Egypt went on as usual, as though nothing unusual had happened. The exodus-flight under Moses never qualified as "history" in Egyptian annals, and we possess very many of these; it would have been buried and forgotten in the sands of the Sinai desert, were it not for later developments.

Biblical religion began with an event that was insignificant, ahistorical and secular — the liberation of a small number of slaves. Yet, we must also emphasize a less visible, yet very important religious factor. The leader Moses was convinced that he had been summoned by God who had "witnessed the affliction of my people in Egypt and heard their cry of complaint against their slave drivers" (Exod 3:7). Moses acted in the name of a personal savior God who revealed the divine name as Yahweh, "the One always there [with you]." According to this explanation of the divine name Yahweh (adopted earlier in some form by Gerhard von Rad, *Old Testament Theology*. 1:180, and later in the commentary on *Exodus* by Brevard S. Childs, 69), God is promising to be always present. Herein lies the important intuition of God as a Savior who intervenes in space and time, especially in times of crisis like the Egyptian slavery.

(II) The second stage, once Israel had been liberated from slavery, again turned out to be insignificant, ahistorical and secular. If we read correctly between the lines of the biblical account about grumbling and the people's concern for "the fish we used to eat without cost in Egypt, and the cucumbers, the melons, the leeks, the onions, and the garlic" (Num 11:5), the liberated slaves celebrated their freedom and turned at once to their physical needs — and to complaints whenever these were not properly attended to. There were, nonetheless, a few religious-minded people like Moses and Miriam who praised God. One of the most ancient hymns of the Bible is the Song of Moses in Exod 15. The relevance of stage two lies in the fact that the liturgical actions in the next stage are forms of secular celebrations, stylized and religiously enhanced: i.e., eating becomes a sacred meal, fleeing out of Egypt becomes a sanctuary procession.

(III) The third stage marks the beginning of religion —religion in the technical sense of an organized way of worshipping God with symbolic actions and credal formulas, with song and sacred narrative, around a sacred object or at a sacred place, under the supervision of priests and ministers. The "Bible" originates at this point from the need of prayers, instructions, etc., in worshipping God the Savior. The Bible is not the product of a desire to record events.

This stage becomes necessary, first when a new generation no longer remembers the liberation, in this case, from slavery in Egypt, and second when *God's* presence in the liberating act is brought to center stage and becomes the important visible factor. Israel's religion, therefore, enabled future generations of people to relive the initial act of liberation in its spiritual significance. The migration out of Egypt becomes a sacred journey from sin to grace and is called by the sacred name of exodus. The people seek rest in the Lord (*cf.*, Deut 5:14; 12:10). Religion was intended, first to worship "the Lord ... your God, who brought you out of the land of Egypt, that place of slavery" and second to "remember that you too were once slaves in Egypt" (Deut 5:6, 15). Israel's religion assured the people that within their secular origins and development Yahweh, the liberating God, had acted out of personal compassion for the afflicted. In this transition from the secular to the sacred, liberation is transformed into the theological title of a redeemer God. By accentuating God's presence in Israel's secular origins, religion sharpened the people's faith in God's continuous presence in their contemporary secular life.

Religion made history! What had been insignificant, secular events, now became so important as to be the center around which scattered groups of Canaanites clustered with the invaders led by Joshua across the River Jordan to become the twelve tribes of Israel. Liturgy thus became the major factor in the formation of biblical material. What we read in the Bible, accordingly, is not so much an account of what really happened in coming out of Egypt as it is the way by which the reality of the exodus continued to be a real moral and religious force in the lives of later generations of people, by worship and instruction, by organization and hope.

The first appearances of prophecy stretched between stages two and three. Prophecy attempted to maintain the heroic origins of Israel as a force for liberating persecuted people and as an effective means of maintaining human justice and supplying basic human needs. Balaam the prophet in Num 22-24 could not be bought off by the wealthy presents of Balak, king of Moab; instead of cursing he blessed Israel. When elders were needed to assist Moses in meting out justice to the people (*cf.*, Exod 18 — note their secular, common-sense origin *before* the theophany of Sinai in chap. 19 of Exodus), "the spirit came to rest on them [and] they prophesied" (Num 11:25). This latter verse is textually difficult, but the translation of the *New American Bible* is fully justified, particularly in view of a later verse where Moses defends the right of others to prophesy, even if they had not been at the ordination ceremony (Num 11:16-17, 24-30). When Joshua complained against them, Moses replied, "Are you jealous for my sake? Would that all the people of the Lord were prophets!" (Num 11:29). Not only do we perceive an inherent danger of jealousy among prophets, but we observe Moses' defense of prophets who were directly chosen by God out of the rank and file without human authorization.

When prophecy appears again in the person of Deborah, Samuel, Elijah and Elisha, we meet individuals, fully engaged in the liberation of Israel from the threat of powerful kings at Hazor (Judg 4:2), from the iron chariots of the Philistines (Judg 1:19; 1 Sam 8-17), from the land grabbing greed of Israelite kings like Ahaz (1 Kgs 21), from hunger and sickness in the family (1 Kgs 17:17-24; 2 Kgs 4). In these popular forms of piety miracles occur. Prophets are associated with miracles, however, not to prove anything, nor to advance their own career, nor to exhibit extraordinary power, but rather to feed the hungry and cure the sick.

(IV) When liturgy forgot its insignificant, secular origins and degenerated into salaried careers for its personnel, prophets stormed upon the scene. Micah lashed out:

> Her leaders render judgment for a bribe,
> her priests give decision for a salary,
> her prophets divine for money,
> While they rely on the Lord, saying,
> "Is not the Lord in the midst of us?

No evil can come upon us!"
Therefore, because of you,
Zion shall be plowed like a field...
(Mic 3:11-12)

In fact God introduces a new kind of prophet. We call them the classical prophets, no longer functioning as advisers to kings like Nathan and Gad, certainly not depending upon miracles and the extraordinary presence of the spirit like Elijah and Elisha, not officially associated with temple or sancturaries like Samuel, not even using the name of prophet. As Bruce Vawter wrote in one of his latest works on prophecy, the first of the classical prophets, Amos of Tekoa, categorically denied belonging to those "prophets who were in the hire of courts, sanctuaries, and the like, prophets for favorable oracles, who could be dismissed at will," as the high priest Amaziah desired to do with Amos (*cf.*, Amos 7:12-15 — *Amos, Hosea, Micah* 68). Amos lashed back at the high priest Amaziah: "No *nabi* I, nor son of *nabi*. I was a herdsman and a dresser of sycamores, till Yahweh took me from behind the flock and told me: 'Go, prophesy to my people Israel'" (Vawter's translation from *The Conscience of Israel*, 75).

(V) The classical prophets' challenge to liturgy, in what is our fifth and final stage, itself evolved into its own liturgical texts. The preaching of the prophets became the books of the prophets. While religion recoiled from the sting and rebuff of prophets, religion was also responsible for some of the final editing of prophetical material, as we see in the final chapter of Habakkuk, or the overall shape of the prophecy of Micah. Prophecy as a book can be arranged and edited, it can be read selectively in discreet segments and it can always be put back on the shelf — or as a scroll, rolled up and placed again in the ark of the covenant. No living prophet could ever be returned to a proper place on the shelf, to be heard at a time more convenient to the congregation.

Still another example of prophetical impact upon liturgy is visible in Ps 22. While its first major section, vv. 2-22, was written under a strong presence of the prophet Jeremiah (see especially vv. 10-11), it modulates into a liturgical song of thanksgiving in vv. 23-27. Again under the possible influence of prophecy, this time Isa 40-66, the thanksgiving song was extended in vv. 28-32 to include the foreigners at the end of the earth, the sick and possibly the dying, finally the unborn. Those persons whom the Torah explicitly excluded from liturgical participation (Lev 21:16-23; Deut 23:1-9) are granted a place in the prophetical liturgy of Ps 22.

According to this five stage rubric in the formation and development of Israel's religion, prophecy kept religion in touch with its original purpose, liberation from oppression. Paradoxically, prophecy enabled religion to be genuinely religious in the biblical sense by bringing religion back to its secular origins. In this way prophecy maintained the intuition of God as Savior, against a momentum in organized religion to overemphasize the wonders of God Creator. With the flip of the coin we recognize that religion by transforming the fast dying secular memory of the flight out of Egypt into a sacred ceremony made history out of what would have been buried in the sands of Sinai. Without organized religion prophecy would never appear; without prophecy religion would not be worth surviving.

2. Who is Israel?
(See Bibliography numbers 2, 3, 7, 8, 9, 16, 17, 20, 24, 27)

In the second section of our study we focus upon the basic religious spirit of the Mosaic covenant at the core of prophecy. In seeking an answer to the question, "prophet, who are you?" we need to explore the implications of another, still more elementary question: *Who is Israel?* By getting to the heart of this query, we appreciate what prophecy was defending against false external forms in Israel's late religious and civil society.

We pursue the question, "Who is Israel?" according to three principal moments of Israelite history: in Egypt, in the wilderness, and in the period of the settlement in the land.

In Egypt "Israel" was a mixture of *'apiru* (outlaws or refugees, uprooted from their Asiatic habitat, tending from their origins to be politically centralized) and *shosu* (marauders, bonded in clans or individual tribes but otherwise politically decentralized, living in Edom and northward, harassing caravans). These were the conglomerate of Asiatics who fled or migrated into Egypt before and during the Joseph period (Gen 37-50).

During the exodus, "Israel" consisted of these *'apiru* and *shosu* along with the mixed multitude, which Exod 11:38 and Num 11:4 called *'ereb rab* and *ha'sapsup*, riffraff as the very sound of these Hebrew words connotes.

In the land of Canaan "Israel" emerged from a blend of many groups who had suffered oppression and deprivation. Roland de Vaux (*The Early History, 375*) refers to groups, some expelled from Egypt who had centered around Kadesh in the lower Negeb desert and then entered Canaan by the south; others who fled from Egypt, experienced the miracle of the Sea, camped at Sinai and eventually entered Canaan from the east or Transjordania. Still others in Canaan around Shechem never migrated into Egypt but were related to the Joseph tribes and quickly formed treaties with them (Josh 8:30-35; Judg 6-9); other local people, disenfranchised or reduced to slavery in Canaan, gravitated towards the invaders from the east in common cause against oppression.

Only under the organizational skill of David and Solomon was this motley group united, so that all claimed to be inheritors of patriarchal promises and so could consider themselves blood-bonded or fellow *go'alim.* If there be any common bonds, uniting the people as "Israel," it is summarized in two of the ten commandments: "I, the Lord, am your God, who brought you out of the land of Egypt, that place of slavery... Remember that you too were once slaves in Egypt" (Deut 5:6, 15). Israelite common bonds are those of oppression and liberation, of radical discontinuity from royalty and empires. "Israel" meant a rejection of the more centralized, stratified and controlled forms of life. Negatively, "Israel," according to an important position in this thesis, did not emerge from natural, biological, social or geographical bonds.

"Israel" consisted of people bonded in the belief that their liberation was ultimately due to God's free choice and covenant, to God's compassion for the oppressed, to a relation of equality among peoples and to a differentiation due to God's charismatic gifts which reached for the intuitive, secret potential within people.

Israel's leadership, therefore, was first entrusted to charismatic leaders whose spirit and attitude were institutionalized within: (a) priesthood who like early nomads possessed no land, never mourned the dead and were entirely dependent upon the Lord (Lev 23; Num 18:20; Deut 10:9); (b) Nazirites who appeared as desert warriors with hair unshorn, without alcohol or any contamination with the dead (Num 6:1-21); (c) the major judges with extraordinary exploits to their name in the Book of Judges, individuals specially gifted with the *ruah yahweh*; (d) ecstatic prophets, also strongly gifted with the spirit (1 Sam 10:5-6). Even other, more organizational types of leaders appear, like the elders, but these, as we saw already, were said to prophesy under the impact of the spirit (Num 11:24-30).

From this background we can summarize important aspects about the inner quality of Israel and of Israel's religion, that show up prominently in earlier and later prophecy.

(1) Israel emerged out of many, divergent forces and groups with no distinctive racial or cultural background. What they had in common was their liberation from oppression, which religion enabled them to recognize as the action of a Savior God. Through Yahweh's presence they were accustomed to face overwhelming opposition and to react with heroic strength. Even though prophecy bore a strong attachment to the earliest origins of Israel, nonetheless, it was bound to no single culture nor even to any style of government, civil or religious. It could be a

force for dramatic change — as when Samuel anointed the first two kings, Saul and David (1 Sam 10:1; 16:13), or when Nathan granted eternal promises to the Davidic line (2 Sam 7:14-15), something until then unheard of in Israel — or when a drastic reversal cut the tree of David to the ground, leaving only a dry stump on the surface (Isa 11:1) — or again when the privileges were returned to all the people, evident in the plural sense of the word "you" in the Hebrew text of Isa 55:4-5.

Prophecy thrived among the communities that clustered at such places as Jericho (2 Kgs 2:5-7), Gibeah (1 Sam 10:10), Rama (1 Sam 19:23), Bethel (2 Kgs 2:3) and Gilgal (2 Kgs 4:38). Here it organized itself familially by clan and by loyalty to the Sinaitic covenant. These groups were not friendly towards royalty, urban life and centralization, as we notice in the anti-monarchic traditions in 1 Sam 8 or in the activity of Elijah (1 Kgs 17-21). Even when prophets appear as royal chaplains in the person of Nathan and Gad (2 Sam 7:1-2; 2 Sam 24:13) and possibly led liturgical functions in the temple or at sanctuaries (possibly the case with Habakkuk and Nathan — see Lawrence Boadt, 165-7, 240-1) they also exercised an extraordinary independence in correcting kings, not simply in a formalistic cultic ceremony as happened with the Babylonians on their New Year's ceremony or *akitu*, but in secular, everyday life. Prophecy made heroic demands, almost without flinching, such as Isaiah's demand for faithful waiting instead of any alliance with Assyria in Isa 7 (see also Isa 30:15-18). Prophecy also announced Israel's reduction to slave status as *'anawim* (Zeph 2:3; 3:12) out of whose remnant a new people of Yahweh would emerge.

(2) Throughout prophecy Yahweh will appear primarily as savior rather than under the title of creator. The first clear announcement of Yahweh as creator did not come until the preaching of Jeremiah (Jer 27:5), yet even here in a context of Israel's salvation history. Jeremiah attributed creation to the same "outstretched arm," by which Yahweh brought Israel out of Egypt and led them through the wilderness (Deut 4:34). Prophecy ensured that biblical reli-

gion never focused too strongly upon first creation and the
initial foundation of city and dynasty at Jerusalem. If creation enters into prophecy, as in Amos' book, it appears
more as fragmentary hymns added by the later editor to
the preaching of the prophet (Amos 4:13; 5:8-9; 9:5-6).

(3) Prophecy was far more willing to take risks for the
future than to stabilize the ancient forms within religion
and politics. Jerusalem can be certainly destroyed as was
the ancient sacred city of Shiloh (Jer 7; 26); the dynasty can
be reduced to a hidden root whose life will be revived by
the spirit in God's own time (Isa 11). Prophecy could look
behind the several centuries of development in the Davidic
monarchy and see its restoration and reformation through
the lowly, forgotten city of Bethlehem where Jesse, the
father of David, once lived (1 Sam 16; Mic 5:1). The present moment, at times seemingly affluent, was risked for a
future of poverty. According to the prophets only just,
God-fearing people had a right to life and its prosperity
(Isa 11).

(4) Prophets remained "devoted Israelites," as Bruce
Vawter stated in an earlier quotation. Normally their reaction to non-Israelites was neutral at best, most often hostile, almost always suspicious even about friendly treaties
with them. Samuel sanctioned a herem war against the
Amalekites (1 Sam 15). From Amos onward almost every
prophetic book included a section called "oracles against
the nations," where some of their most brilliant writing
occurs. In fact, the most gifted of all prophets, Nahum, has
provided us with a book entirely against the foreign nation
of Assyria. At the same time prophecy could appeal to the
secular origins of Israel as a riffraff conglomerate of many
peoples to challenge one of Israel's most sacred traditions,
the exodus. We hear the fiery voice of Amos, asking the
people:

> Are you not like the Ethiopians to me,
>   O people of Israel, says the Lord?
> Did I not bring the Israelites from the land of Egypt
>   As I brought the Philistines from Caphtor
>   and the Arameans from Kir? (Amos 9:7)

Amos has reduced the exodus to its secular meaning, a migration from one place to another for sake of a better, more secure life. Every nation, the prophet reminds Israel, has had its migrations. What makes Israel's unique remains unanswered here in 9:7, but in another passage where the same liturgical formula is quoted, "I brought [you] up from the land of Egypt," Amos provides an answer. He turns to Yahweh's compassionate love for Israel: "You alone have I favored, more than all the families of the earth" (Amos 3:2). Yet where orthodox tradition would then add, "Therefore I will bless you," Amos declares, "Therefore I punish you."

Another unanswered, or better, unanticipated question comes to our mind. Is Amos implying that the migrations of other nations could be considered a sacred exodus, provided they would recognize by faith Yahweh's "outstretched arm"? Can we conclude that the symbols of the Bible can be reexpressed in the different histories of other peoples? Prophecy, even if it did not think of these questions in precisely this way, still endorses our right to ask them. This' prerogative is very clearly acted upon by prophets like Habakkuk and Jeremiah. In their preaching the questioning of God becomes the word of God for us!

It is interesting to note that Amos' radical questioning in 9:7 has been relegated to an appendix of one-liners. Each of the four statements in Amos 9:7, 8a, 8b-9, 10, may have some attachment to Amos' fifth vision in 9:1-6, as Hans Walter Wolff has shown. Yet the one-liners are clearly fragmentary and undeveloped, unlike the other oracles and discourses in Amos. Perhaps the implications of 9:7 were too radical and too disturbing to Israel's religious system, initially rejected from the editing of Amos' preaching and then later reinserted in this appendix.

In a number of other places prophecy borders on universal salvation, or at least on providing a message to foreigners (i.e., Isa 2:2-4 and Jer 1:5 before the exile; Isa 49:6 during the exile; Isa 56 & 66 after the exile) yet the intuition is never developed. The prophetical book of Jonah is the only exception to this observation. (See the book of Senior-Stuhlmueller, chap. 4.)

Prophecy, because of Isreal's mixed and confusing origins, exercised the freedom to challenge, condemn and even doom to destruction all external forms of Israel's religious and political establishment. These institutions, we must note, were already gifted with divine promises of everlasting survival! Prophecy could take dramatic risks for the sake of the poor, as God did in bringing ex-slaves and other riffraff out of Egypt. Prophecy worshipped a God who revealed the divine presence primarily as Savior, interacting at crucially difficult moments in Israel's history. Yahweh, therefore, was not venerated principally as a Creator God who must maintain the golden age, the royal city and sacred dynasty.

Because prophecy challenged Israel's religion (a) from its pre-religion stages when the people were struggling with mammoth secular problems and (b) from Israel's pre-national stage when the people were still a mixture from many ethnic, racial and social points of origin, prophecy was frequently tempted to recognize a universal scope to Israel's mission. The temptation was generally resisted, for only in the book of Jonah does prophecy formally address the question of universal salvation, and here only in four short chapters which are hardly a developed and integrated theology about the role of the nations in biblical religion.

3. The Names of the Prophet
(See Bibliography numbers 4, 10, 13, 23, 25)

We now take another approach: a study of the various words used for prophet in the Hebrew Bible. In view of the diversity just encountered, it is difficult to speak of a clearly defined office of prophet, nor can we oversimplify the matter by declaring the prophet to be an ecstatic or an occasional person summoned by God at a time of crisis. Prophets are seen in various roles, sociologically and psychologically, at times very involved, at other times on the periphery, at times closely associated with liturgy and the government of Israel, at other times seriously condemning these institutions. We approach this aspect by investigating the use of various terms or titles for prophecy.

Surely the most important one, at least in the long run, is *nabi'*. The word may have originated from an ancient Akkadian word, "to announce or to call out." Grammatically, the verb occurs only (a) in the passive (niphal) form, even though it is translated in the active sense in English translations, i.e., "you commanded the prophets not *to prophesy*" (Amos 2:12); or (b) in the intensive-reflective (hithpael) form, as in the example to be studied below (1 Sam 10:5-13). The noun form, *nabi'*, consisting of the a-i vowel sequence, would indicate again the passive state of the person, as in other instances, *mashiah* (Messiah or anointed one) *'ani* (the poor or afflicted one), *nazir* (Nazirite, one totally dedicated interiorly and exteriorly to the Lord — Num 6:1-21).

Though passive to the spirit of the Lord, these prophets were intensively active, as we noticed in 1 Sam 10:5-13. In this account Samuel is offering various signs to Saul that Yahweh has chosen him as king:

> After that you will come to Gibeath-elohim, where there is a garrison of the Philistines. As you enter that city you will meet a band of prophets, *in a prophetic state* — or as the *Bible de Jérusalem* (ed. 1974) translates the phrase, "et ils seront en délire" — coming down from the high place preceded by lyres, tambourines, flutes and harps. The spirit of the Lord will rush upon you, and you will be changed into another man. When you see these signs fulfilled, do whatever you judge feasible, because God is with you (1 Sam 10:5-7).

Samuel's reference to these prophets as a sign from the Lord surrounds them with respectability. However, the sequence of events when Saul joins them temporarily (1 Sam 10:9-13), even stripping himself and lying naked all that day and night (19:22-24), shows, as Bruce Vawter wrote in the *Jerome Biblical Commentary* (12:7), that this "profession [of *nabi'*] was regarded as hardly in keeping with responsible, respectable citizenship." Undoubtedly, the ecstatic fervor was contagious, surrounded as it was with music and dancing; the spirit of the Lord so transformed the person that they could be considered even a stranger to themselves, or as 2 Kgs 9:11 expressed it, "a madman."

The title, *nabi'*, seems more at home in northern traditions, as in the original nucleus of stories in 1 Sam. The references in the northern prophet Hosea are favorable (Hos 6:5; 9:7-8; 12:11, 14). When *nabi'* occurs in early southern traditions, we encounter a more negative evaluation. Amos refused the title (Amos 7:14). Isa 3:2-3 seems to link the *nabi'* with fortunetellers, magicians and charmers, while Isa 28:7 is a devastating attack upon the drunken priest and *nabi'*. Finally, Mic 3:5, 6, 11 cites the prophets as flagrant examples of greedy, venal leadership:

> Thus says the Lord, regarding the prophets
>   who lead my people astray;
> who, when their teeth have something to bite,
>   announce peace,
> But when one fails to put something in their mouth,
>   proclaim [literally, sanctify] war against him
>   (Mic 3:5).

We recognize in such passages as 1 Kgs 22, that prophets began to argue among themselves; this fact indicates a serious decline and disintegration in their leadership (see Simon John DeVries). The same conflict between the *nabi'*, as we saw already, occurred in Jer 28.

Another term for prophet, also accepted favorably in the north, is *ro'eh* or seer, an archaic term which has to be explained in 1 Sam 9:11 by means of *nabi'* and does not occur again till the postexilic age in the two books of Chronicles (except for the single reference in Isa 30:10). From the incident in 1 Sam 9, the *ro'eh* was a holy person, highly respected, who was associated with the official worship of the town and on occasion offered information for a fee.

From the north we derive another term, *'ish (ha) 'elohim* — *man of God*. We learn from such passages as 1 Sam

9:6-10 that it was a substitute for *ro'eh*, and from the Elijah story in 1 Kg 17:17-24 or the Elisha narrative in 2 Kgs 4:42-44, this person was peripheral to the mainline of society and worship, subject like Elijah to persecution, associated with fringe groups, called prophetic guilds, and (as Petersen adds) at times amoral, as when Elisha summoned a bear to massacre forty-two children who jeered at him as a "Baldhead!"

Finally there is the word *hozeh,* again to be translated *seer*. Isa 30:10 links *hozeh* and *nabi'* and speaks favorably of each; Amos from the southern city of Tekoa seems willing to accept the title of *hozeh* (7:12-15). Therefore, *hozeh* seems to have a particularly southern or Judahite focus. As the word implies, *hozeh* stresses the visionary aspect while *nabi'* the aspect of the spoken word. In such passages as Isa 1:1; 2:1; 13:1; Amos 1:1; Mic 3:1; Hab 1:1 the prophet is said to "see" the words which they speak. The vision, moreover, is associated with the prophet's mystical presence within the divine council of Yahweh, as we see in the inaugural visions of Amos (7:1-9; 8:1-3), Isaiah (chap. 6), and Ezekiel (chap 1-2). Commissioned within the divine council, the prophet spoke forthrightly to kings and nations about the morality of their political actions. Even the prophet Jeremiah appealed to 'the authority of having stood within the divine council in arguing against false prophets (Jer 23:18-22).

While these various titles for prophet, which we have just investigated, tended to blend and merge, still their early use individually enables us to draw some conclusions about prophecy. First, prophecy was not a distinctive office like levite or elder but rather a role which various persons assumed or were called to. The roles of prophet varied greatly, some like Samuel, the *ro'eh* or seer, acted in leadership roles in formal liturgical functions and were highly respected; others like Elijah, the *'ish [ha] 'elohim* or man of God, lived more on the periphery, possesed no recognized public place of authority yet acted mightily, even miraculously for the poor and oppressed. Another *'ish[ha] 'elohim.* Elisha, was closely associated with bands of prophets and their commune or families. Here we see miracles to provide for the needy and a style of living somewhat separate from the big cities and the government structure. Because the northern kingdom was far less centralized than the southern kingdom at Jerusalem, these prophetic communes are associated with the north. The *hozeh* or seer is a title of function given to southern prophets like Isaiah, Micah, and Habakkuk. These prophets are seen in their lore of being commissioned from the most high council of Yahweh and each of their words are buttressed with the authority of having been seen in a vision. The *hozeh* prophets are divine heralds, addressing, instructing and scolding kings from a strong moral stand in favor of Israel and in favor of decency and uprightness.

If there are any common elements among these roles of prophets, we detect: a strong sense of being designated by God to speak out or to act forcefully in the name of the ancient covenant (particularly with northern prophets) or in the name of decency and honesty (with southern prophets); a fearlessness in standing up against any human authority, even though it be divinely validated as priest or king, and not only correcting it but also declaring its demise, should it not reform. These prophets, consequently, are close to the common person, the type who is easily oppressed and taken advantage of. The slavery of Israel in Egypt became a type of oppression and liberation of the poor; the holy city of Jerusalem with its dynasty and temple became a type of risking all for the sake of a people united in justice and adoration before Yahweh, with extraordinary hopes for the future. If prophecy was not an office but a calling, individually received by anyone whom God finds to the divine choice, then the spirit of Moses remains intact. Yahweh called Moses out of the lowest of the tribes (Levi), a person who did not speak distinctly, to speak before kings and to deliver Yahweh's dispossessed motley group of people.

Last of all, after this investigation into the various titles for prophet, we have to admit that normally those individuals whom we call prophets with books to their names did

not call themselves prophets. The reverse is true only with
Ezekiel. They were not concerned with who they were but
with what they were to do in the name of the Lord. We
remember Amos' words, "I am no prophet ... but the
Lord said, 'Go! Prophesy to my people Israel.'" As
"devoted Israelites" they dreamed and labored for the people whom he chose and dearly loved, and for whose sake
the Lord was willing to lose everything they had gained
through divine blessing and help (city, dynasty, temple,
homeland) that Israel may be determined, as Micah
expressed it, to "do the right, to love goodness, and to walk
humbly with your God" (Mic 6:8). These words were
addressed to 'adam, the Hebrew word in Gen 1-2 for
humanity, male and female, without any racial, ethnic,
social or geographic distinctions. Prophecy inevitably finds
itself with the type of people whom Yahweh led out of
Egypt.

4. True and False Prophecy
(See Bibliography numbers 5, 6, 12, 16)

In this final section, we approach the question, *prophet,
who are you?* with a new specification. The question is
rephrased: true prophet, how do we distinguish you from
others who are false? Following the position of scholars like
G. von Rad and G. Quell, James A. Sanders agrees that
"the *exousia* [or convincing power] of the true prophet ...
simply is not subject to scientific analysis." Sanders then
quotes from L. Ramlot, to the effect that prophecy is "*mys-
tique en un sens large*" (Sanders, 29). True and false mysti-
cism is a very delicate line to detect, as we know biblically
from the extensive discussion, reaching back into pre-
Christian times, about the acceptability of the book and
the person of Ezekiel. Canonically this book hung on the
cliff for quite some time.

The question of true and false prophecy is raised often
enough in the Bible and of late has been addressed by
scholars.

In the Old Testament various criteria are advanced as a warning or condemnation against false prophecy. Each norm is correct, yet none of them is sufficient, and even altogether they do not provide a sure determinative of true prophecy. Perhaps the ultimate reason for the insufficiency lies in the fact that the Bible does not clearly and convincingly stand by a single interpretation even in quoting other biblical passages; on the face of it the Bible can even contradict the biblical statement which it is quoting. Compare the prophetical texts about beating swords into plowshares (Isa 2:4; Mic 5:3). and plowshares back into swords (Joel 4[3]:10). Still other related passages come to mind: i.e., relating Ps 68:19 with Eph 4:8; or Mic 5:1 with Matt 2:6; or again Hos 11:1 with Matt 2:15, and Hos 13:14 with 1 Cor 15:54-55. From the viewpoint that each biblical text is infallibly true and its meaning eternally the same, we are faced with the conclusion that the Bible is erroneous in places and attempted to correct itself. If, however, we view the problem according to the suggestion here, each biblical passage was a pastoral attempt to refine the will of God at different moments and for different circumstances. As the wise preacher expressed the dilemma in the book of Ecclesiastes: "There is an appointed time for everything . . . a time to be born, and a time to die; . . . to kill and to heal . . ." (Eccles 3:1-8). We are dealing more with various pastoral moments than with speculative statements of orthodox theology.

Beneath our discussion lies the assumption that the person(s) arriving at a judgment of true or false prophecy need to be gifted with more than systematic orthodox theology. Two most important ingredients in deciding true or false prophecy can be identified as (a) intuition into the complex psychological situation and (b) common sense to determine how the best is humanly possible. These two qualities provide anyone making use of the following set of criteria with an insight into what enables people to respond *pastorally* to God's presence, especially at times of crises. Prophetic ministry leads people to react prayerfully, peacefully, uprightly, humbly, and even heroically.

True and false prophecy then may amount to the charism of pastoral effectiveness. Sanders expressed this idea in a striking way: "The false prophets invoked an otherwise decently good theology but at the wrong time..." (p. 31). He comments with this example: "Deutero-Isaiah said Yes to what Ezekiel fifty years earlier had said No." Each prophet referred to God's promises to Abraham and Sarah (Ezek 33:24; Isa 51:2). Ezekiel concludes that "the mountains of Israel shall be so desolate that no one will cross them" (Ezek 33:28), while Deutero-Isaiah assures Zion that "the Lord shall ... have pity on all her ruins; her deserts he shall make like Eden, her wasteland like the garden of the Lord" (Isa 51:3). Both are true prophecies even though directly opposite in their application of God's earlier promises to Abraham in Gen 12:2-3; 17:3-8.

Each of the following criteria has its own validity for specific occasions. As the situation modulates, so must the criteria.

(1) Among the least frequently cited criteria for true prophecy is the moral argument. It is adopted by Mic 3:5-12. This passage, quoted earlier in this study, condemns the greedy prophets. Ezek 13:17-21 excoriates prophetesses "who prophesy their own thoughts," and Isaiah angrily lashed at prophets "staggering [from wine and strong drink] in their visions, tottering when giving judgment" (Isa 28:7). Yet a closer reading of each passage leaves us unsure whether or not we have a fail-safe criterion for true prophecy. Micah and Isaiah are denouncing other religious leaders along with prophets; Ezekiel will not tolerate the false claim of the prophetesses over life and death. Finally, the bitter sarcasm of Amos in calling the women of Samaria obese cows (4:1) and Jeremiah's crude sexual reference in 5:8 for the men of Jerusalem ("lustful stallions" in the NAB reads literally "horses with strong testicles") put a few dents on the halo of the canonical prophets.

(2) Another disqualifying mark on a true prophet is identified in "urging you to follow other gods whom you have not known" and speaking in their name (Deut 13:2; 18:20; also Jer 2:8; 23:13). Yet other prophets who spoke in *Yah-*

weh's name were clearly enough condemned, like those in 1
Kgs 22, or the prophet Hananiah in Jer 28. The question of
monotheism and polytheism, moreover, was not as crucial
in the pre-exilic days as during the exile; Deut 4:19; 29:25
& 32:8-9 somewhat quietly leave the other gods to the
other nations. In the days of Jeremiah the problem became
more subtle; "Baal" prophets were clothed in the mantle of
"Yahweh" prophets. Only during the exile does a prophet
determinately argue the case that Yahweh alone is God (Isa
41:4, 21-24; 43:9-12; 48:11-13).

(3) Can we distinguish the true from the false prophet by the
manner of their receiving revelation and hidden knowledge? Dreams are frequently a genuine means for Yahweh
to communicate with his servants, as far back as Abraham
(Gen 15:12), Joseph (Gen 37:5; 40:4-8), and Balaam, one of
the first prophets in the Bible (Num 22-24). Yet in Num
12:6-8 we are told that dreams while acceptable are nonetheless to be judged by Moses and Mosaic tradition. Jer
29:8-9 explicitly warns the people against being "deceived
by the prophets and diviners who are among you; do not
listen to those among you who dream dreams. For they
prophesy lies to you in my name." Yet these verses like v.
15 seem to be later, albeit inspired additions to Jeremiah's
words and are juggled around into a different arrangement
of verses in the NAB.

(4) A frequent enough criterion in the career of a true
prophet like Isaiah (chap. 6) and Jeremiah (Jer 23:18, 22) is
seen in their presence within the heavenly council of Yahweh. However, in 1 Kgs 22:19-23, the [true] prophet sees a
vision of "the Lord seated on his throne with the whole
host of heaven standing by to his right and to his left."
Among the hosts are those who ask to "go forth and
become a living spirit in the mouths of all his [King Ahab's
false] prophets." "The Lord replied, "You shall succeed in
deceiving him. Go forth and do this." It is interesting that
the very throne from where Isaiah receives his call is the
place where the lying spirits originate! Evidently, no matter
how important this criterion may have been for Jeremiah,
it is not sufficient by itself.

(5) The fulfillment of prophecy is another important criteri-

on, at least for Deut 18:21-22 and in a battery of texts about Yahweh first and last in Deutero-Isaiah (Isa 41:1-5; 41:21-29 + 42:8-9; 43:8-13, 16-21; 44:6-8; 45:18-22; 46:8-13; 48:1-11, 12-19). This way of judgment would be more generally applicable for our problem of true and false prophecy if the main purpose of prophecy was prediction, which it is not. In fact, the innovative study of Robert P. Carroll shows how the non-fulfillment of prophecy, even for the early church in the non-return of Jesus in glory, became a most important factor in the theological reorganization and brilliant expanse of a religious group. We have examples, already in Old Testament times, of prophecy-predictions never fulfilled: like the return of the northern tribes announced by Jeremiah in chap. 31; or the everlasting dynasty of David through an heir to come from the seed of David's loins (2 Sam 7:12-16). Ultimately this criterion's weakness shows up in the simple consideration: is a prophet like Jesus proven to be false because his hopes and announcements are not fulfilled within the lives and times of any group of Jesus' disciples?

We are offered then a number of criteria for determining true and false prophecy. To make effective use of these we need insight and good judgment as to how the ideals of God, expressed in crucial, creative moments of Israel's history, can be realized with the greatest amount of peace for the community of God's people. These criteria may at times be applicable to other offices in Israel, like elder or priest (Mic 3:11), yet prophecy does not have the benefit of more visible signs of authenticity: by birth within tribe and family for priests; or formal acceptance in the case of elders (*cf.*, Num 11:16-17, 24-25).

Conclusion

Our answer to the question, *prophete, qui es-tu?* may seem as elusive as in the beginning. If any clues emerge, the following may offer some assistance. Prophecy continues *the heroic moments* of Israel's origins, as we saw in Israel's evolution from nomads fleeing from oppression to a people settled in their own land. Later when the great moments were to be celebrated liturgically as the *mirabilia Dei*, these wonders tended to be submerged beneath rubrics, temples, priestly careers and wealth. Liturgy forgot its origin and purpose, to liberate slaves from oppression, and had become the oppressor of its own people. Even the early bands of prophets were co-opted into this scheme. Here is where the classical prophets were summoned out of the desert like Amos to shout in God's name, "I hate, I spurn your feasts" (Amos 5:21). Liturgy was not to be corrected by better rubrics, but as Isaiah pointed out, people were told to:

> Put away your misdeeds...
>   cease doing evil; ...
> make justice your aim; redress the wronged,
>   hear the orphan's plea, defend the widow
>   (Isa 1:16).

Prophets reached behind religion's ritual and organization to the pre-religion stage of Israel. Prophets were so difficult to deal with because they challenged religion on its non-religious or secular basis!

In the second stage of our study we saw that prophecy instinctively drew upon the origins of Israel which were not rooted in race, social strata, and geography. Israel was a royal mixture! In the name of a savior God who was compassionately willing to work within any human situation, even the most desperate, prophecy went to the brink of glimpsing the salvation of the nations.

Prophecy was not an office nor a specific state. It was a role to which anyone, regardless of sex or social position, could be summoned by God. The various titles for this role, we saw in the third section, tended to highlight a special or individual commissioning by God, an ability to peer deeply into reality, the association with the poor and needy, an exceptional sense of living and acting under divine compulsion, a dedication to ancient tradition and to the community of God's people.

In pursuing the norms for judging true and false
prophets, we were given many pieces of advice, like speaking in the name of the true God, not being greedy or
immoral, a perception of the future within the agony of the
present moment, awesome presence in the divine assembly.
Yet, to use these criteria properly, we not only need to
choose the one(s) more appropriate to the situation but we
also have to act with particular insight into the human
setting and to call upon solid common sense.

We ask if all this can be summarized still more succinctly. Years ago we attempted this definition: prophets
are those persons, 1) so fully and consistently members of
their community and in touch with its charism and founding inspiration, 2) so perceptive and articulate that 3) as a
result they bring the internal challenge of the community's
conscience — its hopes and ideals — to bear upon the
external form of the community's life-style and work. By
challenging the present moment with the finest, divinely
inspired ideals, prophets were announcing the future —
eventually that future when the divine word became flesh
and dwelt among us.

Bruce Vawter capsulized the entire discussion in the title
to his book, *The Conscience of Israel.* With this book and
his other works on prophecy, coupled with his exceptional
clarity and insight, we can proceed onward and hopefully
blend other studies into the task for each generation to
answer, *prophète, qui es-tu?*

BIBLIOGRAPHY

1. Blenkinsopp, Joseph. *A History of Prophecy in Israel.*
Philadelphia: Westminster, 1983.

2. Boadt, Lawrence. *Jeremiah 26-52, Habakkuk, Zeph-
aniah, Nahum.* Wilmington: Glazier, 1982.

3. Brueggemann, Walter. "Trajectories in Old Testament
Literature and the Sociology of Ancient Israel." *JBL* 98
(1979) 161-85.

4. Buss, Martin J. "The Social Psychology of Prophecy." *Prophecy. Essays Presented to Georg Fohrer.* Berlin; New York: de Gruyter, 1980. 1-11.

5. Carroll, Robert P. *When Prophecy Failed.* New York: Seabury-Crossroad, 1979.

6. Crenshaw, James L. *Prophetic Conflict.* Berlin & New York: de Gruyter, 1971.

7. Gottwald, Norman K. *The Tribes of Yahweh.* Maryknoll, NY: Orbis, 1979

8. Gottwald, Norman K., and Frank S. Frick. "The Social World of Ancient Israel." *Seminar Papers 1975.* Society of Biblical Literature. Missoula, MT: Scholars Press, 1975. I:165-78.

9. Halpern, Baruch. *The Emergence of Israel in Canaan.* Chico, CA: Scholars Press, 1983.

10. Koch, Klaus. *The Prophets.* Vol. 1. Philadelphia: Fortress, 1983.

11. Monloubou, L. *Prophète qui es-tu?* Paris: Cerf, 1968.

12. Munderlein, Gerhard. *Kriterien wahrer und falscher Prophetie.* Bern: Peter Lang, 1974; 2 ed. 1979.

13. Petersen, David L. *The Roles of Israel's Prophets.* Sheffield: Sheffield UP, 1981.

14. Rast, Walter E. *Tradition History and the Old Testament.* Philadelphia: Fortress, 1972.

15. Sanders, James A. "Hermeneutics in True and False Prophecy." *Canon and Authority.* Eds. George W. Coats & Burke O. Long. Philadelphia: Fortress, 1977. 21-41.

16. Senior, Donald, and Carroll Stuhlmueller. *Biblical Foundations for Mission.* Maryknoll, NY: Orbis, 1983.

17. Spina, Frank Anthony. "*Israelites* as *gerim*, 'Sojourners,' in Social and Historical Context." *The Word*

of the Lord Shall Go Forth. Philadelphia: American Schools of Oriental Research, 1983. 321–35.

18. Stuhlmueller, Carroll. "History as the Revelation of God in the Pentateuch." *Chicago Studies* 17 (1978) 29–43.

19. —————. *Psalms.* Wilmington: Glazier, 1983.

20. de Vaux, Roland. *The Early History of Israel.* Philadelphia: Westminster, 1978.

21. Vawter, Bruce. *Amos, Hosea, Micah.* Wilmington: Glazier, 1981.

22. —————. *The Conscience of Israel.* New York: Sheed & Ward, 1961.

23. —————. "Introduction to Prophetic Literature." *Jerome Biblical Commentary.* Eds. Raymond E. Brown, et al. Englewood Cliffs, NJ: Prentice-Hall, 1968. 223–37.

24. Vogel, Walter. *Le Prophète, Un Homme de dieu.* Montréal: Bellarmin, 1973.

25. de Vries, Simon John. *Prophet Against Prophet.* Grand Rapids: Eerdmans, 1978.

26. Wilson, Robert R. *Prophecy and Society in Ancient Israel.* Philadelphia: Fortress, 1983.

27. Wolff, Hans Walter. *Joel and Amos.* Philadelphia: Fortress, 1977.

THE WRITINGS

Roland E. Murphy, O. Carm.
The Divinity School — Duke University

The *Ketubim*, or Writings, are the third and final division of the Hebrew Bible, the Tanak. This seems to have been an open-ended collection of disparate works in the intertestamental period. The process by which it was formed, and how it came to be a closed canonical collection, remains a mystery. It contains *nova et vetera*, Daniel and Psalms, and in the Hebrew and Greek traditions the deviations in the sequence of the books can be seen as symbolic of their variety and acceptance in the community. It would be impossible to do justice to all of them in a survey. Hence we will concentrate on a limited area: the so-called wisdom literature, Psalms, the Chronicler, and Daniel.

1. Wisdom Literature (See Bibliography numbers 3,5,10,12,14,17,18,22-30,35-37,39-40)

Although some are of the opinion that wisdom literature is a misnomer for the books it is used to characterize, the phrase has caught on, and it well serves to designate Proverbs, Job, Ecclesiastes, and among the so-called apocrypha, Sirach and the Wisdom of Solomon. It has even been borrowed by Egyptologists and students of Mesopotamian literature to designate the type of literature in the ancient Near East that is comparable to these works. In general there has been a startling upswing in wisdom studies since World War II.[1] Roman Catholic tradition had always tended to emphasize wisdom literature, since it included Sirach and Wisdom in the canon. While Protestant and Jewish scholarship gave due emphasis to Job and Qohelet, there was less of a tendency to see the wisdom movement as a whole. This has now changed, so that an area that was once regarded somewhat as an orphan, and even set apart from "true" biblical theology, has become an exciting field. Now the question is, one may somewhat facetiously say, what is not wisdom? Several reputable scholars have claimed that wisdom influence can be detected in the primeval history (Gen 2–3), the Joseph story (Gen 37–50), the Succession Narrative (2 Sam 9–20 and 1 Kgs 1–2), Amos, Isaiah, Esther, and several Psalms. This aspect of research has perhaps gone overboard, and there is a need to establish satisfactory criteria for judging proper wisdom "influence."[2]

The landmark study in the field is Gerhard von Rad's *Weisheit in Israel.*[3] The German scholar has long been a successful exponent of salvation history in Israel, and then towards the end of his life he produced a study of Israelite wisdom (including Sirach) that is full of insights. It is perhaps more provocative than definitive, but it stands as the most successful synthesis to date.

Under the influence of the great discoveries of Egyptian literature in the twentieth century, it was thought that a book like Proverbs must be the result of a royal court

[1]This is documented in Murphy, "Hebrew Wisdom" (**Bibliog. no. 27**), where one can find a more complete bibliography and statement of issues. Cf. the representative articles in the collection edited by Crenshaw (**Bibliog. no. 10**).

[2]See article, "Method in Determining Wisdom Influence upon 'Historical' Literature" in Crenshaw 481-94 (**Bibliog. no. 10**).

[3]See **Bibliog. no. 39.**

school in Jerusalem. The argument was based upon parallel phenomena in the ancient Near East. The Egyptian "teachings" (*Sebayit*), so remarkably similar to the counsels and sayings in Israel, were authored and transmitted in the scribal school of the Egyptian court. Similarly, the bilingual (Sumerian and Babylonian) sayings and compositions were seen to be attached to the kind of school that the Sumerians called "e-dubba," or "house of tablets." But it soon came to be realized that this was too narrow a basis for the setting of Israelite wisdom. Rather, tribal and family wisdom and training played a basic role in the origin of the sayings that become current in Israel. Schools and scribes doubtless assisted in the development and transmission of traditional Israelite wisdom. But there is a dearth of knowledge about the precise setting of the wisdom teachers before or after the Exile. We know from Eccl 12:9 only that Qohelet "taught the people knowledge, and weighed, scrutinized and arranged many proverbs," and that Ben Sira could issue an invitation, "take up lodging in the house of instruction" (Sir 51:23). But the precise life setting of the sages is difficult to establish.

Progress has been made, however, in determining the typical literary genres employed by the sages: proverbial sayings (Prov 10–21), rather lengthy consecutive wisdom poems (Prov 1–9; Sirach, *passim*), admonitions (Prov 22–24, which bears striking similarity to the teaching of the Egyptian sage, Amenemope), disputation speeches (the debate between Job and the three friends in Job 3–31), reflections (characteristic of the observations found in Ecclesiastes), hymns (Sir 42:15–43:35), and even midrash (Wis 11–19).[4]

The striking characteristic of the wisdom literature is its consistent indifference to the sacred traditions of Israel: the promises to the Fathers, the Exodus, Sinai and Moses and the covenant. It is only at the end of the movement that they appear (in the "praise of the fathers" in Sir 44–50, and

---

[4]For a full discussion of sapiential literary genres, see **Bibliog. no. 30.**

the midrash on the plagues in Wis 11–19). This fact ties in with the international stamp which wisdom has. It is with the wisdom of the people of the East and of Egypt that the wisdom of Solomon is compared (ET, 1 Kgs 5:9–10). Although Solomon is the sage *par excellence* in the Israelite tradition (in the sense that he is a patron, rather than author), the wisdom of non-Israelites is included: Agur in Prov 30:1–6 and Lemuel in Prov 31:1–9. Job is described as a foreigner from the land of Uz, and his three friends are non-Israelites. None of them have recourse to the episodes of traditional salvation history; their dialogue is played out against the background of experience and traditional teaching, but in an Israelite style.

What is the stuff of Israelite wisdom? G. von Rad has described it as "a response made by a Yahwism confronted with specific experiences of the world" (p. 307). This dynamic relationship in which the Israelite stood in relation to environment, the experience with other humans, with animals, with the entire creation, created a search for what was called "wisdom" (*hokmāh*). It is essentially a practical wisdom, how to cope with the vicissitudes of life. But the lessons which experience communicated came to be phrased in catchy sayings and cautious admonitions; such formed the "teachings" of the sage.

Another way of putting this is to say that wisdom theology is creation theology. Israel looked to God's creation for insights into the problems of living. The ant can teach diligence (Prov 6:6–8); although the bee is the least of winged creatures, it reaps the choicest of harvest (Sir 11:3); even the mountain goats teach human beings about God's care (Job 39:1–4). What might seem to be the least of creatures, such as rock-badgers, locusts and lizards, can communicate wisdom lessons (Prov 30:26–28).

Creation includes other people—how is one to live with them? If the Decalogue set down some general rules of morality, the advice of the sages is aimed at broad moral formation: what kind of character is one to have? The virtues of diligence, honesty, self-control (especially of the tongue), are among the most frequently inculcated. There is a steady contrast in Prov 10–16 between the wise/virtuous and the foolish/wicked. "Fear of the Lord," an umbrella term which ranges from a basic awe before the numinous to a practical moral observance, is the "beginning" of wisdom, i.e., it leads to wisdom.

Although the sages were aware of ambiguities and hence of the limitations of wisdom (Prov 21:30–31), they worked on the principle that true wisdom brought life, while folly or wickedness yielded destruction (Prov *passim*; Ps 37, etc.). A fateful dialogue developed: how is one to understand the suffering of one who is wise and virtuous, and the prosperity of the foolish and wicked? The book of Job was written precisely to broaden the question, to put down the over-simplification represented by Job's three friends.

If the author was without an answer, as human beings have been ever since and before, he brought to bear all that the Israelite tradition had to say on the topic. One of the most important questions raised in the Bible is found in the mouth of the "Satan," no less: "Is it for nothing that Job is God-fearing?" (1:9; cf. 2:3). Indeed, questions tinged with irony flow through the work.[5] Although the speeches of Elihu (a sorry figure?) remain a problem for the unity of the work, recent commentators[6] have wisely decided to explain the book as it stands. This is true even for the enigmatic disappearance of Zophar and the unlikely views of Job in chaps. 25–27. The various attributions of parts of these chapters to Bildad, Zophar, and Job—as posed by scholars of every hue—have met with little success. Something is wrong with the text, surely one of the most difficult in the Hebrew Bible, but the surgical operation is likely to kill the patient.

Qohelet was not insensitive to the issue of the suffering of the innocent (4:1–3; 9:1–3). But he takes up an even more fundamental issue: is there any meaning to life? His verdict is well-known: "vanity of vanities" (1:2; 12:8, the

[5]See Janzen (**Bibliog. no. 18**) 17-22.
[6]See **Bibliog. nos. 3, 18.**

inclusio for the book). This is not an idle and easy conclusion in the style of traditional Christian asceticism which
counts the world as nothing in view of the glory to come. It
is a fundamental assertion about *this* world, a world which
made no sense to Qohelet. And the reason is clearly given:
no one (not even the wise!) knows what God is doing (3:11;
8:17; 11:5). As in the case of the book of Job there has been
a growing tendency among scholars[7] to explain Ecclesiastes as all of one piece instead of resorting to glosses by
various later hands that would have softened the harshness
of Qohelet's views. These alleged glosses turn out to be
singularly unsuccessful; Ecclesiastes is a genuinely disturbing book to any fundamentalist interpretation of Scripture.
Qohelet critiqued the insights of traditional wisdom, but he
was recognized as a "wise man" (12:9) even if he admitted
that wisdom was beyond his reach (7:23). The dialogue of
wisdom with the world continued beyond him into Sirach
and the Wisdom of Solomon, without stripping the ways
of God with humans of their mystery—even asserting the
primacy of wisdom as a way of life.

The most engaging, if mysterious, theological development is the personification of Wisdom as a woman (Job 28;
Prov 1,8,9; Sir 24; Wis 7-9). Personification is no stranger
to the Bible, but the extent to which wisdom is personified
is quite unusual, so much so that many authors prefer to
speak of hypostasis, but without explaining how this fits
into postexilic monotheism. It has long been customary to
identify personified wisdom as a divine attribute, and some
scholars still maintain this. But divine attribution does not
do justice to the development of the figure of wisdom
throughout the literature. In a well-researched monograph
B. Lang[8] has concluded that Lady Wisdom is a personification of Israelite school wisdom; the didactic style of the
teacher is reflected in her discourse (Prov 1, 8, 9). Gerhard
von Rad explicitly denies that wisdom is merely an attrib-

[7]See **Bibliog.** no. 14.
[8]See **Bibliog.** no. 22.

ute of God, and in a somewhat mystical vein he wrote of her as the "self-revelation of creation."[9]

In the most general sense personified wisdom is a divine communication; she finds her delight with both God and humans (Prov 8:30–31). This divine communication could be identified with the Law which the Lord covenanted with Israel. The author of the Wisdom of Solomon stressed more her divine origin and nature; she is "an aura of the might of God and a pure effusion of the glory of the Almighty...the spotless mirror of the power of God" (Wis 7:25–26). The figure of wisdom moves also into the New Testament, serving as a background to the logos doctrine in the first chapter of the Gospel of John; Paul is able to describe Christ as the supreme communication, "the wisdom of God" (1 Cor 1:24).

The wisdom "apocrypha," Ecclesiasticus and Wisdom of Solomon, have always received due attention in Catholic scholarship, since they are considered to be part of the canon. But they were also important among Jews and Protestants as examples of currents of thought in the intertestamental period. The wisdom of Ben Sira may have received the name "church book" (*Liber Ecclesiasticus*) from its extensive use in the early Church. There was a renewed interest on all sides in this work when most of the original Hebrew text became known to the western world by the discovery of Solomon Schechter in 1896. The Hebrew text had dropped out of sight since the time of St. Jerome (about 400, although it was known to the Jews, and it seems to have been a medieval text of the Jewish Karaite sect that Schechter recovered in the old Cairo synagogue. This discovery kindled new studies of Ecclesiasticus at the time, but the interest faded until recently. Then the discovery of more Hebrew fragments of Ben Sira in one of the Dead Sea caves, and also at Masada, has spurred what can be called a veritable renaissance in Sirach studies.

[9]This is the title of a chapter in *Wisdom in Israel* (144–76) (**Bibliog. no. 39**). I think von Rad was more on target in *Old Testament Theology* I.441-53 (**Bibliog. no. 38**), where he stresses that wisdom is a revelation of God, even if through creation. See now Murphy, "Wisdom and Creation" (**Bibliog. no. 29**).

Among these may be singled out the monographs of J. Marböck, L. Prato and J. Haspecker concerning wisdom, theodicy, and fear of the Lord in Ecclesiasticus.[10] There is no longer any credence in the view that Ben Sira represents a religious decline. His emphasis on legal piety is not legalism. He offers a decidedly optimistic, and sane,view of life, even if he does not confront reality in the style of Job and Ecclesiastes.

A good modern commentary on this lengthy work is still a *desideratum*, and the forthcoming Anchor Bible commentary by A. Di Lella and the late Patrick W. Skehan should remedy this lack. Skehan's pioneer work on the text of Ecclesiasticus prepared for the excellent translation which is found in the New American Bible. This is at present the best English translation available, because it works critically with both the Hebrew and the Greek texts, not to mention the Syriac. Most vernacular translations are simply a version of the Greek text, without the necessary text-critical work.

The Wisdom of Solomon is an unusual Jewish work in that it is written in Greek, probably by an Alexandrian Jew of the first century B.C. It is a remarkable example of the coming together of Judaism and Hellenism. On the one hand, it reflects such a Greek commonplace as the four cardinal virtues (Wis 8:7); on the other hand it is an intensely Jewish work which arrives at a doctrine of immortality, not from the nature of the soul or the human composite, but from the relationship of humans to God ("justice is undying" [Wis 1:15]). It provides an interesting combination of salvation history and wisdom, a phenomenon strange in the sapiential tradition, when it describes wisdom as a savior figure in the history of the patriarchs and Moses (chap. 10), and then presents a midrashic exposition of the plagues of Egypt. As in Ben Sira (chap. 24), wisdom has broadened to include the old traditions of the

[10]See **Bibliog. nos. 25, 35, 17,** respectively.

covenant. The best introduction to the work is the volume by C. Larcher, whose commentary has started to appear.[11]

The Song of Songs deserves attention here. It is not technically wisdom literature; it is a collection of love poetry, without doubt.[12] But there is an increasing tendency among recent scholars (E. Würthwein, B. Childs, et al.) to recognize that the assembling and preservation of the poems were probably due to Israelite sages who found here values that were in harmony with the way of wisdom. In other words, the canonical form raises the question of the hermeneutical level of understanding that is appropriate to the work.

The Song has had an importance in history out of all proportion to its size. More "commentaries" were written on it in the Middle Ages than on any other book in the Old Testament; from the 12th century alone we have some thirty works. Over the centuries one could count on Roman Catholic scholars to be on the side of the traditional (or "allegorical" so-called) interpretation fixed by Origen, Gregory the Great, Bernard of Clairvaux and a host of writers. But over the last thirty years there has been a remarkable change of direction in Catholic understanding of the book.[13] The literal sense is now generally recognized to be concerned with love between man and woman. The change can be dramatically illustrated by the splendid commentary of Pere A. Robert of the Institut Catholique of Paris. In 1956 he published an annotated translation of the Song in the French "*Bible de Jérusalem*" (from which the popular English translation derives, the Jerusalem Bible). After his death in 1955 a first-class scholarly commentary by him was published by A. Feuillet and R. Tournay (1963). Robert had worked out a scholarly argument

---

[11]See **Bibliog. nos. 23, 24.**

[12]See **Bibliog. no. 12.**

[13]This is well-documented in the summary of the history of interpretation in Pope (89-229) (**Bibliog. no. 34**). The most recent study, by Fox, (**Bibliog. no. 12**), firmly anchors the Song against the background of Egyptian love poetry. His illustration of the love themes and the nature of the love relationship is very much on target.

for the traditional interpretation, based on the recognition of "anthological composition" in the Song. "Style anthologique," as the French scholar viewed it, is a midrashic method in which the choice of words and images in a composition is deliberately made, to suggest the level of meaning intended by the writer. Words from earlier biblical writings are re-used. The terms are repeated in a context which express the same or analogous thought. For example, the "mountains of *btr*" in Cant 2:17 is translated as "mountains of the covenant" by Robert. He reasoned that *btr* which means "cut in two," recalls Abraham's separation of the covenantal sacrifice related in Gen 15. Hence the "mountains of the covenant" are those of the country promised to Abraham when he offered the sacrifice which sealed the covenant. It must be confessed that these and other arguments have not really succeeded in winning any consensus. Despite the fact that "anthological composition" is a recognizable feature in late postexilic writings such as the Qumran *Hodayot*, and Wisdom of Solomon, its application to the Song seems to be mistaken. It is noteworthy that the notes for the second edition of the French *Le Bible de Jérusalem* (1974) have been entirely rewritten, and replaced by what one may call the current Catholic interpretation: the Song deals with love between a man and a woman.

But that is not the end of the matter. The history of the exegesis of the Song poses an interesting hermeneutical question to present day exegetes: what is the validity of the traditional understanding? Is it possible to mount arguments, other than mismatched allegorical considerations, in favor of the view that the Song indeed bears on human love, but also on the love between God and humans?

The present writer thinks a case can be made for the traditional view, but not by way of allegory or anthological composition or by the "fuller sense."[14] The first argument

---

[14]The scholar whom this volume honors wrote an article early on concerning the inadequacy of the fuller sense in general. See **Bibliog. no. 36.**

stems from the *fact* that any text comes to have more meaning than the literal historical sense meant by the author(s). The Bible is not an exception to the fate of any literary text; a surplus of meaning is acquired as the text is handed down among the community. Secondly, historical methodology can serve to correct the vagaries in surplus meaning, and at the same time perhaps provide support for it. In this case the symbolism of sex in the Bible, particularly the metaphor of married sexual union to convey the covenant relationship (Hos 1–3; Isa 65:5, etc.), is significant. In biblical thinking sex was seen to have the intrinsic potential of expressing divine love. The traditional interpretation, aside from its penchant for allegory, is basically in line with the biblical evaluation of sex. Finally, with some caution, one may find in 8:6 the characterization of human love as "a flame of Yah" (*salhebetyāh*, which is rendered in various ways by translators). The function of Yah (or Yahweh) can be seen as an indication that human love is somehow related to divine love. This interpretation is somewhat moot, but it deserves consideration.[15]

2. The Psalms (See Bibliography numbers 1,2,6,9,11,13,19,20,33,38)

The most significant twentieth century contribution to the study of the psalter is the form-critical studies of Herman Gunkel (*Einleitung*, 1933; *Kommentar*, 1926). Through a study of linguistic formulae and comparison with extra-biblical "psalms" in Egypt and Mesopotamia, he firmly established the characteristic of various literary genres: song of praise or hymn, thanksgiving (individual and collective), lament (individual and collective), royal, liturgical, etc. His basic categories have been modified and sometimes improved upon by later scholarship: Sigmund Mowinckel called attention to the liturgical setting of the

[15]See **Bibliog 28.**

psalms, even if his views on a feast of the Lord's enthrone-
ment may be exaggerated; C. Westermann contributed
important studies on the lament and the hymn.[16] But it was
Gunkel who cut through the welter of historicizing commentary (e.g., the alleged "Maccabean" psalms), and who
raised the right questions. All subsequent study of the
Psalms is dependent upon his pioneering work.

The Pontifical Biblical Institute in Rome has contributed in an important way to the ongoing study of the
psalter. In 1945 the Jesuit professors of the Institute published the so-called *Psalterium Pianum*, a Latin translation
ordered by Pope Pius XII. It is based on a careful assessment of the Hebrew text and the ancient versions, and its
text-critical work formed the basis of the English translation found in the current Catholic American version, the
New American Bible. One of the Jesuit professors of the
Biblical Institute, the late Mitchell Dahood, became the
leader in the new and developing trend which was establishing historical and literary associations between the
Bible and the literature of ancient Ugarit. The decipher-
ment and study of the Ugaritic language since its discovery
in 1928 has provided exciting insights into biblical poetry.
Dahood's basic study is a three volume commentary,
Psalms, which appeared in the Anchor Bible series, 1966-
1970. The work is less a commentary (although this dimension is not absent) than a learned translation of the Hebrew
text in the light of new philological and grammatical
insights. This is a pioneer work, but it calls for considerable caution in its use, which only a person skilled in the
pertinent languages can exercise.[17] It remains for future
research to determine how much of Dahood's hypothetical
rendering of the Hebrew will bear up under scholarly scru-
tiny. At one important juncture Dahood moved into bibli-

---

[16]See **Bibliog. 40.** Cf. Mowinckel (**Bibliog. no. 26**). In light of the categories
derived from P. Ricoeur, W. Brueggemann has recently spoken of psalms of
orientation, disorientation, and reorientation — see **Bibliog. no. 5.**

[17]See the appreciative but critical use of Dahood's approach by Peter Craigie
(**Bibliog no. 9**).

cal theology and he claimed to find at several points evidence for a belief in a personal immortality. The most effective refutation of this view is the study published by the scholar in whose honor this *Festschrift* is written.[18]

At the present writing there is no outstanding commentary on the Psalms by a Roman Catholic scholar. The best were done by E. Podechard (in French, and incomplete, 1949-1954), and by G. Castellino (in Italian, 1955). Probably the best recent commentary is by H. J. Kraus, but it is becoming rapidly antiquated and Kraus' *Theologie der Psalmen* did not move much beyond his commentary.[19] However, one must not expect everything from any one commentary on a biblical book. Inevitably they all have their respective strengths and weaknesses.

Because the psalter constitutes the heart of prayer within the liturgy of both ancient Israel and Christianity, it is to be expected that this dimension would be served in modern studies, whether in commentaries of a more popular nature or in spiritual works. Here personal judgment as well as theological principle inevitably plays a role. How is the Christian to relate to the Old Testament? How do Israelite kingship, national violence, personal vengeance fit into modern prayer? Innumerable studies, reflecting many differences of opinion, could be mentioned, but we will note here only one, which approaches the psalter from an exegetical as well as an esthetic point of view. Notker Füglister, O.S.B., recognizes that the Psalms are poetry that is open and dynamic.[20] Biblical imagery is not simply a noetic experience; it is evocative and invites the reader to yield self to the poem or psalm. He borrows from Rainer Maria Rilke the idea that every experience of a poem has a purely personal factor, for the poem is colored by our own mood and background. Nonetheless he emphasizes the literary genres in which the psalms are written, and uses them as an

[18]See **Bibliog. no. 37.**

[19]Cf. Kraus, *Psalmen; Theologie* (**Bibliog. nos. 19, 20**).

[20]See **Bibliog. no. 13.**

entrée into the thought and mood of an individual psalm. He stresses the power of a psalm to give rise to deeper feelings, the poetic and theological aspects which are proper to it. In this way the psalter becomes not simply a prayer book that is utilized by the community of faith (do we need more prayers?), but a veritable school of prayer, which leads one into confrontation with the divine.

3. The Chronicler
(See Bibliography numbers 31, 32, 41)

We are using the term "Chronicler" as a code name for the books of Chronicles and Ezra-Nehemiah, without pronouncing on their ultimate unity.[21] The original sequence of these works within the *Ketubim* seems to have been 1-2 Chronicles, Ezra-Nehemiah. Only during the Christian era were Ez-Neh separated into two books and placed before 1 Chron. There are still many unanswered questions concerning the sources, canonical and non-canonical, especially the "memoirs" of Ezra and Nehemiah, and the Aramaic passages. The dating of Ezra and his reform (cf. Ez 7:8; Artaxerxes I, 458? Artaxerxes II, 398?) is a perennial problem ever since the Louvain scholar, A. von Hoonacker published his study in 1890 in favor of the 398 date. Since then another proposal was made by the late W. F. Albright, who corrected the text of Ez 7:8 to yield the date of 428. A consensus on this point is still lacking, and hence the relationship of the reform of Ezra to the activities of Nehemiah remains unclear. Our knowledge of postexilic Israel is sadly deficient because of the lack of sources. Here we will deal with only one aspect: the Chronicler as theologian — what values did he choose to emphasize in his presentation of Israel's history?

The work of the Chronicler represents in fact the third great historical corpus in the Hebrew Bible. The Torah or

---

[21]The arguments adduced in Williamson (**Bibliog. no. 41**) make it difficult to attribute Ez-Neh to the author of Chronicles.

Pentateuch covers the period of the Fathers down to Moses; the Deuteronomistic history (from Joshua to Kings) covers the period from the Conquest to the Exile. The Chronicler begins with Adam (no less!) and by means of genealogies (1 Chron 1-9) arrives quickly at the period of Saul-David-Solomon, and then concentrates on the Kingdom of Judah to the exclusion of the northern kingdom. The issue of his theological perspective is more complex than it appears to be at first sight. It is not easy to analyze the reasons for the differences between his presentation and the sources he worked with. But he has his own perspectives which emerge from the particular manner in which he presents the history. The bulk of the narrative deals with the reigns of David and Solomon (1 Chron 10-2 Chron 9). Here the emphasis is on the temple and organization of worship (especially the role of the Levites). This interest is further served by the reorganization after the exile, described in Ezra 1-6, and by the description of Ezra's reform. From this point of view the Chronicler seems to be intent on authenticating the religious life of his own day (end of fourth century). In his presentation of the history of the pre-exilic people the theme of faith and apostasy, obedience and disobedience, is set out according to the traditional law of retribution (see also the Deuteronomist).

In sum, the views of the Chronicler are highly selective and interpretive. He has certain particular interests: the Temple and all that involves (priests, Levites, worship); David (rather than Moses!). He is concerned about establishing the continuity of his community with the past as portrayed in the kingdom of David. It may be with some exaggeration that Robert North sees the Chronicler as asserting the superiority of the Davidic covenant over the Mosaic covenant, but the Chronicler has equivalently de-emphasized the covenant and law in an age that was devoted to the Torah![22]

[22]See **Bibliog. nos. 31, 32,** where North's views are expressed. For a broader interpretation of the Chronicler against the background of the post-exilic community, see Williamson (**Bibliog no. 41**), especially his summary of scholarly views on pages 132-40.

4. Daniel
(See Bibliography numbers 4, 7, 8, 15, 16, 21)

It is significant that in the Christian canon Daniel is ranked among the four great prophets, whereas in the Jewish tradition the book is found among the *Ketubim*. Doubtless the late date of the work, in the Maccabean period, is a reason for this. In an era that has become more aware of its own apocalyptic manifestations the book of Daniel has received due attention. The book presents several problems that still call for solution: its unity and literary form is particularly complicated by the mixture of Hebrew and Aramaic (2:24-7:28), and by the contrast between the stories (in third person) in chaps 1-6, and the visions (in first person) in chaps 7-12. A fairly broad consensus has been reached that the book dates to the time of Antiochus Epiphanes (*Circa* 165), although the stories in chaps 1-6 are earlier and eventually were brought together so as to be pertinent to the Maccabean period. The most spectacular evidence for the "pre-history" of chapter 4 is a Qumran fragment, the Prayer of Nabonidus (4QPrNab). The fragment relates how Nabonidus, king of Babylonia and Assyria, living in Teima, has recourse to an anonymous Jew in order to recover from his illness. Historical record shows that Nabonidus did sojourn in Teima; the book of Daniel transfers the story of Nabonidus to Nebachadnezzar. There is no question of direct literary influence; rather both the fragment and chapter 4 represent variant traditions about Nabonidus' sojourn in Teima.

The shift in the understanding of the book of Daniel is put delicately by the late Louis Hartman: "Having lost sight of these ancient modes of writing [the reference is to the apocalyptic and haggadic genres], until relatively recent years Jews and Christians considered Dn to be true history, containing genuine prophesy ... it was natural to assume that the Daniel in chs. 1-6 was a truly historical character and that he was the author of the whole book. There would be few modern biblical scholars, however, who would now seriously defend such an opinion."[23] The literary forms used in the book of Daniel have been illuminated in recent years by study of the non-canonical apocalypses, and in some cases by the Dead Sea Scrolls. Once scholarship extricated itself from trying to defend the "historical" character of the book, attention could be more profitably given to its message. A recent study of John J. Collins does just that. In the book of Daniel old motifs are taken up into a "new vision of life and reality," which nonetheless takes its beginning from the persecution of the Jews by Antiochus Epiphanes. At the same time the vision transcends this particularity to point to the perennial conflict between good and evil. Collins singles out two distinctive features: 1) polarization, the antithesis between heaven and earth, end-time and present; 2) an emphasis on wisdom, the wise or "elect" are those who have a vision from on high, but who are involved in the real world, from which there is no retreating. "It is not a philosophy for all seasons. Its relevance is greatest in times of change and uncertainty when the beasts of chaos seem again to rise from the sea."[24]

It is in Dan 7 that the beasts rise from the sea, and there appears "one like a son of man coming on the clouds of heaven." The precise identification of the son of man is still subject to some dispute.[25] But it is certain that the traditional messianic interpretation cannot be sustained, despite G. Beasley-Murray.[26] Similarly the sequence of the world kingdoms in Dan 9 is now seen to climax in the Greek (not Roman) power, which is dominant at the time of the composition of the book. There is no justification for the messianic interpretation of the cutting down of an "anointed"

---

[23] Hartman, "Daniel" (**Bibliog 15**) 448.

[24] Collins, *Apocalyptic Vision* (**Bibliog. no. 7**) 223. The association of apocalyptic and wisdom is meant differently than in the famous claim of von Rad that wisdom is the "mother of apocalyptic."

[25] Hartman, Di Lella (**Bibliog. no. 16**) 85-102.

[26] Beasley-Murray (**Bibliog. no. 4**) 44-58.

(Dan 9:26; actually the reference is to the high priest,Onias III). The loss of these time-honored interpretations is really a gain: the vitality of the book of Daniel in its Maccabean milieu is recognized and appreciated.

At the outset it was remarked that the Writings provided a (lively) variety to the biblical canon. That variety is the secret of the appeal which Writings have had for both Jewish and Christian tradition. It is not an accident that the five scrolls (Megillot) which came to be read on key Jewish feasts were taken from this collection: Ruth, Song of Songs, Lamentations, Ecclesiastes, and Esther. The *Ketubim*, like the many works (apocrypha and pseudepigrapha) which did not find their way into the canon, open up perspectives that are but faintly seen in the Law and the Prophets. Perhaps the verdict of Rabbi Akiba concerning the Song of Songs, when its canonical status was questioned, can be extended to all of the *Ketubim* — that the day of creation was not greater than the day on which the Song was written (M. Yadayim, 3:5).

BIBLIOGRAPHY

1. Alonso, Schökel L. *Salmos.* Madrid: ediciones cristiandad, 1966.

2. _____. *Treinta Salmos.* Madrid: ediciones cristiandad, 1981.

3. Andersen, Francis I. *Job.* Tyndale OT Commentaries. Leicester: Inter-Varsity, 1976.

4. Beasley-Murray, G.R. "The Interpretation of Daniel 7." *CBQ* 45 (1983) 44-56.

5. Brueggemann, Walter. *The Message of the Psalms.* Minneapolis: Augsburg, 1984.

6. Castellino, G. *Libro dei Salmi.* La Sacra Bibbia. Rome: Marietti, 1955.

7. Collins, John J. *The Apocalyptic Vision of the Book of Daniel.* HSM 16. Missoula, MT: Scholars Press, 1977.

8. _____. *Daniel, With an Introduction to Apocalyptic Literature.* Forms of Old Testament Literature 23. Grand Rapids, MI: Eerdmans, 1984.

9. Craigie, Peter. *Psalms 1-50.* WBC 19. Waco, TX: Word Books, 1983.

10. Crenshaw, J. L., ed. *Studies in Israelite Wisdom.* New York: KTAV, 1976.

11. Dahood, Mitchell. *Psalms.* 3 vols. Anchor Bible 16-17A. Garden City: Doubleday, 1966-70.

12. Fox, Michael V. *The Song of Songs and Ancient Egyptian Love Songs.* Madison, WI: University of Wisconsin Press, 1985.

13. Füglister, Notker. *Das Psalmengebet.* München: Kösel, 1965.

14. Gordis, R. *Koheleth: The Man and His World.* New York: Schocken, 1951.

15. Hartman, Louis F. "Daniel." *The Jerome Biblical Commentary.* Eds.Raymond E. Brown, et al. Englewood Cliffs, NJ: Prentice-Hall, 1968. 446-60.

16. Hartman, Louis F., and A. Di Lella. *The Book of Daniel.* AB 23. New York: Doubleday, 1978.

17. Haspecker, J. *Gottesfurcht bei Jesus Sirach.* AnBib 30. Rome: Pontifical Biblical Institute, 1967.

18. Janzen, J. Gerald. *Job.* Interpretation Bible Commentary. Atlanta: John Knox, 1985.

19. Kraus, Hans Joachim. *Psalmen.* BKAT XV/1-2. Neukirchen-Vluyn: Neukirchener Verlag, 1960.

20. _____. *Theologie der Psalmen.* BKAT XV/3. Neukirchen-Vluyn: Neukirchener Verlag, 1979.

21. Lacocque, A. *The Book of Daniel.* Atlanta: John Knox, 1979.

22. Lang, Bernhard. *Frau Weisheit.* Düsseldorf: Patmos, 1976.

23. Larcher, C. *Etudes sur le Livre de la Sagesse.* EB. Paris: Gabalda, 1969.

24. _____. *Le Livre de la Sagesse ou la Sagesse de Salomon.* EB. Paris: Gabalda, 1983, 1984.

25. Marböck, J. *Weisheit im Wandel.* BBB 37. Bonn: Hanstein, 1971.

26. Mowinckel, Sigmund. *The Psalms in Israel's Worship.* Oxford: Blackwell, 1962.

27. Murphy, Roland E. "Hebrew Wisdom." *JOAS* 101. (1981) 21-34.

28. _____. "The Song of Songs: Critical Biblical Scholarship *vis-à-vis* Exegetical Traditions." *Understanding the Word: Essays in Honour of Bernhard W. Anderson.* JSOTSS 37. Sheffield: Almond, 1985. 63-69.

29. _____. "Wisdom and Creation." *JBL* 104 (1985) 3-11.

30. _____. *Wisdom Literature.* FOTL XIII. Grand Rapids: Eerdmans, 1981.

31. North, Robert. "The Chronicler." *The Jerome Biblical Commentary.* Eds. Raymond E. Brown, et al. Englewood Cliffs, NJ: Prentice-Hall, 1968. 402-38.

32. _____. "Theology of the Chronicler." *JBL* 82 (1963) 369-81.

33. Podechard, E. *Le Psautier.* 3 vols. in 1. Lyons: Facultés Catholiques, 1949-54.

34. Pope, M. *The Song of Songs.* AB 7C. Garden City: Doubleday, 1977.

35. Prato, L. *Il problema della teodicea in Ben Sira.* AnBib 65. Rome: Pontifical Biblical Institute, 1975.

36. Vawter, Bruce. "The Fuller Sense: Some Considerations." *CBQ* 26 (1964) 85-96.

37. _____. "Intimations of Immortality and the Old Testament." *JBL* 21 (1972) 158-71.

38. von Rad, Gerhard. *Old Testament Theology.* 2 vols. New York: Harper, 1962.

39. _____. *Weisheit in Israel.* Neukirchen-Vluyn: Neukirchener Verlag, 1970. (published in English as *Wisdom in Israel.* Nashville: Abingdon, 1972).

40. Westermann, Claus. *The Psalms: Structure, Content & Message.* Minneapolis: Augsburg, 1984.

41. Williamson, H.G.M. *Israel in the Books Of Chronicles.* New York: Cambridge University Press, 1977.

42. Winston, D. *The Book of Wisdom.* Anchor Bible 23. Garden City: Doubleday, 1979.

JESUS AND GOSPEL

John Dominic Crossan
DePaul University

"One is artist if one experiences as content, as the 'thing itself,' that which all nonartists call 'form.' In so doing one belongs without a doubt to a crazy world: for from now on all content appears as purely formal — our lives included."

Friedrich Nietzsche

When one raises the question of continuity between the historical Jesus and those early and divergent interpretations which first proclaimed him, the answer is usually given in terms of faith, theology, and content. In *This Man Jesus*, Bruce Vawter, for example, asked "what went on in the mind of Jesus himself — what was the connection, if any, between his consciousness of certain realities and the later titles by which the church sought to encapsulate them" (see Bibliog. no. 19, p. 196). I accept completely the validity and importance of that discussion but I intend here to investigate the possibilities of a different approach. My purpose is to raise the question of continuity in terms of language, genre, and form. But even as I do so, it becomes evident that language, genre, and form may be but other names for faith, theology, and content.

A. Jesus and Wisdom

1. Wisdom and Aphorism. (See Bibliography numbers 4, 20).

In Prov 8:22–31 wisdom claims an extremely close relationship with God at the moment of creation. It starts with, "The Lord created me at the beginning of his work, the first of his acts of old. Ages ago I was set up, at the first, before the beginning of the earth. When there were no depths I was brought forth, when there were no springs abounding with water." And it ends with, "When he marked out the foundations of the earth, then I was beside him, like a master workman; and I was daily his delight, rejoicing before him always, rejoicing in his inhabited world and delighted in the sons of men."

Bruce Vawter has drawn attention to the problem with translating the Hebrew verb in Prov 8:22 as "created me." He has argued, most convincingly, that it "retains here the same meaning that it possesses elsewhere in Proverbs, viz., 'acquire,' 'get,' 'take,' ... wisdom appears here as a being existing before all created things, not a creature, therefore, but a prior to creation, which was attainable and attained by God, who then concurred with it in the creation and ordering of the universe ... The wisdom that has thus entered into man's world is now as a consequence attainable by man" (see Bibliog. no. 20, p. 207).

I leave aside here any consideration of the transcendental status accorded creative wisdom in that text, and focus instead on the fact that it is contained in the book of Proverbs, precisely proverbs. Wisdom could, of course, be combined with law, as in Sir 24:23–34, with history, as in Sir 44–49, and with cult, as in Sir 50, but there is a very special connection between wisdom and proverbs or aphorisms which is evident, say, from Proverbs through Sirach to Wisdom. How is this special relationship between creative wisdom and wise saying to be understood?

The prose miniature is a useful term for the entire spectrum of adage, aphorism, apothegm, epigram, fragment, proverb, maxim, sentence, or saying. Within that fluid spectrum the poles may be defined by the proverb, which emphasizes anonymous and ancestral tradition, and the aphorism, which emphasizes individual and personal expression. This produces a creative tension within the prose miniature between the communal and the personal, the group and the individual, and it raises the question of the origins of all such sayings whether of authorship presently known or long, long since unknown. Is aphorism always at the root of proverb and is that the teaching of the prose miniature spectrum? (see Bibliog. no. 4).

To emphasize a positive response to that question, I shall use the single term aphorism hereafter, and repeat the question: what is the special and peculiar connection between creative wisdom and aphoristic saying?

There are three aspects of the aphorism that seem to me quite fundamental to its understanding. First, there is its programmatic isolation. It stands alone, possibly no more than one short sentence, and yet it contains a world in miniature. The dialogue and the discourse, the story and the narrative, need the entirety of their single sentences for completion, but the aphorism stands alone, without before or after, single, complete, adequate, and immaculate. Yet we do know that there was something actually before it. There was the raw experience, the confused and disordered data which is congealed in an ordered sentence. And we know that for all its clarity and security, its accuracy and arrogance, it is but a candle on a dark plain, a consoling but most partial cartography of chaos. Second, and flowing from that first point, is the aphorism's lack of both discourse and narrative dimensions. On the one hand, it asserts without argument, prescribes without pleading, and thereby avoids dialogue, debate, and discourse. On the other, it affirms without anecdote, proclaims without sequence, and thereby avoids account, story, and narrative. It is neither discursive nor narratival. Third, and just as much flowing from the second as from the first, is the aphorism's challenge to creative development. In itself it is neither discursive nor narratival but that precise negativity engenders both dialogue and narrative around it and with it as structural basis.

The creativity of divine wisdom is thus profoundly linked to the prose miniature. It appears at interplay with the raw data of human experience and moving through aphorism towards both dialogue and narrative.

2. Wisdom and Jesus. (See Bibliography numbers 6, 9, 17).

In December of 1945 some farmers from the region of Nag Hammadi in Upper Egypt discovered a buried jar containing Coptic Christian manuscripts copied in the fourth century. Among them was one entitled the *Gospel of Thomas* (see Bibliog. no. 17). Greek fragments of this same gospel had been discovered around the turn of the century at Oxyrhynchus farther to the north along the Nile, and these had been copied much earlier, in the second century.

There are three very fascinating aspects to this newly discovered gospel. There is, first of all, the question of its date, that is, the date of its original composition and not just the date of its later manuscript copies. The two Oxford scholars, Bernard P. Grenfell and Arthur S. Hunt, who discovered those first fragments concluded: "(1) that we have here part of a collection of sayings, not extracts from a narrative gospel; (2) that they are not heretical; (3) that they were independent of the Four Gospels in their present shape; (4) that they were earlier than 140 A.D., and might well go back to the first century" (see Bibliog. no. 9, p. 2). I consider that those four conclusions, published when the excavators had found only the first fragment, POxy 1, are still absolutely correct after we have discovered the complete gospel. Next, there is the question of its form. I leave this aside for the moment but will return to it in some detail below. Finally, there is the question of its content, which is a theology of Jesus as divine wisdom. It looks from the present back to the inaugural moment of beginning and it denies emphatically the value of looking from the present towards the apocalyptic moment of ending. I do not know whether this theology of Jesus as divine wisdom is earlier than that of Jesus as apocalyptic judge. But it is conceptually independent of it and ideologically opposed to it. It also reminds us that Jewish wisdom has at least as much right to be called the mother of Christian theology as has Jewish apocalyptic.

There are three major steps in this theological development. First, Jesus is divine wisdom. In *Gos. Thom.* 28 Jesus speaks in the first person address characteristic of divine wisdom in the Old Testament texts. "I took My place in the midst of the world, and I appeared to them in flesh. I found all of them intoxicated; I found none of them thirsty. And my soul became afflicted for the sons of men, because they are blind in their hearts and do not have sight; for empty they came into the world and empty too they seek to leave the world. But for the moment they are intoxicated. When they shake off their wine, then they will repent." Jesus, like wisdom, is rejected, and yet this saying is more plaintively hopeful than the voice of wisdom, say in Prov 1:24–26, "Because I have called and you refused to listen ... I also will laugh at your calamity; I will mock when panic strikes you." Still, the warning of wisdom in Prov 1:28 that there will come a time too late for repentance, that "they will seek me diligently but will not find me," is repeated by Jesus as wisdom in *Gos. Thom.* 38b, "there will be days when you will look for me and will not find Me."

Second, Jesus as divine wisdom turns the believer's gaze back towards the moment of beginning, towards the creation, and towards Gen 1–3. For example, in Gen 1:3, "God said, 'Let there be light'; and there was light." Then, in Wis 7:26, wisdom is "a reflection of eternal light, a spotless mirror of the working of God, and an image of his goodness." And so in *Gos. Thom.* 77a Jesus declares, "It is I who am the light which is above them all."

Third, this theology of Jesus as divine wisdom is directly and polemically anti-apocalyptic. Stevan L. Davies, who may well have written the best book presently available on the *Gospel of Thomas*, notes that "Thomas contains a variety of logia which are in the form of questions and answers, questions by the disciples as a group and answers by Jesus. The questions predominantly are about the end of time or about the nature of Jesus. In both cases the disciples' questions seem to indicate a failure to understand" (see Bibliog. no. 6, pp. 82–83). Corrections about the end of time appear in *Gos. Thom.* 18, 51, 113, and corrections about the nature of Jesus appear in *Gos. Thom.* 24, 37, 43, 52, 91. Both sets of corrections coalesce to say that what they seek is already before their eyes if they can but see it. The polemical overtones of those corrections are also quite evident, in fact derisively so, in *Gos. Thom.* 3a, "If those who lead you say to you, 'See, the Kingdom is in the sky,' then the birds of the sky will precede you. If they say to you, 'It is in the sea,' then the fish will precede you. Rather, the Kingdom is inside of you, and it is outside of you." The Kingdom is, like wisdom, both inside and outside the believer, both an internal gift and a cosmic presence. But, as Davies reminds us, "the use of Kingdom for Wisdom is certainly not a feature of traditional Jewish Wisdom literature; it is a new move, a creative shift of the tradition" (see Bibliog. no. 6, p. 45). The *Gospel of Thomas* is what Jewish wisdom theology from the Old Testament looks like after it has been integrated with the Kingdom of God from the teaching of Jesus. And since Jesus is divine wisdom, *Thomas* either does not know or does nor need any of those other titles used for Jesus elsewhere in early Christianity, for example, Christ, Lord, Savior, Son of David, Son of Man, or Son of God.

This very early gospel, then, turns the believer's gaze resolutely from the future consummation with Jesus as apocalyptic judge and back to the inaugural creation with Jesus as divine wisdom. Thus in *Gos. Thom.* 18, "The disciples said to Jesus, 'Tell us how our end will be.' Jesus said, 'Have you discovered, then, the beginning, that you look for the end. For where the beginning is, there will the end be. Blessed is he who will take his place in the beginning; he will know the end and will not experience death.'"

B. Jesus and Aphorism (See Bibliography no. 11)

I propose a consideration of creative wisdom appearing in aphoristic sayings before being developed into aphoristic dialogues and aphoristic narratives, and of Jesus as wisdom itself, an early Christian interpretation polemically opposed to apocalypticism. How, then, does Jesus as wisdom relate to that aphoristic tradition?

I choose one single aphorism for study. Others might be better for one or other part of the argument but this one is best for the complete sweep of the developmental process.

The chosen aphorism is that concerning Kingdom and Children, the saying which equates being a child and entering the Kingdom. There are five different and mutually independent versions to be considered: (1) Justin Martyr, *First Apology* 61:4; (2) Matt 18:3; (3) Mark 10:15 = Luke 18:17; (4) John 3:3, 5, 7; (5) *Gos. Thom.* 22a. That high number of independent versions makes it also very appropriate as an example.

You will notice that I have not quoted the saying. This is quite deliberate and intends to remind us that Jesus was an oral not a scribal poet. In an oral sensibility what is remembered, what is retained in memory, is a linguistic structure and not a linguistic sequence. This does not mean that it is vague or imprecise but simply that is a precise structure and not a precise sequence (see Bibliog. no. 11). Oral memory retains the basic aphoristic core but allows a large amount of freedom in its oral or even written realization. The orally retained structural core cannot even be summarized without some decision on linear sequence, for example, Kingdom and Children as against Children and Kingdom. Indeed, it cannot even be diagrammed without a similar decision, for example, Kingdom/Children as against Children/Kingdom. There is no such thing, in other words, as the exact wording of the original aphorism. There is only the exact structure of the original aphoristic core, namely, the equation, however expressed, of Childhood status and Kingdom status. That is why, for example, the core aphoristic structure, which in itself is remembered neutrally, can be realized and expressed either negatively, as in Justin, *1 Apol.* 61:4; Matt 18:3; Mark 10:15; John 3:3, 5, and also positively, as in Mark 10:14b; *Gos. Thom.* 22a; John 3:7.

1. Aphorism and Ritual. (See Bibliography numbers 1, 7).

The first case involves the Kingdom and Children aphorism in Justin Martyr's *First Apology* 61:4.

Justin was born of pagan parents at Flavia Neapolis, modern Nablus, in Samaria, at the start of the second century. He was converted to Christianity around 130, opened a philosophical school in Rome, and became Christianity's first great apologist to both Jews and pagans alike. He was martyred by beheading around 165.

Text. Justin's *First Apology* is addressed to the Emperor, his sons, and the Senate and people of Rome "in behalf of those men of every race who are unjustly hated and mistreated" (see Bibliog. no. 7, p. 9). In *1 Apol.* 61 he explains to them the ritual of baptism as follows:

"Those who are convinced and believe what we say and teach is the truth, and pledge themselves to be able to live accordingly are taught in prayer and fasting to ask God to forgive their past sins, while we pray and fast with them. Then we lead them to a place where there is water, and they are regenerated in the same manner in which we ourselves were regenerated. In the name of God, the Father and Lord of all, and of our Savior, Jesus Christ, and of the Holy Ghost, they then receive the washing with water. For Christ said: 'Unless you be born again, you shall not enter the kingdom of heaven.' Now, it is clear to everyone how impossible it is for those who have been born once to enter their mothers' wombs again."

You recognize immediately the parallel between that quoted aphorism of Jesus and the citation in John 3:3,

"Truly, truly, I say to you, unless one is born anew, he cannot see the kingdom of God," or 3:5, "Truly, truly, I say to you, unless one is born of water and the Spirit, he cannot enter the kingdom of God." But what exactly is the relationship between John and Justin in these texts?

Independence. In his Harvard doctoral dissertation under Helmut Koester, A.J. Bellinzoni noted both the general resemblance and quite specific differences between *1 Apol.* 61:4 and John 3:3, 5. There is for example, the personal second plural as against the impersonal third singular format, the absence as against the presence of "truly, truly," the form *anagennēthēte* as against the beautifully ambiguous *gennēthē anōthen* (born again, or, born from above), and "kingdom of heaven" as against "kingdom of God." He concluded that "Justin has independently preserved a liturgical baptismal text in a form older than that found in John and that John's text is probably based on the same or on a similar tradition" so that "the version of this saying in *Apol.* 61:4 is a fairly accurate reproduction of a traditional liturgical formula used in Justin's church in Rome" (see Bibliog. no. 1, p. 137).

There is, however, one rather obvious objection which he did not consider. As noted at the end of my citation above, Justin glosses the aphoristic citation with "Now, it is clear to everyone how impossible it is for those who have been born once to enter their mothers' wombs again." But, in between the twin citations in John 3:3, 5, poor Nicodemus is made to ask derisively, "'How can a man be born when he is old? Can he enter a second time into his mother's womb and be born?'" Since this dialogue is surely a Johannine creation, does this parallel not prove dependence of Justin on John?

I am still inclined to opt for independence for two reasons. First, there is a general fact that this is the only place in Justin where there is such a parallel to John. If Justin knew and used John here, I would expect to find John elsewhere as well. Second, when the Kingdom and Children aphorism was used in, for, and during a baptismal liturgy, it needed some explanatory gloss, some proof that

Jesus intended baptism by this saying. The logic was that, since the saying could not have been intended literally, it must have been intended liturgically. I consider, therefore, that aphorism and argument first came together in baptismal ritual and thence came down quite independently to both Justin and John.

Ritual. In the first case, therefore, aphorism generated not scripture but ritual, and it evokes the possibility of aphoristic creativity moving towards liturgy rather than literature. In our present data, of course, the aphorism, even as liturgical content, is now extant only in scripture, with John, and in apology, with Justin. This is, however, a salutary reminder that aphorism could live on in engendered riches just as well as in engendered writings. All the other cases to be considered, however, will involve movement from aphorism to scripture.

2. Aphorism and Cluster. (See Bibliography no. 2, 12)

The first and most basic literary way to break the programmatic isolation of the aphorism is by cluster. Indeed, as one moves from oral to scribal modality , this becomes a minimal necessity. One can hardly imagine a book enshrining a single aphorism, no matter how magnificent. And that raises almost as inevitably the need for some principle of clustering, be it by themes or authors, by contents or forms, by patterns or sequences. So, for example, Auden and Kronenberger cluster *The Viking Book of Aphorisms* by themes and sub-themes, but they also begin it with sayings about being human and conclude with sayings about being dead.

(1) Aphoristic Cluster.

The second case involves the Kingdom and Children aphorism in Matt 18:3.

Text. Here is a full text of Matt 18:1-5. As you read it, notice especially how it concludes with a cluster of three sayings, that is, with an aphoristic cluster:

"At that time the disciples came to Jesus, saying,
'Who is the greatest in the kingdom of heaven?' And
calling to him a child, he put him in the midst of them,
and said,
(1) 'Truly, I say to you, unless you turn and become
like children, you will never enter the kingdom of
heaven.
(2) Whoever humbles himself like this child, he is the
greatest in the kingdom of heaven.
(3) Whoever receives one such child in my name
receives me.'"

There are two separate incidents involving aphorisms
about children in Mark 9:33–37 (receiving a child) and
Mark 10:13–16 (receiving the Kingdom like a child):

(1) Mark 9:33–37 = Matt 18:1–5 = Luke 9:46–48;
(2) Mark 10:13–16 = Matt 19:13–15 = Luke 18:15–17.

But those twin parallelisms serve to hide somewhat the
complexity of what Matthew has done. He apparently
noticed the redundancy between Mark 10:14 and 10:15 so
he separated them, leaving Mark 10:14 = Matt 19:14 but
putting a version of Mark 10:15 earlier at Matt 18:3. Thus
the parallels between Matt 18:1–5, with which we are concerned, and his Markan source are as follows:

Matt 18:1 = Mark 9:33–34
Matt 23:11 = Mark 9:35
Matt 18:2 = Mark 9:36
Matt 18:3 = Mark 10:15
Matt 18:4 = -----
Matt 18:5 = Mark 9:37a

Independence. That preceding discussion raises the question whether the Kingdom and Children saying in Matt
18:3 is just his version of Mark 10:15 or whether he might
not have here an independent version.
On the one hand, Rudolf Bultmann states emphatically

that, "Matt. 18:3 . . . is clearly not an independent tradition, but is the Matthean form of Mk. 10:15 in another context" (see Bibliog. no. 2, p. 32). On the other hand, Barnabas Lindars argued persuasively that, "even on the assumption of Markan priority, the version of the saying in Mt. 18:3 must be regarded as equally likely to represent the original as the version in Mk. 10:15" (see Bibliog. no. 12, p. 288). He cites four reasons for his conclusion: (1) the better balance of verb and adverbial clause in both protasis and apodosis of Matt 18:3 over Mark 10:15; (2) the verb "enter" of Matt 18:3 is less redactionally and contextually derivative than the "receive" of Mark 10:15, which comes from the other child aphorism in Mark 9:37; (3) Matt 18:3 uses the plural "like children" despite the fact that Mark 10:15 has a singular, and such a singular would fit far better than a plural with the other singulars in Matt 18:2, 4, 5; the plural is thus presumably a given and unchanged pre-Matthean feature of the saying; (4) the phrase "turn and become" is a Semitism which means "become again." This semitism is for Lindars a final and most important indication that Matt 18:3 is independent of and even more original than the version in Mark 10:15.

Cluster. In Matt 18:3–5 the Kingdom and Children aphorism in 18:3 is immediately followed by two other aphorisms in 18:4 and 5. This is a good example of what I mean by an aphoristic cluster. In the aphoristic cluster the first saying in 18:3 is, as we have just seen, probably an independent version of the traditional Kingdom and Children aphorism. And the third saying in 18:5 is derived from Mark 9:37a. But the middle one in 18:4 has no parallels elsewhere and is a pure Matthean creation. In content, of course, it serves as commentary and interpretation for the preceding 18:3. It tells us that, for Matthew, the "to turn and become like children" in 18:3 means to "humble himself like this child" in 18:4.

One first literary or scriptural development of an aphoristic saying is to group it along with other aphoristic sayings similar to it in form and/or content and thus to create aphoristic clusters. And in such clusters there may be both traditional sayings and redactional creations and the latter may serve to interpret the former.

(2) Cluster Gospels.

Not only can an aphoristic saying be developed into an aphoristic cluster but such clustering can then become the principle for gospel composition. This brings us back once more to the *Gospel of Thomas*.

The units of this gospel, which scholars number as 1–114, usually begin with "Jesus said" or "He said" (1, 8, 65, 74) but sometimes they begin with questions, comments, or requests from the disciples in general (6, 12, 18, 20, 24, 37, 43, 51, 52, 53, 99, 113) or particular disciples such as Mary (21), Salome (61), or Simon Peter (114), or more vaguely from "a man" (72), "a woman" (79), or "they said" (91, 104). It is also worth noting how some sayings have at least minimal narrative features (22, 60, 100).

Internally, the numbered units may be composed of just a single saying but they often have two and sometimes even more separate aphorisms combined in a single numerical unit. Externally, there is no overall compositional design evident in the gospel. Many of the units are linked together verbally and some are linked together formally but only in small groups of two or three units. There is, for example, a verbal clustering in *Gos. Thom.* 73–74–75. The word-linkage is italicized.

> [73]"Jesus said, 'The harvest is great but the laborers are few. Beseech the *Lord*, therefore, to send out laborers to the harvest.'
> [74]He said, 'O *Lord*, there are *many* around the drinking trough, but there is nothing in the cistern.'
> [75]Jesus said, '*Many* are standing at the door, but it is the solitary who will enter the bridal chamber.' "

Besides such verbal clusters, there are also formal clusters, of beatitudes, in *Gos. Thom.* 68–69, and of parables, about "a man" in 63–64–65 or about what "The Kingdom of the Father is like" in 96–97–98. Such predominantly verbal clusters are typical of the *Gospel of Thomas* and they constitute it in the most minimal form of written composition, the cluster gospel.

In summary, then, the *Gospel of Thomas* is the principle of aphoristic cluster writ large as gospel. And, as such, it contains not only aphorisms but dialogues and parables as well. It seems certain that the Synoptic Sayings Source (Q) is also composed by clustering but there may be thematic and even sequential forces at work there as well, for example, the progression from Jesus and the Baptist at the beginning to the apocalyptic consummation at the end. Indeed, Q might well be what the borderline of transition from cluster to narrative gospel looks like.

3. Aphorism and Narrative. (See Bibliography numbers 2, 10, 13, 16)

(1) Aphoristic Narrative.

The third case involves the Kingdom and Children aphorism in Mark 10:14, 15.

Text. Here is the full text of Mark 10:13–16. As you read it, notice the redundant nature of 10:14b (children) and 10:15 (child).

> "And they were bringing children to him, that he might touch them; and the disciples rebuked them. But when Jesus saw it he was indignant, and said to them; Let the children come to me, do not hinder them; for to such belongs the kingdom of God. Truly, I say to you, whoever does not receive the kingdom of God like a child shall not enter it.' And he took them in his arms and blessed them, laying his hands on them."

Rudolf Bultmann had already suggested "treating v. 15 as an originally independent dominical saying, inserted into the situation of vv. 13–14 ... for vv. 13–16 are a complete apophthegm without v. 15" (see Bibliog. no. 2, p. 32).

The saying of Jesus in 10:14b is: "Let the children come to me, do not hinder them; for to such belongs the kingdom of God." This saying could make sense by itself, as its frequent citation within the Christian tradition has proved. But the emphatic and double opening with its positive ("let") and negative ("do not") imperatives bespeaks at least an implicit dialectic with some previous situation. I do not consider, therefore, that Mark 10:13,14,16 is an aphoristic story build up from an originally independent aphoristic saying in 10:14b. Rather is its an integrated story in which saying and setting were always and ever in dialectic with one another.

Leaving aside for the moment the aphoristic saying in 10:15, what about this integrated story in 10:13,14,16? I see no compelling or even persuasive reason to postulate pre-Markan tradition in this integrated story. And there are three reasons that convince me that 10:13,14,16 is a Markan creation composed to frame and contain the pre-Markan aphoristic saying in 10:15. First, structures. The Markan penchant for dualism and especially for a positive followed by a negative appears in 10:14, (let them come / do not hinder them), as Frans Neirynck has noted (see Bibliog. no. 13, pp. 84, 92, 99, 115, 122). Second, expressions. Phrases such as "do not hinder" in 10:14 and "took them in his arms" in 10:16 are derived by Mark from the earlier units in 9:39a and 9:36. Third, words. In his study of Mark's redactional style, E.J. Pryke placed all of 10:13 and 16 in "the redactional text of Mark" (see Bibliog. no. 16, p. 165). I conclude that all of Mark 10:13,14,16 was created by Mark as an integrated story whose primary point was to continue the criticism of the disciples which dominates so much of this entire section in Mark.

Independence. I consider that 10:15 is an independent and pre-Markan aphoristic saying. This is confirmed by comparing it with the preceding Matt 18:3 and succeeding John 3:3, 5. In these three cases there is an aphorism with similar construction: (a) solemn opening: "Truly, I say to you," with the usual doubling of the "Truly" in John; (b) protasis formulated negatively; (c) apodosis also formulated negatively; and (d) the same verb "enter" in all three cases ("see" in John 3:3 but "enter" in 3:5).

Narrative. This shows a second possible development of an aphorism. The originally independent and pre-Markan aphoristic saying in 10:15 was formed into a self-subsistent story in 10:13,14,16 through Mark's doubling of 10:15 into 10:14b. Not only can aphorisms cluster together with other aphorisms, either traditionally given or redactionally created, as in Matt 18:1–5, but they can create aphoristic and even integrated stories as in Mark 10:13–16.

(2) Narrative Gospels.

The four intracanonical gospels are narrative and not just cluster gospels. They are stories. This is most especially true of Mark whose form may well have been normative not only for Matthew and Luke but even for John as well. Although liturgy and exegesis have accustomed us to ponder Mark's units as if they were parts of a cluster gospel, this is to misunderstand its destiny as a narrative gospel. This was well understood by those anonymous scribes and communities who found the harsh negativity of 16:7–8 too difficult an ending to accept and who therefore appended different conclusions to finish the story more traditionally. But, as Werner Kelbner has shown so well, "because we have focused on the individual stories in Mark we have not really come to know the story of Mark" (see Bibliog. no. 10, p. 11). It is almost as if, for both liturgical reading and exegetical study, the power of the cluster gospel whose form had been rejected from the canon, came back to haunt it and thus to dominate over the narrative form which the canon itself had accepted and consecrated.

4. Aphorism and Dialogue. (See Bibliography numbers 12, 15, 17)

The fourth case involves the Kingdom and Children aphorism in John 3:3, 5, 7.

Text. Here is the full text of John 3:1–10. As you read it, notice that the dialogue between Nicodemus and Jesus has three exchanges with the words of Nicodemus getting steadily shorter and those of Jesus getting steadily longer.

Also notice that there are three separate citations of the aphorism acting as the armature of the dialogue in 3:3,5,7. It is given in basic format in 3:3, in expanded format in 3:5, and in contracted format in 3:7.

> "Now there was a man of the Pharisees, named Nicodemus, a ruler of the Jews. This man came to Jesus by night and said to him, 'Rabbi, we know that you are a teacher come from God; for no one can do these signs that you do, unless God is with him.'
> Jesus answered him, 'Truly, truly, I say to you, unless one is born anew, he cannot see the kingdom of God.'
> Nicodemus said to him, 'How can a man be born when he is old? Can he enter a second time into his mother's womb and be born?'
> Jesus answered, 'Truly, truly, I say to you, unless one is born of water and the Spirit, he cannot enter the kingdom of God. That which is born of the flesh is flesh, and that which is born of the Spirit is spirit. Do not marvel that I said to you, "You must be born anew." The wind blows where it wills, and you hear the sound of it, but you do not know whence it comes or whither it goes; so it is with every one who is born of the Spirit.'
> Nicodemus said to him, 'How can this be?'
> Jesus answered him, 'Are you a teacher of Israel, and do not understand this?'"

What John has done with the Kingdom and Children aphorism is quite fascinating. (a) As noted already, the dialogue of Nicodemus and Jesus has three exchanges: 2b/3, 4/5-8, and 9/10. (b) It is structured so that Nicodemus gets one assertion (2b) and two questions (4, 9), while Jesus gets two assertions(3, 5-8) and one question (10). (c) Finally, the unit is framed by the ironic contrast between "teacher" in 3:3 and 3:10.

Independence. Barnabas Lindars has argued that John's version of this aphorism is independent of the Synoptic tradition. He proposed: (a) The "of water and the Spirit" in

3:5a is John's own reformulation of the "anew" in 3:3a, and the "see" of 3:3b is John's own reformulation of the "enter" of 3:5b. That is to say, the "anew" (*anōthen*) and the "enter" are pre-Johannine. (b) "John's (*anōthen*) can bear the meaning 'again,' and so represents a more idiomatic translation of the Aramaic phrase which appears in Matthew's version as *straphēte kai* ['turn and']." (c) In adapting his source and dropping any mention of children, "John intended the meaning 'from above' in verse 3, contrary to the required meaning [anew, again] of the underlying source" (see Bibliog. no. 12, pp. 290, 292).

Hence, there was a pre-Johannine version which said, "unless one is born anew/again, one cannot enter the kingdom of God." John used this thrice but with interpretative variations each time, in 3:3, 5, 7.

Dialogue. Although the general framework of the gospel format turns even John 3:1–10 into a story, and although the arrival of Nicodemus by symbolic night is also something of a narrative, the basic formation of 3:1–10 is that of an aphoristic dialogue. It has three exchanges between the speakers and these arc built around three variations on the Kingdom and Children aphorism in short and long, negative and positive, traditional and redactional variations.

(2) Dialogue Gospels.

I have already mentioned the short dialogues among the predominantly aphoristic structure of the *Gospel of Thomas* recently discovered at Nag Hammadi. In that same collection were other gospels whose entire composition was dialectical, the structure being a series of questions and answers between Jesus and his disciples after the resurrection. Of this form of gospel, so dear to Gnostic Christianity, Pheme Perkins has observed that, "unlike the lively drama of the Platonic dialogue or the more pedantic style of the philosophic dialogue employed by a Cicero or Augustine, the Gnostic dialogue does not aim at an exchange of ideas and an examination of philosophical positions ... The artificiality of some of the questions suggests that the protagonists never represent a real alternative. They

merely provide the revealer with an opportunity to discharge his mission" (see Bibliog. no. 15, p. 19).

Two examples of such dialogue gospels from Nag Hammadi will suffice. The *Dialogue of the Savior* has Jesus
responding to questions and comments by, in this quantitative order, Judas Thomas, Mary Magdalene, Matthew,
and the disciples in general. Even more striking is the case
of the non-Christian treatise *Eugnostos the Blessed* which
was turned into a Christian dialogue gospel, *Sophia of
Jesus Christ*, by the totally artificial insertion of questions
from, in this quantitative order, the disciples in general,
Matthew or Mary Magdalene, and Philip, Judas Thomas,
or Bartholomew (see Bibliog. no. 17).

*5. Aphorism and Narrative-Dialogue. (See Bibliography
numbers 2, 3, 6).*

The fifth and final case involves the Kingdom and Children aphorism in *Gos. Thom.* 22.

Text. Here is the full text of *Gos. Thom.* 22. As you read
it, notice how deftly the aphoristic narrative in 22a is
turned through question and answer into a dialogue with a
single interchange between disciples and Jesus in 22b.
Notice also how this classic compositional hybrid of
narrative-dialogue is bound together by the phrase "enter
the Kingdom" from the aphoristic narrative being twice
repeated in the question and answer parts of the aphoristic
dialogue.

> "Jesus saw infants being suckled. He said to his disci-
> ples, 'These infants being suckled are like those who
> enter the Kingdom.' They said to Him, 'Shall we then,
> as children, enter the Kingdom?' Jesus said to them,
> 'When you make the two one, and when you make the
> inside like the outside, and the outside like the inside,
> and the above like the below, and when you make the
> male and the female one and the same, so that the
> male not be male nor the female female; and when
> you fashion eyes in place of an eye, and a hand in

place of a hand, and a foot in place of a foot and a likeness in place of a likeness; then will you enter (the Kingdom).'"

The content of 22b has been very well explained by Stevan L. Davies. "We find in Logion 22 the idea of the restored image of Adam, no longer male or female. We find there an idea of a new body and of the general unification of above and below, inside and outside, which derive from Thomas' sophiological speculations on the locations of Kingdom and light and Wisdom. Thomas' Logion 22 is a baptismal reunification formula. It is not like such a formula, nor is it merely derived from such a formula; it is such a formula. It is not, of course, the only one in early Christian literature" (see Bibliog. no. 6, pp. 131–132). This means that, especially in the dialogue of 22b, we are dealing with intensively Thomistic redaction.

Independence. My general position on the *Gospel of Thomas* is that it is completely independent of the intracanonical gospels. That, of course, cannot be argued in detail here (see Bibliog. no. 5), but, at least, I see no compelling or even persuasive reason to claim that *Gos. Thom.* 22a is dependent on the versions in Matt 18:3 or Mark 10:15 or John 3:3, 5.

The saying in those three intracanonical locations is a threatening double negative ("unless ... not"), but the story in Mark 10:13,14,16 and *Gos. Thom.* 22a present the saying as a simple and straightforward positive statement. Thus in Mark 10:14b the saying reads, "for to such belongs the kingdom of God," and in *Gos. Thom.* 22a, "These infants being suckled are like those who enter the Kingdom."

Narrative-Dialogue. The section in 22a is a classic example of an aphoristic story, that is, an aphoristic saying developed into narrative. A setting or situation is given with "Jesus saw infants being suckled." But this situation is already verbally contained within the aphorism itself: "He said to His disciples, 'These infants being suckled are like those who enter the Kingdom.'" On the one hand, this adds very little to the aphorism itself, but, on the other, it significantly chooses the narrative mode (situation) over the discourse mode (address) to develop the aphorism. Notice also that the incident begins with Jesus, with something from Jesus rather than something to Jesus. It begins with "Jesus saw." This recalls Bultmann's observation that, "It is characteristic of the primitive apophthegm that it makes the occasion of a dominical saying something that happens to Jesus (with the exception of the stories of the call of the disciples). It is a sign of secondary formation if Jesus himself provides the initiative" (see Bibliog. no. 2, p. 66). But the aphoristic narrative in 22a is profoundly interpreted by the addition of the aphoristic dialogue in 22b. The entire complex of *Gos. Thom.* 22 shows how dialogue is used to interpret the aphorism as demanding return to the androgynous unity of Adam at the dawn of creation.

(2) Narrative-Dialogue Gospels.

Even this hybrid example in *Gos. Thom.* 22, in which dialogue is appended to narrative as its interpretation, finds a similar process writ large as gospel. This is the case of *Epistula Apostolorum*, a hybrid document composed around the middle of the second century as Catholic Christianity counter-attacked both the form and content of its opposing Gnostic Christianity (see Bibliog. no.3).

This text's first quarter is a very summary narrative gospel of Jesus' birth, infancy, miracles, passion and resurrection (3–12). But, then, its last three quarters are taken up by dialogue between the risen Jesus and the disciples. Repeatedly, the "we said" of the apostles presents Jesus with comments or questions to which he responds. The content of the document is quite Catholic but its formal emphasis on post-resurrectional dialogue rather than pre-resurrectional narrative doomed it, presumably, to extra-canonical status.

3. Jesus and Parable (See Bibliography numbers 8,14, 18).

The aphoristic sayings of Jesus are transmissionally developed along three major generic trajectories to become aphoristic clusters, aphoristic narratives, and aphoristic dialogues. Those same three genres are constitutive for three types of early Christian gospels: cluster gospels, narrative gospels, and dialogue gospels.

Over fifteen years ago Helmut Koester spoke of "One Jesus and Four Primitive Gospels" (see Bibliog. no. 18, pp. 158–204). Three of his primitive gospels are basically the same as my cluster, narrative, and dialogue gospels. His fourth one, namely, miracle gospels, has not been discussed here. This is primarily because of the lack of specific extant examples. But I am not at all sure that this lack invalidates Koester's suggestion. It may well be that such aretalogies, which could easily have been organized originally as cluster gospels, were thoroughly rejected and even more thoroughly suppressed because of the danger of Jesus being accepted primarily or even exclusively as a popular magician. For now, however, I focus only on the above three genres of gospel.

If one thinks of Jesus as aphorist, all three of those gospel types are equally valid as generic responses, as literary creations to proclaim Jesus as the aphoristic wisdom of God. But if one thinks of Jesus as parabler, there is only one of those primitive gospel types which is in clear formal continuity with that inception. The narrative gospel, the one type accepted by Catholic Christianity for canonical inclusion, is the formal heir of parable.

In *The Art of Rhetoric* (11, 20) Aristotle divided rhetorical proofs into *enthymemes*, which are general statements which can be used for deductive purposes, such as maxims and proverbs, and *examples*, which are specific narratives which can be used for inductive purposes. Examples are either historical or fictional; and fictional examples are either realistic and possible, such as parables, or unrealistic and impossible, such as fables (see Bibliog. no. 8, pp. 272–279). For Aristotle, then, parables are realistic fictions.

The parables of Jesus fit well into that framework. They are, of course also metaphors of the Kingdom, but their mode is that of realistic fiction. Whether or not they have precise historical incidents or even general historical actualities behind them is irrelevant and but a concomitant of their realism in any case. Thus, for example, the parable of The Evil Tenants could have represented an actual Galilean happening or a permanent Galilean possibility but it certainly plays along the border between the actual and the potential, the anecdotal and the typical.

It should be underlined that Jesus was rather special in this pedagogic use of parable. For example, in comparing him with his contemporary Pharisees, Neusner concluded that "Pharisaic-rabbinic traditions contain few, if any, parables." He continues: "As to similitudes and similar forms, we find no equivalent ... Hyperbole and metaphors are not common. As to such similitudes as master/servant, tower/war, lost sheep/lost coin, the thief, faithful servant, children at play, leaven, seed growing of itself, treasure in the field, pearl of great price, fish-net, house-builder, fig tree, returning householder, prodigal son, unjust steward, two sons, and the like — we have nothing of the sort. It is true that later rabbinic materials make use of similitudes. But the materials before us do not" (see Bibliog. no. 14, Vol. 3, pp. 85–86). A special generic usage does not necessarily establish qualitative superiority but it may well indicate what form a speaker found most appropriate and what form an audience found most memorable.

In formal terms, therefore, Jesus the aphorist fits well into the wisdom traditions of Israel but Jesus the parabler is a more unusual phenomenon.

My suggestion is that the aphoristic heritage of Jesus generated cluster, narrative, and dialogue gospels, but that the parabolic heritage of Jesus focused attention precisely on one of those genres, namely, the narrative gospels. Thus the narrative realism of the parables finds its formal continuity in the narrative realism of those gospels alone accepted as canonical in the ascendancy of Catholic Christianity.

BIBLIOGRAPHY

1. Bellinzoni, Arthur J. *The Sayings of Jesus in the Writings of Justin Martyr.* Leiden: Brill, 1967.

2. Bultmann, Rudolph. *The History of the Synoptic Tradition.* Trans. John Marsh. New York: Harper & Row, 1963.

3. Cameron, Ron. *The Other Gospels: Non-Canonical Gospel Texts.* Philadelphia: Westminster, 1982.

4. Crossan, John Dominic. *In Fragments: The Aphorisms of Jesus.* San Francisco: Harper & Row, 1983.

5. _____. *Four Other Gospels: Shadows on the Contours of Canon.* Minneapolis: Winston-Seabury, 1985.

6. Davies, Stevan L. *The Gospel of Thomas and Christian Wisdom.* New York: Seabury, 1983.

7. Falls, Thomas B. *Writings of Saint Justin Martyr.* New York: Christian Heritage, 1948.

8. Freese, John Henry. *Aristotle: The Art of Rhetoric.* LCL 193. Cambridge, MA: Harvard University Press, 1926.

9. Grenfell, Bernard P., and Arthur S. Hunt. *The Oxyrhynchus Papyri. Part I.* London: Egypt Exploration Fund, 1898.

10. Kelber, Werner H. *Mark's Story of Jesus.* Philadelphia: Fortress, 1979.

11. _____. *The Oral and Written Gospel: The Hermeneutics of Speaking and Writing in the Synoptic Tradition, Mark, Paul, and Q.* Philadelphia: Fortress, 1983.

12. Lindars, Barnabas.   "John and the Synoptic Gospels: A Test Case." *NTS* 27 (1980–81) 287–94.

13. Neirynck, Frans.   *Duality in Mark: Contributions to the Study of the Markan Redaction.* BETL 31. Louvain: Leuven University Press, 1972.

14. Neusner, Jacob.   *The Rabbinic Traditions about the Pharisees before 70.* 3 vols. Leiden: Brill, 1971.

15. Perkins, Pheme.   *The Gnostic Dialogue: The Early Church and the Crisis of Gnosticism.* New York: Paulist, 1980.

16. Pryke, E.J.   *Redactional Style in the Marcan Gospel: A Study of Syntax and Vocabulary as Guides to Redaction in Mark.* SNTSMS 33.   New York: Cambridge University Press, 1978.

17. Robinson, James M., General Director.   *The Nag Hammadi Library in English.* Ed. Marvin W. Mayer. San Francisco: Harper & Row, 1977.

18. Robinson, James A., and Helmut Koester.   *Trajectories Through Early Christianity.* Philadelphia: Fortress, 1971.

19. Vawter, Bruce.   *This Man Jesus: An Essay toward a New Testament Christology.* Garden City, NY: Doubleday, 1973.

20. _____."*Prov 8:22: Wisdom and Creation.*" *JBL* 99 (1980) 205–16.

THE SYNOPTIC GOSPELS

Daniel J. Harrington, S.J.
Weston School of Theology

When I was first becoming interested in biblical studies twenty-five years ago, it did not take long for me to hear the name of Bruce Vawter. One of my best memories will always be the intellectual and spiritual excitement that I experienced in reading the books, articles, and reviews by Vawter and his colleagues in the Catholic biblical movement during the late 1950s and early 1960s. The pioneering and popularizing work done by these scholars found official expression to some extent in Vatican II's Dogmatic Constitution on Divine Revelation, which was promulgated in 1965. This approbation, in turn, led to an even greater enthusiasm for biblical study in Catholic circles and an increasing demand for both scholarly and nontechnical aids in understanding the Scriptures. It also encouraged Catholic scholars to take a more active part in the international and interconfessional dialogue that is biblical scholarship today. Thus the invitation extended by the editors to synthesize scholarship on the Synoptic Gospels since Vatican II is an occasion for me both to repay a personal debt of gratitude to Vawter and his colleagues in the Catholic biblical movement, and to be a witness to the current ecumenical profile of biblical scholarship.

The fifth chapter of the Dogmatic Constitution on Divine Revelation (*Dei Verbum*) deals with the New Testament. When describing the Gospels, the Constitution makes the following statement in section 19:

> The sacred authors wrote the four Gospels, selecting some things from the many which had been handed on by word of mouth or in writing, reducing some of them to a synthesis, explicating some things in view of the situation of their churches, and preserving the form of proclamation but always in such fashion that they told us the honest truth about Jesus.

Using some of the phrases in this long and dense sentence, I will try to indicate where current biblical scholarship stands on the life settings and theological perspectives of the Synoptic Evangelists, the transmission of the Gospel material, and the events behind the Gospels. The order of presentation—from Gospels, through tradition, to events—reflects the approach taken by scholars in recent years and proceeds from the most certain and tangible matters to more difficult and elusive matters.

Life Settings and Theological Perspectives

The Constitution on Divine Revelation describes the work of the Evangelists as "selecting . . . reducing . . . explicating . . . and preserving the form of proclamation." This description assumes that the Evangelists had sources at their disposal but used these sources creatively to speak to situations within their own communities in accord with the good news of Jesus Christ.

Perhaps the most dramatic development in Synoptic gospel studies in the past twenty years has been the clear recognition that, though these three Gospels provide a "common view" of Jesus (and thus are rightly called Synoptic), they had different purposes and spoke to different communities, they presented the story of Jesus in different ways, and they had different theological emphases. Whereas earlier generations sought to fit the Synoptic Gospels into one outline purporting to give us the life of Jesus and busied themselves in producing Gospel harmonies and lives of Jesus, now we try to appreciate the unique perspective of each Evangelist and the particular interpretation and portrait of Jesus that he gave us.

The word "gospel" was used by Paul and other early Christians to describe as "good news" what God has done for humanity in the person of Jesus Christ, especially through his death and resurrection. The three Gospels that we customarily call Synoptic Gospels (Matthew, Mark, and Luke) look something like biographies, or lives, of Jesus. Provided that we avoid using the term "biography" in its modern sense as a scientifically accurate and detailed chronological presentation of a person's life, then the Synoptic Gospels seem to qualify as biographies. In fact, Luke's Gospel employs many of the conventions of the ancient biographical tradition. But even when "biography" is used in its proper ancient sense there is still a problem, for the ancient biography aimed to present its subjects as examples to be imitated or avoided. In some respects, the Jesus of the Synoptic Gospels (especially in Luke) is an example to be imitated. But in other ways, this Jesus bursts the bonds of human possibility and emerges as a revelation from and of God, as the decisive encounter between the divine and the human.

The Gospels are good news from God to us through and in Jesus. They were written by people who believed passionately in the truth of this good news. They were written for believers, for those who already knew something about the gospel and wanted to learn even more. They were (and are) invitations to enter into the story of Jesus more deeply. They are, as the Constitution on Divine Revelation says, "proclamation," and thus something more than the words "life" or "biography" in both their ancient and their modern meanings can convey.

*1. The Synoptic Evangelists had Different Purposes
and Spoke to Different Communities.* (See
Bibliography numbers 2, 16, 19, 27, 30)

As far as we can tell, Mark was the first one to move
from "gospel" (the good news) to Gospel (the literary
genre). He seems to have put together his story of Jesus
around A.D. 70, that is about forty years after the events of
Jesus' public ministry and his death and resurrection. The
traditional site of Mark's activity is Rome, because of several technical Latin terms taken over in his Greek text and
second-century patristic testimony. Other possible sites
suggested by modern scholars include Galilee in Palestine,
Alexandria in Egypt, and Antioch in Syria.

The first and most obvious purpose that Mark had in
creating the Gospel genre was to put order into the various
traditions about Jesus. The words and deeds of Jesus had
been circulating in oral and written forms for some forty
years, and Mark's way of putting them in order was to
incorporate them into the story of Jesus. Thus the gospel
was transformed into the Gospel.

Mark was also responding to some existential needs of
the community for which he wrote. That community was
either already experiencing persecution or expecting it very
soon, and Mark's Gospel set before it the suffering Christ
as a model of fidelity to God and a source of encouragement. That community was also becoming increasingly
non-Jewish in character, and so its new members needed
more comprehensive and formal instruction about Jesus.
Moreover, that community was being challenged to answer
some tough questions being put to it by outsiders: Why did
Jesus die a criminal's death on the cross? Why did Jesus
not claim the title of Messiah more openly and do what the
Messiah was supposed to do? Where do his followers fit in
relation to other Jewish groups? Mark sought to suggest
answers to such questions.

Matthew seems to have known Mark's Gospel and integrated it into his own revised and expanded story of Jesus.
The most obvious source of expansion was Matthew's use

of a collection of Jesus' sayings designated by modern scholars as Q. He also made use of other sources, e.g. in the infancy narratives. Matthew's second edition of Mark's Gospel is generally placed at Antioch in Syria or in some other city in which Jewish influence was strong. It is dated after A.D. 70 on the basis of allusions to the destruction of Jerusalem (see Matt 21:41; 22:7; 27:25).

In addition to revising and expanding Mark's Gospel, Matthew sought to address some of the problems that his predominantly Jewish-Christian community faced. These Jewish Christians needed instruction about their identity as the people of God and about their relationship to the Jewish tradition. They needed encouragement to widen their missionary horizons to include non-Jews. They had to deal with the painful tensions between "old" and "new" without rejecting either.

Luke also had access to Q and to other sources than Matthew had, and so he too set out to provide independently of Matthew a revised and expanded version of Mark's story of Jesus. The composition of Luke's Gospel has been assigned to Rome, Greece, Asia Minor, Syria, and Palestine—in other words, to practically everywhere in the ancient Mediterranean world. If there is no certainty about the place of composition, there is some consensus about the date, certainly after A.D. 70 (see Luke 19:43–44; 21:20–24) and probably about the same time as Matthew's Gospel.

In his preface (Luke 1:1–4), the Evangelist tells us that he wished to provide an orderly account of "the things which have been accomplished among us," that is, the life, death, and resurrection of Jesus, as well as the spread of the Christian mission from Jerusalem to Rome (in the Acts of the Apostles). By using the conventions of the didactic biography, Luke put forth Jesus as a model of right attitudes and behavior before God, even though the biography framework is sometimes strained to the breaking point by the unique character of Jesus. Whoever Theophilus to whom Luke dedicated his work really was, Luke had in mind an audience that knew something about Judaism but was largely Gentile Christian in constitution. This community seems to have had a special problem regarding wealth, and so Luke took pains to encourage the rich to share their goods and to console the poor by reminding them of God's special care for them.

In sketching the Synoptic Evangelists' purposes and life settings I have said nothing about the apparent references to them in the New Testament (for Mark, see Acts 12:12, 25; 15:37–39; Col 4:10; 2 Tim 4:11; Phlm 24; 1 Pet 5:13; for Matthew, see Matt 9:9; 10:3; for Luke, see the "we" passages in Acts as well as Phlm 24; Col 4:14; 2 Tim 4:11). Nor have I dealt with the early patristic traditions that Mark was Peter's interpreter, Matthew was one of the Twelve, and Luke was Paul's companion. The reason for the silence is that, when these references and traditions are examined critically, they raise more problems than they solve and are not very reliable guides in interpreting the Gospels.

2. The Synoptic Evangelists presented the story of Jesus in Different Ways.

In moving from gospel to Gospel, Mark brought the traditions about Jesus into the framework of a narrative. These traditions included a wide variety of literary types: sayings (proverbs, warnings, prophecies, etc.), parables, narratives, controversies or conflicts, healings, and nature miracles. Some of these small units had already been joined together to form larger blocks, and a connected account of Jesus' passion and death may also have been available to the Evangelist.

Mark took these blocks of tradition and imposed upon them a geographical and theological outline. He showed how Jesus the miracle-worker and teacher received a mixed reception in Galilee (1:1—3:6) and how he was misunderstood and rejected by people in his home area (3:7—6:6). As Jesus travelled in Galilee and beyond, Jesus was even misunderstood by his own disciples (6:7—8:21). On the way up to Jerusalem, he instructed the disciples about himself and their relationship to him (8:22—10:52). Jesus' brief activity in Jerusalem begets more hostility and misunderstanding (11:1—13:37), and the opposition to Jesus reaches its climax in his suffering and death in Jerusalem (14:1—16:8). Within this geographical and theological framework, Mark used a variety of literary devices (contrast of characters, irony, paradox, the "sandwich" technique of telling two stories at once, etc.) to produce a tense and dynamic narrative.

In his revision and expansion of Mark's Gospel, Matthew did not disregard the geographical-theological outline entirely. But he began by extending Mark's outline backward with the addition of the infancy narrative (Matt 1:1—2:23) and forward by including the risen Lord's commission to the eleven disciples in Galilee to preach the gospel to all nations (Matt 28:16–20). As a way of introducing the teachings of Jesus not available to Mark, Matthew constructed five speeches: the Sermon on the Mount (chaps. 5—7), the missionary discourse (chap. 10), the parables (chap. 13), the advice to the community (chap. 18), and the eschatological discourse (chaps. 24— 25). Within the general framework provided by the infancy narrative and the five speeches, Matthew recounted the beginnings of Jesus' ministry (3:1—4:25), the powerful deeds of Jesus (8:18), the decisive significance of Jesus and his rejection (11:1—12:50), his miracles and controversies on the way to the cross (13:54—17:27), the growing opposition to Jesus (19:1—23:39), and his death and resurrection (26:1—28:20).

Like Matthew, Luke sought to provide a richer portrait of Jesus by including sources not available to Mark. He also wished to clear up som obscurities, set aside some potentially offensive points, and improve on Mark's style. The result of Luke's expansion and revision is a narrative in which Markan material appears in three blocks: Luke 3:1—6:19 = Mark 1:1—3:19; Luke 8:4—9:50 = Mark 3:20—6:44 and 8:27—9:50; Luke 18:15—24:12 = Mark 10:1—16:8. The copy of Mark's Gospel used by Luke may have lacked Mark 6:45—8:26, or perhaps Luke omitted this section for a reason. Most of the Q material appears in Luke

6:20—8:3 and 9:51—18:14, which also contain many traditions found only in Luke's Gospel.

The result of Luke's redactional activity is a geographical and theological outline that differs somewhat from
Mark's outline. It reaches back into Jesus' infancy and
describes the preparation for his public ministry (1:5—
4:13). Then it describes Jesus' healing and teaching in Galilee (4:14—9:50). The most striking feature in Luke's
outline is the amount of space given to the journey of Jesus
and his disciples from Galilee to Jerusalem (9:51—19:44;
cf. Mark 8:22—10:52). Then Jesus exercises a farily extensive ministry in Jerusalem (19:45—21:38). Not only do the
passion and death take place in Jerusalem, but so also do
the appearances of the risen Lord (22:1—24:53). In the
course of telling the story of Jesus, Luke alone includes
beautiful hymns, memorable stories (the good Samaritan
and the prodigal son), and extraordinary characterizations
(Mary, the disciples, Jesus, the people of the infancy
narrative).

*3. The Synoptic Evangelists had different theological
emphases. (See Bibliography numbers 5, 9, 13, 29)*

As should be abundantly clear by now, the Synoptic
Evangelists used traditional material and thereby transmitted the beliefs and emphases of the early Christian communities. They agree that Jesus is the Messiah, the Son of
Man, the Son of God, Wisdom, etc. They agree that Jesus
gathered disciples who accompanied him during life and
bore witness to him after death. They agree that the Christian community has an identity and a mission within salvation history. But for all their agreement on these matters,
they approached Christology, discipleship, and salvation
history in different ways.

For Mark, Jesus was the suffering Messiah. Some of the
traditions that Mark used suggest that the idea of Jesus the
miracle-worker was very popular in early Christian circles.
Mark took over that idea and placed it beside another
popular understanding of Jesus—the teacher. But Mark

demanded that Jesus' miracles and his teaching be understood in light of the cross. Everything in his Gospel suggests that the cross is the key to understanding Jesus.

While not denying the centrality of the cross, Matthew shows how Jesus brought to fulfillment the promises of the Old Testament and went beyond them. He frequently points out how this or that event in Jesus' life fulfilled an Old Testament passage. He portrays Jesus as the authoritative interpreter of the Old Testament Law and therefore as the revealer of God's will. He focuses on christological titles having rich Old Testament backgrounds (Son of David, Messiah, Wisdom) and gives particular attention to the Son of Man (See Dan 7:13–14) and the Son of God (see Pss 2:7; 110:1). Nevertheless, the significance of Jesus is not exhausted by any of these titles; they only highlight certain aspects of it and never adequately.

In his portrait of Jesus, Luke too was heavily dependent upon the Christian tradition for his titles of Jesus. But Luke's major contribution to our understanding of Jesus comes with his presentation of Jesus as the prophet and as the martyr. In his first public action at the synagogue in Nazareth (Luke 4:16–30), Jesus' mission is defined in terms of Isa 61:1–2 (see 58:6) and the Old Testament prophets, Elijah and Elisha. He not only acts as a prophet (see Luke 7:16, 39), but he also dies as a prophet (see Luke 13:33–34) and in accordance with prophecy (see Luke 24:25–27). In his death, Jesus bears witness to his special relationship to God and remains faithful to his own principles of forgiveness and love of enemies (see Luke 23:34, 46). Innocent of all the political charges hurled against him, Jesus suffers the death of a martyr.

The different ways in which the Synoptic Evangelists treat discipleship and salvation history are closely related. In the first half of his Gospel, Mark presents the disciples of Jesus in a relatively positive way, thus encouraging readers to identify with them. But as the story of Jesus proceeds, the disciples misunderstand Jesus and even betray him in Jerusalem. Now the readers are forced to choose between the faithful Jesus and his foolish and cowardly disciples. Thus the disciples serve as a negative example for the community in its own efforts to understand the mystery of the crucified Messiah. On the other hand, the portrait of Jesus the wonder-worker and teacher who fulfills God's will by accepting the cross gives the community a better sense of its own place within God's saving plan: It too must accept the cross and live its life under the sign of the cross.

Matthew's presentation of the earliest followers of Jesus is a bit more positive: They have "little faith"—some faith but certainly not perfect faith. They need instruction in the way of Jesus as well as encouragement to entrust themselves to Jesus' power (see Matt 8:18–27; 14:22–33). They need to understand that Jesus who is Emmanuel ("God with us," see 1:23) is with the Christian community "always, to the close of the age" (28:20). They need to recognize that they as the community of Jesus Christ are now God's people (see 21:41, 43) and that they have a duty to share that identity even with people who are not Jewish by birth (see 28:19).

While not entirely suppressing the negative aspects of the disciples, Luke develops the idea that the Twelve Apostles were the principles of continuity between the time of Jesus and the time of the church (as described in Acts). Those who were with the earthly Jesus bear witness to his death and resurrection, and carry on the message and ministry that he began. In the time of the church, which extends from the ascension of Jesus to the end of the world, the Holy Spirit guides the community of Jesus standing in continuity with the first followers of Jesus. Yet for all the positive significance that Luke attributed to the Twelve Apostles, they are not the only examples of discipleship in his Gospel. The disciples include figures from the time of the Old Testament (Zechariah and Elizabeth, Simeon and Anna, John the Baptist), figures from the time of Jesus (the poor, the seventy disciples, etc.), and from the time of the church (those who accept the apostles' message). The one figure spanning all three periods in salvation history is Mary, the ideal disciple who hears God's word and keeps it (see Luke 8:19–21; 11:27–28).

The following chart illustrates the distinctive theological emphases of the Synoptic Evangelists regarding Jesus, the disciples, and salvation history:

	Mark	Matthew	Luke
Jesus	Suffering Messiah	Fulfillment of OT	Prophet and Martyr
Disciples	Foolish, cowardly	"Little Faith"	Twelve Apostles
Salvation History	Life under the cross	God's people through Christ's abiding presence	The Spirit-guided Church

The Transmission of the Gospel Material

When Vatican II's Constitution on Divine Revelation described the work of the Evangelists, it spoke of them as "selecting some things from the many which had been handed on by word of mouth or in writing." Thus the document asserts that the final product of the Gospels came at the end of an extended period in which traditions from or about Jesus had been handed on in oral or written forms. Of course, the ecclesiastical document does not specify the precise nature of the sources available to Evangelists. It merely states (as fact) that oral or written sources were available to them.

The scholarly discussion about the sources of the Synoptic Gospels has been intense and necessarily speculative. The three areas that are most important are the Synoptic problem, the nature of Q, and the existence of other sources.

1. Matthew and Luke used the Gospel of Mark and Q. (See Bibliography numbers 3, 15, 17, 24, 25, 32)

The so-called Synoptic problem concerns the relationship among the Gospels attributed to Matthew, Mark, and

Luke. The fact that these three Gospels provide such a common view of Jesus (as opposed to that of John's Gospel) that there must be a genealogical relationship was recognized in patristic times. Augustine thought that Matthew wrote the earliest Gospel, that Mark composed a rather poor imitation of Matthew's work, and that Luke used the other two Synoptic Gospels. In the late eighteenth century, the German New Testament scholar Johann J. Griesbach proposed that Matthew's Gospel was used by Luke and that Mark used the Gospels of Matthew and Luke.

As investigation of the Gospels became more critical in the late nineteenth and early twentieth centuries, scholars began to recognize that Mark's Gospel was most likely the earliest. This theory of Markan priority was accompanied by the realization that Matthew and Luke independently had access to a collection of Jesus' sayings designated by the letter Q. They also used special sources designated by the letters M (Matthean) and L (Lukan). This explanation of the Synoptic problem is called the Two-Document hypothesis or Two-Source theory. It asserts that the Synoptic Gospels are related in the following way:

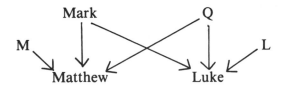

The terms "hypothesis" and "theory" are crucial, for this diagram is simply   the most economical and currently satisfying way to explain the evidence in the Synoptic Gospels. It is not without problems.

Until fairly recently, Catholic scholars usually defended Matthean priority along the lines of Augustine's solution. But during the 1950s and 1960s, Catholics increasingly came to accept the classic formulation of the Two-Document hypothesis, to the point that now the staunchest defenders of this hypothesis are based at the Catholic University of Louvain in Belgium. However, the increasing acceptance of Markan priority and the existence of Q does not mean that all Catholic New Testament scholars agree. Some Catholic scholars (e.g., Bernard Orchard) have been prominent in the revival of the so-called Griesbach hypothesis, and others (e.g., M.-E. Boismard) have developed more sophisticated and complex explanations of the Synoptic problem. Thus the most popular Gospel commentaries written by Catholic scholars now take for granted the Two-Document hypothesis, while individual researchers try to develop even more adequate and comprehensive solutions to the Synoptic problem.

The quest to understand the relationship among the Synoptic Gospels is an important undertaking, for on its solution depends the way we look at the development of early Christianity. In the first section of this article, I followed the majority of scholars in assuming the validity of Markan priority and the use of Q by Matthew and Luke. What I said about the life settings, outlines, and theological emphases of the Gospels would stand up no matter what solution to the Synoptic problem I chose. But if I tried to sketch out the history of early Christianity on the basis of the Griesbach hypothesis, or the Two-Document hypothesis, or Boismard's explanation, I would necessarily produce three very different scenarios.

2. Q was a collection of Jesus' sayings written in Greek during the 50s. (See Bibliography numbers 11, 14)

The letter Q has been used since the 1890s to designate the collection of sayings used independently by Matthew and Luke in addition to Mark's Gospel. The cipher Q bears some relationship to the German word *Quelle,* meaning "source," though exactly how it first came to be used among New Testament scholars has been a topic of recent controversy. The existence and content of Q is a hypothesis. The source has been reconstructed by investigating those passages in which Matthew and Luke agree and Mark has nothing at all. Once possible Q material has been isolated (e.g. Matt 3:7–10; Luke 3:7–9), one must distinguish the Evangelist's peculiar contributions from the wording of the source and argue about which Evangelist (usually Luke) better preserved the form of Q.

When the possible Q material is sifted out along these lines, what emerges is a collection of Jesus' sayings without a passion narrative. Among the theological emphases of the Q material are preparation for the return of Jesus as the Son of Man, and need to carry on Jesus' proclamation of God's kingdom, and the preparation for hostility and persecution. Though based on oral material expressed in Aramaic or Hebrew, Q most likely came to Matthew and Luke in written form and in Greek. Because the sayings in Q seem more "primitive" than Mark's Gospel, the written Greek form of Q is usually dated to the 50s or early 60s of the first century A.D.

3. Other Written and Oral Sources about Jesus were available. (See Bibliography numbers 1, 4, 8, 10, 12, 18, 23)

The neatness of the Two-Document hypothesis should not obscure the fact that in the early days of Christianity there were many sources about Jesus. In the preface of his Gospel (see 1:1–4), Luke talks freely about "many" who have provided information concerning Jesus and proposes to write "an orderly account" on the basis of such information. Among the "many" were surely Mark and the compiler of Q. But Luke (and Matthew) included other sources (L[and M]) and the infancy story. Whether all the special material in Luke (or Matthew) came from a single source or (what is more likely) from several sources, investigation of those passages pushes us back even further into the Jesus tradition.

When describing Mark's achievement in moving from gospel to Gospel, I listed the kinds of traditions about

Jesus that were available to the first Evangelist: sayings (proverbs, warnings, prophecies, etc.), parables, narratives, controversies or conflicts, healings, and nature miracles. It was the achievement of the so-called form critics in the 1920s to sensitize us to the ways in which the Jesus tradition was shaped and handed on before it was integrated into the larger Gospel framework. The assertions of the form critics about the precise life settings of these literary forms may be open to serious questioning. But there can be no doubt regarding their accomplishment in isolating the chief literary packages in which the Jesus tradition was transmitted.

Were the traditions in M and L and in the pre-Markan material in written or oral form? Although it is hard to be certain, it does seem that most, if not all, of this source material was in writing. But the predominantly written character of the Jesus tradition does not preclude an oral stage. In fact, some oral tradition is a logical necessity. The real question concerns how extensive and how organized the oral tradition was.

Twenty years ago the general reliability of oral tradition as evidenced by anthropologists and the process of oral transmission developed by Jewish rabbis were often cited as part of an apologetic defence of the historicity of the Gospels. Since then doubts have grown about the applicability of the anthropological evidence and the analogy of rabbinic tradition. We are learning to live with a less neat and simple picture of the early tranmsmission of the Jesus tradition. We are also reckoning with the possibility that in second- and third-century documents like the *Gospel of Thomas* or the *Secret Gospel of Mark* there may be some very early traces of the Jesus tradition that have escaped inclusion in our canonical Gospels.

Gospel interpreters must also reckon with the possibility that some materials attributed to Jesus in the Synoptic Gospels were the product of the creative activity of unknown early Christians or the Evangelists. This possibility arises from the fact that our modern distinction between the historical Jesus and the Christ of faith was unknown to the early Christians. The form critics argued that some sayings and stories attached to Jesus in the Gospels originated in connection with various situations confronted by the church only after Jesus' death. In other words, such sayings or actions represented what Jesus would have said or done if he were still present physically. Another possible source of Jesus' sayings could have been the activity of early Christian prophets who spoke in Jesus' name under the guidance of the Holy Spirit. A third source could have been the creation of teachings or events connected to Jesus on the basis of Old Testament models. Although it is always difficult to be certain in particular cases, readers of the Synoptic Gospels should at least be aware of the possibility of creative activity on the part of the early church.

The Events Behind the Gospels

The last part of the Constitution on Divine Revelation's description of the Evangelists' work states that "they told us the honest truth about Jesus." This phrase raises the issue of the historical reliability of the Gospels and the relation of the Gospel texts to the events that they describe. The assumption that the Evangelists told the honest truth about Jesus does not demand a fundamentalist reading of the Gospels from Catholics. In fact, such a reading hardly does justice to the nature of the Gospels and the purpose of the Evangelists. This section of our survey considers the possibility of writing a life of Jesus on the basis of the canonical Gospels, the ways in which we can reach some certainty about the teaching of the earthly Jesus, and the special problems posed by the virginal conception and resurrection accounts.

*1. The Gospels do not Allow us to Write the
Biography of Jesus.* (See Bibliography numbers 34–36)

That somewhat shocking statement is not really very radical when it is explained. No biblical scholar of any stature doubts the existence of Jesus of Nazareth as a historical figure in Palestine in the early part of what has come to be known as the Christian era. Neither does any reputable scholar doubt certain historical facts about this Jesus of Nazareth: He was raised in Nazareth of Galilee, was baptized by John the Baptist, carried out a ministry of healing and teaching in Palestine, gathered disciples around him, went up to Jerusalem, was crucified around A.D. 30 by the Roman officials there, and was said to have appeared alive again to his disciples. Granting the historical existence of Jesus and the basic outline of his life in the Gospels, we still cannot write a detailed biography in the modern sense or even a didactic biography in the ancient sense.

In moving from gospel to Gospel, Mark imposed on his disparate sources his own geographical and theological outline. This outline was taken over and developed in various ways by Matthew and Luke. That the Markan outline corresponds to the actual outline of Jesus' life is not impossible. Nevertheless, it remains necessary to explain how Mark could present Jesus' public activity as taking place in the span of one year with only one journey to Jerusalem, and John could extend it over three years and have Jesus make several trips to Jerusalem.

A more promising and less anachronistic model for understanding the Synoptic Gospels is the didactic biography popular in antiquity. This analogy accounts for many features in the Gospels; e.g. the presentation of characters as examples to be imitated or avoided, the freedom shown in rearranging material in order to make a point, and the emphasis on moral significance. As helpful as the didactic biography analogy is, it is still too limited a framework for containing the extraordinary claims that the early Christians were making about the person of Jesus. It also fails to do justice to the activity of the believ-

ing community in its memory of Jesus and to the kerygmatic character of the Gospels which speak "from faith to
faith."

For such reasons, it no longer seems possible to write
Jesus' biography. The difficulties involved in this task only
became clear in liberal Protestant circles in the early twentieth century. In Catholic circles the tradition of lives of
Jesus (a hybrid of the harmony of the Gospels, historical-
geographical information about Palestine, and meditative
comments) remained alive into the early 1960s. While well
intentioned and often inspiring, these Catholic lives of
Jesus were basically exercises in religious imagination and
too often functioned as substitutes for personal contact
with the Gospel texts.

The Jewishness of Jesus has emerged as an attractive
theme in recent years. Jewish religious thinkers and historians have been reclaiming Jesus as one of their own, and
Christians have been rediscovering Jesus' Jewishness as a
sign of his humanity. Jesus the Jew was born, lived, and
died in first-century Palestine. He stood for the great religious ideas of Israel as expressed in the Hebrew Bible and
the Jewish tradition. Through him, Israel's great heritage
has been transmitted to all nations.

Although both Jews and Christians welcome the attention to the Jewishness of Jesus, it is nevertheless important
to face some problems associated with this topic. First of
all, our increased knowledge of the diversity within Palestinian Judaism in Jesus' time makes it difficult to know what
kind of Jew that Jesus was and against which background
we should try to interpret him. Second, Jewish sources
about Jesus are either late or suspect on other grounds.
Christian sources have passed through a complicated process of transmission. Those who try to get behind those
sources often end up either interpreting Jesus entirely
within the confines of Judaism or in taking him out of
Judaism entirely. Finally, while both Jews and Christians
can agree that Jesus the teacher was a victim of oppression,
the ultimate theological assessment of Jesus made by

orthodox Christians goes beyond what is acceptable to Jews.

2. The Gospels do Allow us to Reconstruct the Teaching of Jesus. (See Bibliography numbers 20, 21, 26, 31, 33)

Given the difficulties involved in proceeding from the analysis of any text to a statement about history and given the special problems involved in using the Synoptic Gospels as historical sources, the task of trying to rediscover the teaching of Jesus may appear doomed to fail. But New Testament scholars have developed some criteria for determining what was distinctive in the teaching and related activity of the earthly Jesus. With these criteria as keys, they are then able to attain some reasonable certainty about the content of that teaching as a whole.

The criteria used in rediscovering the teaching of Jesus can be expressed under four headings: (1) the criterion of discontinuity or dissimilarity; that is, a teaching that for some strong reason cannot be attributed either to Judaism or to the early church may be attributed to the carthly Jesus; (2) the criterion of multiple attestation; that is, a teaching present in a wide spread of sources (Mark, Q, M, L, John, Paul) probably echoes the voice of the earthly Jesus; (3) the criterion of Palestinian setting; that is, teachings whose language or content demand a setting in first-century Palestine have a good chance of reflecting the words of Jesus; and (4) the criterion of coherence; that is, those teachings that are consistent with the first three criteria may be authentic teachings of Jesus.

There are some obvious problems connected with the logic of these so-called authenticating criteria. After all, Jesus was a first-century Jew, and the early church deliberately stood in continuity with him. The appearance of a teaching in several different Gospel sources does not necessarily imply that it goes back to Jesus, since someone else could just as easily have created the teaching. The earliest

Christians were Aramaic-speaking Palestinian Jews just as Jesus was. The criterion of coherence depends for its ultimate validity on the other three criteria.

Despite such problems of logic, the application of these criteria has resulted in a reasonably clear and certain picture of Jesus' teaching. Basic to Jesus' words and deeds seems to have been a relationship of special intimacy with God as Father—a status and style of piety that he invited others to share. The focus of Jesus' life and teaching was the coming kingdom of God—when God's reign over all creation would be manifest and acknowledged by all. There are hints that even in the ministry of Jesus this kingdom had been anticipated or inaugurated. Jesus extended the offer of forgiveness and reconciliation with God to the outcasts of society—the poor, tax collectors, sinners, women, etc. To them he held out the possibility of a new relationship with God as Father and of a life lived in response to the divine forgiveness. Jesus' free attitude toward the traditions surrounding the Old Testament Law and perhaps even the Law itself strained his relationship with the Jewish officials and may even have contributed to his death.

3. The Virginal Conception and Resurrection Accounts pose Special problems for the Historian. (See Bibliography numbers 6, 7, 22, 28)

A few years ago it became fashionable to describe the stories of Jesus' infancy as "midrash," with the implication that hardly anything in Matthew 1—2 and Luke 1—2 qualifies as history. That description is not very accurate, since in Jewish circles "midrash" refers to the interpretation of biblical texts, not to the sort of events described in the New Testament infancy narratives. But the term "midrash" at least makes the point that in these infancy narratives there are serious attempts at placing the birth of Jesus in line with those of Moses (Matthew) and Samson and Samuel (Luke). Yet they are not simply exercises in religious imagination for they tell about real historical figures (Jesus,

John the Baptist, Mary, Herod the Great) and real places (Bethlehem and Nazareth). They also contain "theological" elements in the sense that what was believed about Jesus as an adult (his messiahship and his universal mission) is said to have been present even from his birth.

The infancy stories in Matthew and Luke combine Old Testament elements, historical facts, and theological ideas. The problem is to know which is which—a problem that serves as the background for the debate about the virginal conception of Jesus; that is, the belief that Jesus was conceived in the womb of the virgin Mary without the intervention of a human father. Matthew (see 1:20) and Luke (see 1:31–35) believed that this was so, and in this case they provide independent witnesses to an early tradition about Jesus' virginal conception.

Among the arguments raised against the ultimate historicity of the virginal conception tradition are its "high" Christology, the silence of the other New Testament writers, and the rejection of this tradition in some second-century Jewish-Christian circles. Modern critics also pose questions about the physical impossibilities of such an event. The traditional response to such criticism is the appeal to the personal testimony of Mary. But it is now considered very dubious that Mary's reminiscenses formed the basis for the New Testament infancy stories. And even if they did, they would only be her testimony. I am not denying the historical character of the virginal conception, but I am suggesting that historians can only go so far in affirming or denying its historicity because of the nature of the sources at their disposal.

A similar problem is encountered in the resurrection accounts, for dead people are not normally restored to life. In fact, there is no description of the resurrection of Jesus in the New Testament. What we do have are stories about the empty tomb (Mark 16:1 –8; Matthew 28:1 –15; Luke 24:1–12) and the appearances of the risen Lord (Matthew 28:16–20; Luke 24:13–53; see 1 Cor 15:3–8). At best, they only prove that the tomb was empty and that Jesus' disciples experienced him as alive after his death. They do not constitute solid historical proof that God raised Jesus from the dead. Indeed, such a statement bursts the framework of assumptions on which modern historiography is based— the assumptions that everything must be explained on the basis of our present-day experience of the world and in terms of human cause and effect.

In the cases of the virginal conception and the resurrection, what emerges is a problem of historiography. Modern historians proceed on the basis of assumptions that by definition cannot make room for Jesus' virginal conception or resurrection; these events are beyond the scope of so-called scientific history, which operates according to the principles of analogy and cause-and-effect. Furthermore, the ancient writers responsible for the infancy narratives and the empty tomb and appearance stories were not modern newspaper reporters concerned only with the bare facts (Who? What? When? Where? Why?). The problem of historiography encountered in the virginal conception and the resurrection is due to the different assumptions and expectations of the people in the first century A.D. and the twentieth century.

Conclusion

This panoramic view of scholarship on the Synoptic Gospels ends as it began—with a personal reminiscence of Bruce Vawter. One of the first books that I read about the Bible was his *The Bible in the Church* (New York: Sheed and Ward, 1959). One idea in that little book which especially excited me was the contribution of the early church in shaping and producing the book that we call the New Testament. The idea of the Bible as the church's book was new to me at the age of nineteen, and I recall vividly what intellectual vistas Vawter opened up for me then.

Many years have passed, and the idea is no longer new to me precisely because it was so true and because it arises at almost every juncture in contemporary biblical scholarship. But perhaps at no point is it more appropriate and illuminating than in reflecting on the life settings and theological perspectives of the Synoptic Evangelists, the transmisssion of the Gospel material, and the events behind the Gospels.

BIBLIOGRAPHY

1. Aune, David E. *Prophecy in Early Christianity and the Ancient Mediterranean World.* Grand Rapids, MI: Eerdmans, 1983.

2. Best, Ernest. *Mark: The Gospel as Story.* Edinburgh: T. & T. Clark, 1983.

3. Boismard, M.-E., and Pierre Benoit. *Synopse des quatres Evangiles en français, Tome II: Commentaire.* Paris: Cerf, 1972.

4. Boring, M. Eugene. *Sayings of the Risen Jesus: Christian Prophecy in the Synoptic Tradition.* New York: Cambridge University Press, 1982.

5. Bornkamm, Günther, Gerhard Barth, and Heinz Joachim Held. *Tradition and Interpretation in Matthew.* Philadelphia: Westminister; London: SCM, 1982.

6. Brown, Raymond E. *The Birth of the Messiah: A Commentary on the Infancy Narratives in Matthew and Luke.* Garden City, NY: Doubleday, 1977.

7. _____. *The Virginal Conception and the Bodily Resurrection of Jesus.* New York: Paulist, 1973.

8. Bultmann, Rudolph. *The History of the Synoptic Tradition.* Oxford: Blackwell, 1963.

9. Conzelmann, Hans. *The Theology of Saint Luke.* Philadelphia: Fortress, 1982.

10. Crossan, John Dominic. *In Fragments: The Aphorisms of Jesus.* San Francisco: Harper & Row, 1983.

11. Delobel, J., ed. *Logia: Les Paroles de Jésus—The Sayings of Jesus.* Leuven: Peeters—Leuven University Press, 1982.

12. Dibelius, Martin. *From Tradition to Gospel.* New York: Scribner's, 1934.

13. Dunn, James D.G. *Christology in the Making.* Philadelphia: Westminster, 1980.

14. Edwards, Richard A. *A Theology of Q: Eschatology, Prophecy, and Wisdom.* Philadelphia: Fortress, 1976.

15. Farmer, William R. *Jesus and the Gospel: Tradition, Scripture, and Canon.* Philadelphia: Fortress, 1982.

16. Fitzmyer, Joseph A. *The Gospel According to Luke.* AB 28 Garden City, NY: Doubleday, 1981, 1985.

17. _____. *To Advance the Gospel: New Testament Studies.* New York: Crossroad, 1981. 3-40.

18. Gerhardsson, Birger. *Memory and Manuscript.* Lund: Gleerup, 1961.

19. Harrington, Wilfrid. *Mark.* Wilmington, DE: Glazier, 1979.

20. Jeremias, Joachim. *New Testament Theology: The Proclamation of Jesus.* New York: Scribner's, 1971.

21. _____. *The Parables of Jesus.* New York: Scribner's, 1963.

22. Kee, Howard C. *Miracle in the Early Christian World. A Study in Socio-historical Method.* New Haven, CT; London: Yale University Press, 1983.

23. Kelber, Werner H. *The Oral and the Written Gospel.* Philadelphia: Fortress, 1983.

24. Koester, Helmut. *Introduction to the New Testament. Volume Two: History and Literature of Early Christianity.* Philadelphia: Fortress, 1982.

25. Kümmel, Werner Georg. *Introduction to the New Testament.* Nashville,TN: Abingdon, 1975. 38–80.

26. Lambrecht, Jan. *Once More Astonished: The Parables of Jesus.* New York: Crossroad, 1981.

27. LaVerdiere, Eugene. *Luke.* Wilmington, DE: Glazier, 1980.

28. Léon-Dufour, Xavier. *Resurrection and the Message of Easter.* New York: Holt, Rinehart & Winston, 1975.

29. Marxsen, Willi. *Mark the Evangelist: Studies of the Redaction History of the Gospel.* Nashville, TN: Abingdon, 1969.

30. Meier, John P. *Matthew.* Wilmington,DE: Glazier, 1979.

31. Meyer, Ben F. *The Aims of Jesus.* London: SCM, 1979.

32. Orchard, Bernard. *Matthew, Luke and Mark.* Manchester: Koinonia, 1976.

33. Perrin, Norman. *Rediscovering the Teaching of Jesus.* New York: Harper & Row, 1967.

34. Sanders, E.P. *Jesus and Judaism.* Philadelphia: Fortress, 1985.

35. Schweitzer, Albert. *The Quest of the Historical Jesus: A Critical Survey of its Progress from Reimarus to Wrede.* New York: Macmillan, 1959.

36. Vermes, Geza. *Jesus the Jew.* Revised ed. Philadelphia: Fortress, 1981.

PAULINE LITERATURE

Robert J. Karris, O.F.M.

Catholic Theological Union, Chicago

Since it is impossible to do justice to all thirteen letters which bear Paul's name in the New Testament, I will limit myself to examples representative of contemporary currents in Pauline research. The social world of Paul the Apostle will be illustrated primarily from 1 Corinthians. The quest for the heart of Paul's theology will be exampled from Romans. Finally, the distinction between the scholars' Paul and the Church's Paul will be highlighted from 1–2 Timothy and Titus (the Pastoral Epistles).

1. 1 Corinthians and the Social World of Paul the Apostle

1. 1 Paul the Tentmaker (See Bibliography no. 1).

Investigations into Paul's social context have enriched our understanding of Paul and the communities he founded. In the past it was known that Paul was a tentmaker (see Acts 18:35), but little scholarly effort was expended on relating Paul's tentmaking to his missionary preaching and to his society. Sufficient, it seemed, was the explanation that as a rabbi Paul had to have a trade to earn his living.

Recent research by Ronald Hock has set Paul the tentmaker in his social context. Paul, the Roman citizen, who seems to have come from a moderately well-to-do family, went through two to three years of a very disciplined apprenticeship, so that he could preach the gospel free of charge and not be a burden to or be misunderstood by any community. Society had other options available to Paul, the wise man and teacher. Like other teachers in his society, he could have supported himself by begging, by finding a rich patron, or by charging fees for his teaching. But Paul chose the option very few teachers selected: working at a skilled or unskilled job.

As a leather worker — tentmaking is a specialization of leatherworking just as cabinetmaking is a specialization of carpentry — Paul made thongs, gourds for water and wine, harnesses, saddles, shields, as well as tents, tents which were used on ships, by the army, and at festivals. He worked at a trade forbidden by the Rabbinic oral tradition because the unclean substance, urine, was used to tan leather. His equipment of knives and awls was very light and enabled him to move freely from place to place. As Paul narrates in 1 Thess 2:9, he had to work from before sunrise to sunset to make ends meet. He labored in a shop that was 12' high, 12' deep, and 9–12' wide. And since Paul traveled so much, he had not time to establish a reputation which would bring new customers to his shop and offset competition. He was almost always the new leatherworker on the block of shops. Like other teachers who worked with their hands Paul's main audiences were folks who dropped into his shop, either on business or to hear his wisdom. In contemporary imagery, Paul was not the stadium preacher of Billy Graham's stature with many advance people; rather he was like Eric Hoffer, the longshoreman-philosopher who taught for those who would listen.

And as 1 Cor 9 (see also 2 Cor 11:7–15 and 12:13–16) shows, the Corinthians were not pleased with Paul who did not make full use of his right in the gospel to be paid for his spiritual services. The Corinthians gladly gave financial support to Paul's opponents, the "superlative apostles" (2 Cor 12:11). In contemporary terms, they trusted the professional who charged $100 rather than the one whose services were free. But Paul will not allow himself to be put on a par with these apostles and will not accept money from the Corinthians (although he does accept money from the Philippians), lest they mistake him for them.

The social context of Paul the tentmaker allows us to garner rich insights into Paul the apostle. The former zealot for the law, Paul the Pharisee, engages in a trade forbidden by Pharisaic oral law. With knives and awls in his knapsack Paul travels 10,000 miles from city workshop to city workshop to spread the gospel. Paul, the Roman citizen and person of means, labors side by side with social inferiors, from sunrise to sunset to support himself. His preaching is mainly to those one or two people who can crowd themselves into his shop. He does all this, lest people mistake him for a sophist whose purpose in teaching is to become rich. He does all this, to show his paternal and maternal love for his converts (see 1 Thess 2:1–12)

1. 2 Paul The Athlete of Jesus Christ
(See Bibliography no. 2).

In 1 Cor 9:24–27 (see also Phil 3:11–14; Phil 1:27; 4:3) Paul uses the imagery of running and boxing to illustrate his call. Oscar Broneer has made the intriguing suggestion that Paul's sports imagery was drawn from the Isthmian games, one of the four panhellenic games. Sponsored by Corinth and located some 10 miles from Corinth, the Isthmian games were held every two years in the Spring. Paul could have attended the Isthmian games of either 49 or 51. There he would have been able to sell his leather goods and preach the gospel to some of the thousands who flocked to the games; he also would have been able to renew contacts with some of his converts and fellow workers.

While Broneer's suggestion about Paul's social context is

plausible, one need not restrict the possible sources for Paul's sports imagery to the bi-annual Isthmian games. As H.W. Pleket and H. A. Harris have shown, every Greek city had a stadium; there were some 300 important athletic contests at Paul's time; the athletes were handsomely rewarded and were heroes of their cities; the athletic contests were the greatest spectator attractions in the Greek world. Paul did not have to go to Isthmia to discover the athletic imagery. It was available to him in every city he went as he plied his trade of tentmaking.

Paul adopts the sports imagery of his social context and transforms it into a vehicle of the gospel. Paul and his fellow male and female Christian athletes have been called to enter the race of spreading the gospel. The goal is not a finish line some 100, 400, or even 4800 yards away. The goal is a life-long one, the spread of the gospel. Paul did not want to get into this race. He was seized for it, and responded vigorously to his call to be Christ's athlete. Gerald F. Hawthorne comments insightfully on Phil 3:12–16:

> Like an athlete with every nerve and muscle taut, with body thrust forward, with eyes firmly fixed on the goal, so Paul pictures his own ceaseless exertion, his own intensity of desire to reach the end of life and gain the prize. Every part of his existence is thrust wholly into the contest to win. Just as the victor in the Olympian games was called up to the judges' stand to receive the crown at the hands of the Agonothete, so Paul hoped to be called up to receive from God the award he coveted: full knowledge of Christ Jesus (p. 158).

There may also be a deeper dimension behind Paul's use of the athletic imagery of his social context. Why does this once staunch Pharisee use the race imagery anyway? From the time at least of the Maccabean revolt against Antiochus Epiphanes IV and his hellenization of Judea, there was opposition to sports in Judea. An anwer to our query about the whence of Paul's sports imagery may be found in the philosophy of sports. Michael Novak has observed that the victories of sport are ritual triumphs of grace, agility, perfection, and beauty over the process of aging and death (p. 48). On the one hand, Paul seems to use sports imagery to underline the dynamism of his call and response. On the other hand, he employs it to stress that the victory over aging and death which is symbolized in the victory crown Paul strives for is not his accomplishment, but has been won by God's conquest of death in Jesus Christ.

1.3 Paul and the Christian Community at Worship: 1 Cor 11-14 (See Bibliography no. 3).

It seems that most authors on the social world of Paul isolate what Paul says about the Eucharist in 1 Cor 11:17-34 from what he says about other aspects of Christian worship in the rest of 1 Cor 11-14. The operating hypothesis seems to be that Paul is dealing with two different worship gatherings: one for Eucharist, the other for prophecy, glossolalia, interpretation of glossolalia, etc. In what follows I will develop a different hypothesis: in 1 Cor 11-14 Paul addresses problems associated with one worship service. The heart of my hypothesis will be the idea that Paul treats of a worship service which is built on the symposion model. The symposion has two basic parts: the meal; drinking accompanied by discussion. I will develop my hypothesis in three stages.

1.3.1 Problems which Paul encounters in Christian worship at Corinth

It seems that many of the problems with which Paul has to deal in 1 Cor 11-14 stem from the confrontation of Christian values with the values inherent in the Graeco-Roman symposion. Paul may have preached one thing, but the Corinthians heard another.

In 1 Cor 11:2-16 Paul raises the question of the role of women in worship. He will return to this subject in 1 Cor 14:33b-36. As a general rule, one can say that women were excluded from symposia. Their presence at the Christian symposia created problems as Christian values came into conflict with cultural expectations and fears of possible improper conduct. It should be noted that women pray and prophesy at the Christian worship service (1 Cor 11:5).

In 1 Cor 11:17–34 Paul addresses the well-to-do members of the community who host the Lord's Supper, perhaps on the model of the symposion, and provide their peers with more sumptuous fare than the mere bread and wine they supply for the rest. In following accepted social customs, these relatively rich Christians fail to recognize the Christian value of the Body and humiliate, in Paul's eyes, the have-nots. Moreover, these well-meaning Christians, upon entering the drink phase of the symposion, imbibe too freely and get drunk.

1 Cor 12–14 address many issues which were also subjects in treatments of symposia, especially the symposion's second part of drinking and discussion. Paul has to remind the community that its powerful gifts stem from drinking of the one Spirit (1 Cor 12:13) and not from drinking from an amphora of wine. Like the moralist Plutarch, Paul in 1 Cor 13–14 is concerned with those who exalt themselves and their personal gifts over fellowship. For Paul love and the building up of the Body are more important than ecstasy, whether generated by the Spirit or by spirits. In 1 Cor 14:33b–36 Paul returns to the troublesome Christian value of the presence of women at worship. And in 1 Cor 14:40 Paul states explicitly what has been implicit throughout 1 Cor 14: let all be done in order. In insisting on good order at the symposion, Paul echoes the repeated concern of Plutarch and other moralists.

1.3.2 Physical Structure of the House in which the Community met

The research of Jerome Murphy-O'Connor has been most helpful in trying to reconstruct the actual physical setting for 1 Cor 11:17–34. His basic model is the house or villa of a rich person found in the Anaploga section of

Corinth. The dining room or triclinium of this villa is roughly 41 square yards and has couches. The couches on which the diners reclined were 3' wide, 6' long, and 1' high. Adjacent to the triclinium was the atrium which was about 30 square yards. The remaining rooms were bedrooms and other private quarters. Murphy-O'Connor argues that in the triclinium and atrium of this villa, whose size is typical almost throughout the Roman Empire, 30–40 people could be accommodated.

Drawing upon the model from the house of Anaploga and also from the house of the Vettii at Pompeii, Murphy-O'Connor argues that the house in which the Christian community at Corinth met was that of a rich member of the community and would have been similar to the models proposed. When the sub-groups in the Corinthian community gathered together to eat, space in the triclinium was adequate. But for those instances when the entire community gathered together (some 50 people at a minimum), Murphy-O'Connor goes on to postulate tht the wealthy peers of the owner of the villa would have reclined with the owner in the triclinium and would have eaten finer fare than the Christians who sat in the atrium adjacent to the triclinium and supped on bread and wine.

Murphy-O'Connor's reconstruction is an attractive one for 1 Cor 11:17–34, and may even illumine the rest of 1 Cor 11–14. For think of the order one would have to bring to bear on one community gathered in two different rooms trying to listen to revelations, prophecies, teachings, speaking in tongues, and interpretation of tongues as the symposion moved into its second stage. A slight modification of Murphy-O'Connor's reconstruction might be proposed here. From the houses of the Vettii and of the Fawn at Pompeii one knows that a house of a wealthy person might have had a number of triclinia and that during the summer people took their meals in the garden or peristyle. If one would follow the model of houses from Pompeii, one would not need to have so many Corinthians sitting squashed in the atrium. Nevertheless, even in the proposed scenario, the problem of superior food for the wealthy and inferior fare for the have-nots as well as the problem of maintaining order among the groups would still be present.

1.3.3. The Social Customs of the Symposion in the Graeco-Roman Period

Since we anticipated many of these social customs in section 1.3.1 above, we can be brief in this section. The common structural elements in the symposion were: food; a religious ritual, e.g., libation as a transition from food to drink; drink and the symposion proper which consisted of discussion, entertainment, and usually the presence of a flute girl (prostitute). These symposia began at 3 or 4 in the afternoon and usually lasted a minimum of three hours. The average person would attend two a month. In Latin circles there would be six or nine or twelve people present. In Greek circles there could be 36 or more. Upright women were normally not present.

Some of the problems connected with the symposia were: feuds over social status and places of honor at table; lewd conduct of various kinds; drunkenness; lack of order; discrimination in the amount and kinds of food served. This last point deserves further treatment.

Gerd Theissen has called attention to texts from Martial and Juvenal as illuminative parallels to 1 Cor 11:17-34. These authors criticize discriminatory practices which they have experienced at symposia:

> Since I am asked to dinner, no longer, as before, a purchased guest, why is not the same dinner served to me as to you? You take oysters fattened in the Lucrine lake, I suck a mussel through a hole in the shell; you get mushrooms, I take hog funguses; you tackle turbot, but I brill. Golden with fat, a turtledove gorges you with its bloated rump; there is set before me a magpie that has died in its cage. Why do I dine without you although, Pontus, I am dining with you? the dole has gone: let us have the benefit of that; let us eat the same fare (Martial, *Epigrammata*, 3, 60).

On p. 158 Theissen summarizes Juvenal's description of Virro's symposion in *Satura* 5:

> While the host helps himself to good and old wine, fresh bread, plump liver and all kinds of delicacies, the guest must be content with bitter wine, moldy bread, cabbage which smells like lamp oil, suspicious-looking mushrooms, an old hen, and rotten apples. The result is a violent squabble among those invited.

1.3.4 Conclusions

Analysis of Paul's social world aids us in appreciating Christian worship at Corinth. The abuse at the Corinthian Eucharist was not an unworthy reception of Holy Communion in general. The social contest suggests that the reception of Holy Communion was unworthy because the well-to-do Christian hosts could not extricate themselves from their cultural perspectives and were discriminating against the Christian have-nots who belonged to the same Body. They were eating finer food and drinking superior quality wine in intoxicating amounts. Moreover, good order and decency were in short supply. Some men did not want the women to participate actively at worship. To this latter point we turn in our next consideration, that of the role of women in the Corinthian congregation.

1.4 Paul and Women: 1 Cor 14:33b-36 (See Bibliography no. 4).

1.4.1 Paul and Women: the General Social and Religious Context

Within the last ten years or so there has been intense interest in the subject of Paul and women. While there still may be considerable misunderstanding among lay people about the role of women in the Pauline communities, among professionals it has become quite clear that women played a prominent role in Paul's ministry and in the churches he established.

While exceptions existed, it is generally true that women had an inferior status and role in antiquity. As Elisabeth Schüssler Fiorenza observes:

> It was a rhetorical commonplace that Hellenistic man was grateful to the gods because he was fortunate enough to be born a human being and not a beast, a Greek and not a barbarian, a free man and not a slave, a man and not woman. This cultural pattern seems to have been adopted by Judaism in the first or second centuries C.E. and found its way into the synagogue liturgy. Three times a Jewish man thanked God that he did not create him a gentile, a slave, or a woman. This is not a misogynist prayer but an expression of gratitude for religious male privilege...(p. 217).

Pauline statements about the role of women in the church and in ministry must be seen within the above general social context of male religious privilege. Truly revolutionary is the baptismal impetus of Gal 3:28: in Christ Jesus there is no Jew or Greek, no male or female, no slave or free. As Rom 16:1–16 and Phil 4:2–3 indicate, Paul had female co-workers. And as we have seen above, women not only participated in the Christian symposion, but also assumed the important posts of prophet and pray-er (1 Cor 11:5).

It was not easy for new converts, especially men, to assimilate this Christian and Pauline value of equality of male and female in community, worship, and ministry. The dominant cultural and religious values of male superiority could not be stripped off overnight — perhaps not even by Paul himself! An analysis of 1 Cor 14:33b–36 will allow us to see this conflict in Christian and cultural values in operation.

1.4.2 Paul and Women in 1 Cor 14:33b–36: Christian and Cultural Values in Tension

We first treat general isssues. This context is authentic, that is, it is not interpolated into 1 Cor at the end of the first century when 1 Tim 2:8–15 was written. Moreover, this text fits its context: the words, "speak," "be silent," "be subject," and "learn," found in 1 Cor 14:33b–36 also occur in their immediate context. Also, it must be recalled that Paul in 1 Cor 7 highly favors virgins and that in 1 Cor 11:5 he states that women prophesy and pray during worship. Then, too, the Greek of 1 Cor 14:33b–36 indicates that Paul is not talking about women in general, but about wives; that 1 Cor 14:36 begins with a strong adversative particle, é ("What!" in the Revised Standard Version), which is also found in 1 Cor 11:22; and that "the only ones" (1 Cor 14:36 in RSV) can be exclusive and refer solely to men. Furthermore, it must be noted that Paul's society was very insistent that wives not speak in public. Even Plutarch, who championed the equality of women and presented Eumetis as participating at a symposion, has her respond to Cleodoros through Aesop. In addition, as we noted above in 1.3.1 and 1.3.3, an important value to be maintained at a symposion was good order. Finally, there is scholarly consensus that Paul does quote from his opponents in 1 Cor 6:12, 13; 7:1; 8:1 and 10:23. After quoting from their positions, he refutes them.

From the above general observations two interpretations have been fashioned. Both of them show the difficulty Christians had in assimilating Christian values in the face of strong cultural norms. The first interpretation maintains that the cultural value of public order and decency was a stronger value for Paul in this instance than equality of male and female in worship. Wives should not ask disruptive questions during the second part of the symposion. Some scholars who champion this interpretation are quick to add that Paul does not say that wives should subordinate themselves to male community leaders or to their husbands.

The second interpretation is a very recent one and builds upon the accepted thesis that Paul often quotes from his opponents in 1 Corinthians. These opponents are generally seen to espouse the "spiritual" over the "fleshly." Women, especially because of giving birth to the fleshly, could be seen as people to be avoided (see 1 Cor 7:1: "It is well for a man not to touch a woman"). These "gnostic" opponents, whom Paul confronts in 1 Corinthians, would not tolerate women prophets and pray-ers at worship. This interpretation maintains that in 1 Cor 14:34–35 Paul quotes the position of these gnostic opponents as he has quoted their positions in 1 Cor 6:12, 13; 7:1; 8:1 and 10:23. In 1 Cor 14:36 Paul refutes his opponents' view as found in 1 Cor 14:34–35. What follows is the translation of David W. Odell-Scott of 1 Cor 14:33–36:

> For God is not a God of chaos, but of peace as is maintained in all the churches of the saints. Let our women be silent, for it is not fitting for them to speak. But let them be subject in the Spirit as we men interpret it for them, as even the regulations of the churches maintain. If they want to learn anything, let them ask their own husbands at home, for it is shameful for a woman to speak in the public assembly of the church. I don't agree with you men at all. Has the word of God originated with you? Are you men the only ones to whom it has come?

In this second interpretation it is some of the Corinthian men, not Paul, who cannot assimilate Christian values. They bypass the values of the incarnation and that of co-equality of male and female in Jesus Christ.

While this second interpretation is attractive, it needs more scholarly testing. More solidly established in the text and in the social context of Paul's time is the first interpretation. In this interpretation we discover that not even the great apostle Paul can, at all times, transcend his culture. Paul, whose vision of the church in Gal 3:28 remains a challenge to this very day, would not allow any and all explanations of that vision. For him that vision had to conform to the cultural norm of good order and thus of public respectability.

The study of Paul's social context has increased our knowledge of Paul. The title, St. Paul: Apostle to the Gentiles, takes on new meaning when we envision Paul as doing much of his preaching to one or two people in a tentmaker's shop. A new angle of interpretation is given to that same title when we realize that much of Paul's proclamation of the Gospel was done by his establishment of inclusive communities. The fact that men and women, well-to-do and have-nots were gathered together at the Christian symposion spoke eloquently of the nature of the Gospel and of Paul's vision of humanity. And Paul had been seized by Jesus Christ to be an athlete in the race of proclaiming this Gospel to the ends of the earth. Paul's own words about the challenge and demands of this race form a fitting conclusion to this section: "I focus on one thing only; while forgetting what is behind me, and stretching out to what lies before me, I keep running towards the goal-marker, straight for the prize to which God calls me up, the prize that is contained in Christ Jesus" (Phil 3:13–14 in the translation of Gerald F. Hawthorne).

2. Romans and the Quest for the Heart of Paul's Theology (See Bibliography no. 5).

From investigations into the social world of Paul we move into the question of what motivated Paul the tentmaker and athlete of Jesus Christ. We ask questions about the heart of Paul's theology and do so from an examination of Romans, Paul's most important letter.

Although discussion about the occasion and nature of Romans continues in "The Romans Debate," that debate will not be our concern in this section. Rather, we will concentrate on the theme of the righteousness of God, the function of chaps. 9–11 in Romans, and the paradigm of the story of God's acts of righteousness as a key to Paul's theology.

2.1 The Theme of the Righteousness of God (See Bibliography no. 6).

Over the last twenty years or so much progress has been made in understanding the phrase "the righteousness of God," which occurs so frequently in Romans. Although the Reformation debates still linger on in some quarters, there is much agreement on three aspects of the meaning of "the righteousness of God." First, "the righteousness of God" is not a doctrine which defines a static God. Rather, "the righteousness of God" refers to a God active in creation and history for salvation; it is event-oriented. As Marion L. Soards says, after surveying Paul's use of "the righteousness of God": "*'the righteousness of God' in the writings of Paul means the saving power of God that is at work in the world unto salvation*'" (p. 107; emphasis in original).

A second point of agreement is that the theme of "the righteousness of God" stems from the universe of discourse called apocalyptic. Apocalyptic thought interprets reality from the perspective of God's plan for salvation. The theme of "the righteousness of God" enables Paul to interpret the realities of the Christ event, of vast Jewish unbelief in the Christ event, of the reign of Sin and Death in the cosmos, and of creation's incomplete status. The sub-title of J. Christiaan Beker's book captures this dimension of "the righteousness of God" succinctly: *Paul the Apostle: The Triumph of God in Life and Thought.* From observed reality it would seem that Sin and Death are in control of the world. From Paul's apocalyptic perspective he knows in faith that God is in control and has shown his definitive plan for the salvation of the cosmos in the Christ event. In his righteousness God has triumphed over Sin and Death in the death and resurrection of Jesus, the Messiah. Faith in God's act of righteousness in Jesus Christ enables the

Christian to move from the realms of Sin and Death into those of grace and life.

A third and final point of agreement is that "the righteousness of God" has universal dimensions and should not be privatized. It is not just God's mercy for the tortured "introspective consciences" of individual Western men and women. It is not just God's action for the liberation of oppressed believers. God's righteousness is God's salvific action for both Jew and Gentile, that is, for all people. It is God's salvific action for liberation from all oppression, even that caused by Christians themselves. It is God's action not just for humanity, but for all creation which groans for its liberation (Rom 8:18–25).

Paul the Apostle labored day and night as a tentmaker, strove day after day as an athlete towards the goal of proclaiming to the whole world the Gospel of God. And in Romans he defines that Gospel which motivated him as the gospel of God's righteousness, manifested in Jesus Christ: "For I am not ashamed of the gospel. For it is God's saving power for every one who believes, both for Jew and for the Greek. For in it God's righteousness is being revealed from faith to faith, even as it is written: 'But he who is righteous by faith shall live'" (Rom 1:16–17 in Cranfield's translation).

2.2 Romans 9–11 is Integral to Paul's Development of the Theme of the Righteousness of God (See Bibliography no. 7).

In Rom 9–11 Paul deals with the reality that the vast majority of God's elect people have not believed in Jesus as the Messiah. But before delving into how Rom 9–11 fits into Paul's overall argument in Romans, I deem it very important to clear up one matter. It is this: the position commonly held by lay and professional alike that Judaism believed that it could earn its salvation by storing up merit through good works. As E.P. Sanders has shown, this view, although widely held, is not based on a careful reading of Jewish sources. This view is based, it seems, on a reading of some sources, a reading biased by the Reformation debate between Protestants and Catholics about justification by faith or by works. After a lengthy examination of the Jewish sources, E.P. Sanders maintains that covenantal nomism is the pattern of religion of Palestinian Judaism. He defines covenantal nomism thus:

> The 'pattern' or 'structure' of covenantal nomism is this: (1) God has chosen Israel and (2) given the law. The law implies both (3) God's promise to maintain the election and (4) the requirement to obey. (5) God rewards obedience and punishes transgression. (6) The law provides for means of atonement, and atonement results in (7) maintenance or re-establishment of the covenantal relationship. (8) All those who are maintained in the covenant by obedience, atonement and God's mercy belong to the group which will be saved. An important interpretation of the first and last points is that election and ultimately salvation are considered to be by God's mercy rather than human achievement (p. 422).

From E.P. Sander's assessment of Judaism it is clear that the Jews of Paul's time believed that the covenant, the law, and salvation are God's free gifts. Thus, Paul's arguments with Jews did not revolve around an imaginary Jewish doctrine that the Jews could earn their salvation. But Paul did have an argument with the Jews, and it was radical. The gist of that argument has been expressed well by E.P. Sanders: "*Paul in fact explicitly denies that the Jewish covenant can be effective for salvation, thus consciously denying the basis of Judaism*" (p. 551; emphasis in original).

Having cleared up the commonly held misconception that the Jews of Paul's time held that they earned their own salvation, we are now in a position to understand more easily why Paul had to devote three chapters in Romans to "The Jewish Question."

In Rom 1–8 Paul argued that God's righteousness is

God's action in history for salvation and that God's righteousness has been definitively revealed in Jesus Christ and in the Gospel for all who believe. And in developing his argument in Rom 1–8, Paul gave clues that he would subsequently relate his understanding of God's righteousness in Jesus Christ to God's past acts of righteousness for God's chosen people, the Jews (see esp. Rom 3:1–8). In Rom 9–11 Paul returns to and explains that relationship. Put another way, Paul's apocalyptic thought about God's righteousness in Rom 1–8 is not complete until he deals in Rom 9–11 with the realities that God has elected Israel and that the vast majority of Israel has not believed that Jesus is the Christ and God's definitive act of righteousness.

In addressing the Jewish question in Rom 9–11, Paul is adamant in maintaining three convictions. First, Paul loves his Jewish brothers and sisters deeply and would like to pray that he might be accursed and cut off from Christ for the sake of his Jewish kinsfolk (see Rom 9:3). Secondly, Christ, who is God's act of righteousness, has put an end to the law as a way of salvation (Rom 10:4). God's acts of righteousness in the exodus, in passing through the Red Sea, and in the giving of the covenant and law, all have been superseded by God's act of righteousness in Jesus Christ. Salvation comes from believing that God's definitive righteousness has been revealed in Jesus Christ and continues to be revealed in the preaching of the Gospel. To believe in this Gospel, the chosen people are called. Paul's third conviction is that God will maintain his covenant fidelity and righteousness to those whom God has elected, "for the gifts and the call of God are irrevocable" (Rom 11:29). "All Israel shall be saved" (Rom 11:26).

In summary, if we are to understand Paul and Romans, we must always remember the Jewish dimension of his life and thought. Paul related his Gospel of Jesus Christ to God's past mighty deeds of righteousness for God's elected people. Although other Christians in New Testament times might turn their backs on the unbelieving Jews, Paul works intensely that his kinsfolk in belief in the God of Abraham, Isaac, and Jacob might also believe in the Gospel "concerning his Son, who was born of David's seed according to the flesh, who was appointed Son of God in power according to the Spirit of holiness from the resurrection of the dead, even Jesus Christ our Lord" (Rom 1:3-4).

2.3 The Paradigm of the Story of God's Acts of Righteousness as a Key to Paul's Theology (See Bibliography number 8).

In the past and even today scholars have found the key to Pauls' theology in the Damascus Event or Paul's conversion. That may be a legitimate avenue provided stress is placed on the apocalyptic dimension of Paul's thought and thus on the fact that it was God's apocalypse/revelation of God's Son that led Paul to a radically new view of Jesus the Messiah (see Gal 1:16).

A more fruitful way of fashioning a key to Paul's theology has been hinted at above in the discussions of righteousness as event and of God's righteousness manifested in the Christ event as the culmination of God's acts or righteousness. That way is the avenue of story, the story of God's acts of righteousness.

Despite what some have taught in the past, in Romans Paul is not writing a theological tractate and proposing doctrine as such, doctrine which he hopes the Roman Christians will accept and which the Church of today must accept. Rather, in Romans Paul is proclaiming a new and definitive act in the ongoing story of God's dealings with God's rebellious creation and people. In Rom 1-4 Paul shows that this new and definitive act is Jesus Christ, "who was delivered up for our trespasses and was raised for our justification" (Rom 4:25). The story of how God has acted in Jesus the Messiah shows God's purpose for all creation. In Rom 5-8 (and Rom 12-15) Paul shows how Christians participate in and continue the story of God's new act of righteousness against Sin and Death in Jesus Christ. And in Rom 9-11 Paul strives mightily to show how this new act in the story of God's righteousness accords with God's previous acts of righteousness. Put sharply, if one views

Paul's theology in Romans (and in his other letters) from the perspective of story, his theology is thoroughly theocentric.

In conclusion, the paradigm of story captures the dynamism and the continuity in Paul's theology. God's power is active for salvation: in God's past righteous acts, in the Christ event, and in the Gospel. It invites the obedience of faith.

2.4 Summary

Seen from the perspective of Paul's apocalyptic understanding of God's righteousness, the heart of Paul's theology is God's triumph over Sin and Death in Jesus Christ. Moreover, if one were to compare the righteous God whose story Paul tells with the God whose reign Jesus proclaimed, one would find considerably more continuity between the proclamation of Jesus and that of Paul than is commonly taught.

From Romans, esp. chaps. 9–11, one can draw the conclusion that Judaism is the context in which the lifework of Paul the Jew should be viewed. But from Rom 9–11 one cannot draw the conclusion that Judaism is the major or sole opponent of Paul. Indeed, Paul does have opponents. But Paul's opponents in letters like Philippians 3, Galatians, and 2 Corinthians 10–13 may well be Gentiles who had not understood the apocalyptic dimension of Paul's theology and had become persuaded that observance of the law was necessary for salvation.

3. 1–2 Timothy and Titus and the Distinction between the Scholars' Paul and the Church's Paul (See Bibliography number 9).

In the past it was quite common for scholars to construct the life and thought of Paul from the Acts of the Apostles and from the thirteen letters in the New Testament which bear Paul's name: Romans, 1–2 Corinthians, Galatians,

Ephesians, Philippians, Colossians, 1–2 Thessalonians, 1–2 Timothy, Titus, Philemon. Today it is commonplace for scholars to limit themselves to The Big Seven as they fashion Paul's theology: Romans, 1–2 Corinthians, Galatians, Philippians, 1 Thessalonians, and Philemon. The remaining six Pauline letters are judged not to be authentically Pauline. The primary reason for this judgment is that 2 Thessalonians, Ephesians, Colossians, 1–2 Timothy, and Titus differ significantly in language and theology from the Big Seven. And the result of this judgment is that these six Pauline letters are rapidly becoming The Neglected Six. If scholars do treat these six letters in their books or chapters on Paul's life and thought, they usually do so sketchily and under such rubrics as "The Pauline School" or "Early Catholicism."

While the scholars' Paul is derived from The Big Seven, the Church preaches and teaches from all thirteen Pauline letters as sources for Paul's theology. It is no cause for wonderment that problems arise because of the different views of Paul being presented by the scholars and by the Church, e.g., the role of women in the church and in ministry. It is not our main purpose here to pronounce judgment on whose Paul is the genuine Paul, but to point out some differences between the Paul of The Big Seven and the Paul of the Neglected Six. Representatives of the Big Seven will be the two letters we studied above in sections 1 and 2, namely, 1 Corinthians and Romans. Representatives of The Neglected Six will be 1–2 Timothy and Titus, which are known as The Pastoral Epistles. I will follow the two general categories I used above: social context and theology.

3.1 The Social Context of The Pastoral Epistles

In 1.4 above we discussed Paul and Women and showed how Paul was a proponent of the co-equality of men and women Christians as disciples. We also pointed out how much men had to lose as they abandoned their position of authority in a patriarchal world, joined the Christian movement, and accepted Paul's vision of equality of men and women in Jesus Christ. In The Pastoral Epistles we find that the patriarchal model, in which the man is in charge of the household, has become the dominant model in Pauline churches. This model, the household model (in German, the *Haustafel* model), is evident in Tit 2:1–10 and also in 1 Tim 2–6. For our purposes it is sufficient to sample its occurrence in 1 Tim 2:11–15:

> Let a woman learn in silence with all submissiveness. I permit no woman to teach or to have authority over men; she is to keep silent. For Adam was formed first, then Eve; and Adam was not deceived, but the woman was deceived and became a transgressor. Yet woman will be saved through bearing children, if she continues in faith and love and holiness, with modesty (Revised Standard Version).

While Paul in 1 Cor 14:33b–36 may be concerned about good order in the second part of the Christian symposion and require that wives ask disruptive questions at home, he encourages women as prophets and pray–ers at worship (1 Cor 11:5). Did the same Paul, who wrote 1 Cor 11:5 (and Gal 3:28) and who had woman co-workers, write 1 Tim 2:11–15? The answer is No.

But the answer No to our first question does not answer a second question: why is Paul being presented as a teacher of patriarchal authority in 1 Tim 2:11–15? A plausible answer to this second question is to be found by situating The Pastoral Epistles in the social, religious, and temporal context of the second century apocryphal work, *The Acts of Paul.*

The Acts of Paul seems to take Paul's teaching about the value of virginity in 1 Cor 7 to an heretical extreme. This work describes Paul (and virgin "apostles" like Thecla) as preaching that there is no salvation unless one is a virgin. Male listeners to this preaching see it as subversive of society and its patriarchal model. In *The Acts of Paul* 3.12

we read this of Paul: "And Demas and Hermogenes said to him: 'Who this man is, we do not know.' But he (Paul) deprives young men of wives and maidens of husbands, saying: 'Otherwise there is no resurrection for you, except you remain chaste and do not defile the flesh, but keep it pure.'"

The above analysis of *The Acts of Paul* allows us to reconstruct the social and religious context of The Pastoral Epistles in the following way. What we find in The Pastoral Epistles is an attack against Paulinists, represented by the figures of Paul and Thecla in *The Acts of Paul*, who had taken Paul's teaching in 1 Cor 7 to an heretical extreme and had won over many women to their viewpoint. The Pauline author of The Pastoral Epitsles will not allow these Paulinists and their female converts to teach their doctrine in his churches (1 Tim 2:11-15). Furthermore, he adopts the strong measure of enjoining the patriarchal model of society, lest members of his Pauline churches espouse society-destroying conduct like that propounded in *The Acts of Paul* and cause the Christian name to be dishonored. Thus, he instructs the older women to "train the young women to love their husbands and children, to be sensible, chaste, domestic, kind, and submissive to their husbands, that *the word of God may not be discredited*" (Tit 2:4-5).

In sum, the social and theological context, established from a comparison of The Pastoral Epistles with *The Acts of Paul*, enables us to appreciate why The Pastoral Epistles differ from Paul's teaching about women in 1 Corinthians. The author of The Pastoral Epistles sacrifices Paul's teaching on women's role in worship and ministry to preserve the goodness of marriage and creation (see 1 Tim 4:1-5) and to preserve public respectability. In the heat of combatting the extreme interpretation of Paul's views on virginity represented by *The Acts of Paul*, the author of The Pastoral Epistles finds in the widely accepted patriarchal model of society an effective means of ensuring orthodoxy. It would, however, be a theological shame if the church were not to reinstate the model of coequality of disciple-ship once the heretical threat of extreme views on virginity had faded from the ecclesiastical scene.

3.2 The Theology of The Pastoral Epistles

Within the last decades scholars have come to recognize the extent to which Paul makes use of traditional Christian formulations in fashioning the theology found in The Big Seven. Paul, the creative genius and theologian, freely bor-rowed from those who had preceded him in the faith. Good examples are to be found in the words of institution which Paul quotes for the Christian symposion in 1 Cor 11:23-25 and in Paul's teaching about God's righteousness in Rom 3:21-26. What is distinctive about The Pastoral Epistles in comparison with The Big Seven is the extensive use their author makes of Christian tradition. In every chapter the author is indebted to tradition. An excellent example is Tit 3:4-8:

> But when the goodness and loving kindness of God our Savior appeared, he saved us, not because of deeds done by us in righteousness, but in virtue of his own mercy, by the washing of regeneration and re-newal of the Holy Spirit, which he poured out upon us richly through Jesus Christ our Savior, so that we might be justified by his grace and become heirs in hope of eternal life. The saying is sure.

The last sentence is a certain indicator in The Pastoral Epistles that tradition is being cited. But more important in this context than indicators of tradition is the character of the tradition being quoted. It is surely Pauline. In it we have the contrast between God's mercy and human achievement, familiar to us from our study of the right-eousness of God in Romans (see also the tradition quoted in 2 Tim 1:9). Equally familiar is the emphasis that it is God's grace which justifies and not any deed of ours. So in this tradition we hear the voice of Paul. But what we do not hear in The Pastoral Epistles is the apocalyptic dimension in Paul's voice. The Pastoral Epistles give us Pauline tradition, but do not convey the power of Paul's Christian vision of reality and of God's conquest in Jesus' death and resurrection of the forces of Sin and Death. Put sharply, in The Pastoral Epistles Paul's Gospel of God's righteousness has become part of the church's creed and no longer stands in judgment over the church and its elders and bishops.

3.3 Summary

From our brief analyses of The Pastoral Epistles' teaching on women and the righteousness of God, readers have become somewhat acquainted with the reasons scholars offer for their judgment that these epistles (and the other three epistles among The Neglected Six) were not written by Paul. Our brief survey of The Pastoral Epistles should also have increased appreciation of the tension between the scholars' Paul and the Church's Paul on such sensitive issues as the role of women in worship and ministry. Further, this author is convinced that growth in the tendency to bypass The Neglected Six (and Acts) in reconstructions of Paul's life and theology will only eventuate in an impoverishment of the church's understanding of Paul and of his importance in the first Christian century.

The final word to this section and to this entire article on Paul should be given to a scholar who has been a major influence in our contemporary appreciation of Paul. What Ernst Käsemann wrote of The Big Seven might felicitously, although controversially, be applied to the Pauline Literature in general: "However, whenever Paul is rediscovered — which happens almost exclusively in times of crisis — there issues from him explosive power which destroys as much as it opens up something new" (p. 249). Happy rediscovery!

BIBLIOGRAPHY

1. *Paul the Tentmaker*

Hock, Ronald F.   *The Social Context of Paul's Ministry: Tentmaking and Apostleship.* Philadelphia: Fortress, 1980.

Meeks, Wayne A.   *The First Urban Christians: The Social World of the Apostle Paul.* New Haven, CT: Yale University Press, 1983.

Osiek, Carolyn.   *What Are They Saying About the Social Setting of the New Testament?* New York: Paulist, 1984.

2. *Paul The Athlete of Christ*

Broneer, Oscar. "The Apostle Paul and the Isthmian Games." *Biblical Archaeologist* 25 (1962) 2–31.

Harris, H.A.   *Sport in Greece and Rome.* Aspects of Greek and Roman Life. Ithaca: Cornell University Press, 1972.

Hawthorne, Gerald F.   *Philippians.* Word Biblical Commentary 43. Waco, TX: Word, 1983.

Novak, Michael.   *The Joy of Sports: End Zones, Bases, Baskets, Balls, and the Consecration of the American Spirit.* New York: Basic, 1976.

Pleket, H.W.   "Games, Prizes, Athletes and Ideology: Some Aspects of the History of Sport in the Graeco-Roman World." *Arena* 1 (1975) 49–89.

3. *Paul and the Christian Community at Worship: 1 Cor 11–14*

Aune, David E.   "Septem Sapientium Convivium (Moralia 146b–164d)." *Plutarch's Ethical Writings and Early Christian Literature.* Ed. Hans Dieter Betz. Studia ad Corpus Hellenisticum Novi Testamenti 4. Leiden: Brill, 1978. 69–78.

Murphy-O'Connor, Jerome. *St. Paul's Corinth: Texts and Archaeology.* Good News Studies 6. Wilmington, DE: Glazier, 1983. 153–61.

Theissen, Gerd. *The Social Setting of Pauline Christianity: Essays on Corinth.* Ed. and trans. and with an introduction by John H. Schütz. Philadelphia: Fortress, 1982.

4. *Paul and Women: 1 Cor 14:33b–36*

Fiorenza, Elisabeth Schüssler. *In Memory of Her: A Feminist Theological Reconstruction of Christian Origins.* New York: Crossroad, 1983.

Flanagan, Neal M., and Edwina Hunter Snyder. "Did Paul Put Down Women in 1 Cor 14:34–36?" *Biblical Theology Bulletin* 11 (1981) 10–12.

Odell–Scott, David D. "Let the Women Speak in Church: An Egalitarian Interpretation of 1 Cor 14:33b–36." *Biblical Theology Bulletin* 13 (1983) 90–93.

5. *Romans and the Quest for the Heart of Paul's Theology*

Donfried, Karl Paul, ed. *The Romans Debate.* Minneapolis: Augsburg, 1977.

Jewett, Robert. "Romans as an Ambassadorial Letter." *Interpretation* 36 (1982) 5–20.

6. *The Theme of the Righteousness of God*

Baird, William. "On Reading Romans in the Church Today." *Interpretation* 34 (1980) 45–58.

Beker, J. Christiaan. *Paul the Apostle: the Triumph of God in Life and Thought.* Philadelphia: Fortress, 1980.

Reumann, John. *"Righteousness" in the New Testament: "Justification" in the Unites States Lutheran-Roman Catholic Dialogue, With responses by Joseph A. Fitzmyer & Jerome D. Quinn.* Philadelphia: Fortress; New York: Paulist, 1982.

Soards, Marion L. "The Righteousness of God in the Writings of the Apostle Paul." *Biblical Theology Bulletin* 15 (1985) 104–10.

Stendahl, Krister. "The Apostle Paul and the Introspective Conscience of the West." *Harvard Theological Review* 56 (1963) 199–215. Reprinted in Stendahl's *Paul Among Jews and Gentiles and Other Essays.* Philadelphia: Fortress, 1976. 78–96

7. Romans 9–11 is Integral to Paul's Development of the Theme of the Righteousness of God

Cranfield, C.E.B. *Romans, A Shorter Commentary.* Grand Rapids, MI: Eerdmans, 1985.

Sanders, E.P. *Paul and Palestinian Judaism: A Comparison of Patterns of Religion.* Philadelphia: Fortress, 1977.

8. The Paradigm of the Story of God's Acts of Righteousness as a Key to Paul's Theology

Achtemeier, Paul J. *Romans.* Interpretation. Atlanta, GA: John Knox, 1985.

Kim, Seyoon. *The Origins of Paul's Gospel.* Grand Rapids, MI: Eerdmans, 1982.

Sanders, James A. "Torah and Christ." *Interpretation* 29 (1975) 372–90.

9. *1–2 Timothy and Titus and the Distinction between the Scholars' Paul and the Church's Paul*

Käsemann, Ernst. "Paul and Early Catholicism." *New Testament Questions of Today.* London: SCM, 1969. 236–51.

Karris, Robert J. *The Pastoral Epistles.* New Testament Message 17. Wilmington, DE: Glazier, 1979.

MacDonald, Dennis Ronald. *The Legend and the Apostle: The Battle for Paul in Story and Canon.* Philadelphia: Westminster, 1983.

Quinn, Jerome D. "The Pastoral Epistles on Righteousness." Reumann 229–38. (see Bibliography no. 6, above).

Verner, David C. *The Household of God: The Social World of the Pastoral Epistles.* SBLDS 71. Chico, CA: Scholars Press, 1983.

JOHANNINE LITERATURE: FROM TEXT TO COMMUNITY

Pheme Perkins
Boston College

The pioneering efforts of scholars like Bruce Vawter to open up the richness of Biblical studies to the Catholic community have been richly repaid in the area of Johannine studies. It would hardly be an exaggeration to say that while the questions of Johannine research in the period between 1920 and 1970 were dictated by the particular "history of religions" approach of Bultmann and his students, the fastest growing areas of Johannine research in the last quarter of the century have been significantly shaped by Catholic scholars. There is no area of Johannine research in which they have not taken a leading role in the investigation.

Some of the most important lessons that the Catholic community of scholars learned about Biblical scholarship, it learned from the work of Bruce Vawter. We learned to take all efforts at scholarly inquiry seriously. Consequently, the insights and questions of Bultmann and his students are not neglected in the newer synthesis. But we also learned that a Biblical scholar is not a technician trained to handle some narrow area of the Bible. New Testament scholars should be competent in understanding the basic results of research into Hebrew Scriptures and Intertestamental Jewish writings. Persons who specialize in the Hebrew Scriptures should also understand what is going on in the New Testament, though few of us will ever show the breadth of writing on these areas that Bruce Vawter has. In Johannine studies, this breadth has meant that Catholic scholarship has tended to give much more weight to the relationship between the Johannine tradition and its Jewish antecedents than one finds in work from the Bultmannian school.

Finally, in the theological ferment that surrounded Vatican II, the Catholic community began to understand faith and its doctrinal expression as part of a process of developing insight into the revelation entrusted to the church. This understanding of development of faith and church life in all its dimensions was understood to be an organic process of growth. In Johannine scholarship, this central ecclesial insight has borne fruit in a new understanding of the development of tradition within the life-experience of the Johannine community, especially through the work of Raymond E. Brown. But it also represents a rejection of the intellectual schemata of "thesis, antithesis, synthesis" which had governed much of the reconstruction of Christian origins in German Protestant scholarship. Developments in Johannine Christianity do not imply a "hostility" toward the earlier Christian traditions that have been incorporated into the new perspective.

We can hardly do justice to the wealth of scholarship that has been responsible for the growth of Johannine studies in the past quarter century (see Bibliog. no. 1). We will sketch major trends in Johannine scholarship in terms of the "setting" of the Johannine writings in the first century; the "sources" of the Johannine tradition, and the distinctive "theology" of Johannine Christianity. Finally, we will conclude with some brief reflections on the role of Johannine literature in the life and reflection of the church today.

The Setting of Johannine Literature

The distinctive character of the gospel of John, which differs markedly from the synoptics in its outline of events, and persons associated with Jesus, who are not mentioned elsewhere, and in the style and content of teaching attributed to Jesus, has always made it difficult to situate John within the spectrum of early Christianity. The gospel used to be understood as a mid-second century "interpretation" of the type of tradition reflected in the synoptics. The Johannine writings might then be seen as the product of a unique perception of Jesus, whether orthodox or gnostic, that was somewhat "outside" the first century development of Christian tradition. Such views have largely disappeared from scholarly work as both manuscript evidence and study of the traditions within the gospel make it more likely that John reached its present form sometime between 85 and 100 A.D. Thus, Johannine Christianity has emerged alongside that reflected in Matthew and Luke; not as a later reflection on them (See Bibliog. no. 2).

1. First century Judaism in the Background of the Fourth Gospel. (See Bibliography number 3).

One of the most striking features of the gospel, its portrayal of Jesus as the one who reveals God because he has come from and returns to the Father, led Bultmann and his students to look to the myths of a heavenly revealer in later gnostic writings for a parallel understanding of redemption. The sharp dualism between "light" and "darkness" as well as the gospel's picture of "faith" as a "knowledge" of God that is limited to a circle of those around Jesus while others remain in ignorance also seemed to point in a gnosticizing direction. Impressed by the language of "light," "life" and "word," that is both "with God" and active in creation in Jn 1:1–18, others turned to popular versions of stoic and platonic philosophy to suggest that the gospel represented an attempt to render the Christian message in terms that could be understood in the larger "hellenistic" environment. In that connection, the miracle of Cana, turning water into wine, which has no parallel in the synoptics, was seen to be an adaptation of a "miracle" attributed to the god Dionysus. This adaptation would show Christ as the fulfilment of the dreams of salvation in the larger pagan culture.

While no one denies that readers familiar with such currents of thought might find John speaking their language, the foundations of the Johannine tradition do not seem to be set in the cosmological systems of second century gnosticism; in popular stoic or platonic cosmology, or in the idioms of pagan religious myth and cult. The rich pluralism of first century Judaism which has emerged from the study of the Dead Sea Scrolls, the Pseudepigrapha, Jewish writers like Philo and Josephus, and more slowly from the study of archaeological remains, continues to provide new insights into the Fourth Gospel. Suggestive parallels to the "Moses typology" behind the figure of Jesus in John have been found in Samaritan thought. Study of Targumic traditions has played a less striking role in the analysis of the Fourth Gospel, but it continues to provide illuminating parallels to pieces of Jewish legend that appear to be presupposed in the gospel (c.g. the link between Cain and "children of the devil," which appears in Jn 8:44 and in different form in 1 Jn 3:7,10,12).

The case for situating the origins of Johannine tradition within Palestinian Judaism is strengthened by concrete details that presume knowledge of first century Judaea. [Cana in Galilee is the only northern place name mentioned in John that does not appear in the synoptics, while John fails to mention many of the places in Galilee which appear in the synoptics.] The pool of Siloam (Jn 9:7) and the Kidron valley (18:1) are familiar to any visitor to Jerusalem. While "Solomon's portico" (10:23; cf. Acts 3:11) has not been positively identified by archaeologists, Josephus (*Ant,* 20. 9, 7), refers to the oldest portico on the east side as built by Solomon. Excavations of Robinson's arch and its connection to the Royal Portico on the south side have provided details of construction relevant to the arch on the eastern wall of the temple. The pool of Bethesda (Jn 5:2) has been excavated. The structure consisted of five porticoes surrounding a double pool. The pool is also referred to in the copper scroll from Qumran (3 Q 15: XI, 12f.). Finally, the "Pavement" mentioned outside the place of Jesus' trial, (Jn 19:13), which John also refers to by an Aramaic name "elevation," (*Gabbatha*), would seem to refer to the flagstone floor excavated in the vicinity of the fortress of Antonia. If this is an accurate detail, then the trial of Jesus might be definitely located there rather than at Herod's old palace, the site still favored by some scholars.

Archaeological confirmation of particular details in John only establishes the reliability of specific details in the Johannine tradition. It does not support the conclusion that everything in the gospel is an accurate report of Judaea in the time of Jesus. However, the presence of such reliable details in the Johannine tradition does point toward the need to integrate Johannine materials into the study of the early Jesus tradition. Johannine material is not to be "left to one side" as a purely theological reflection on Jesus in the attempt to arrive at reconstructions of the setting of Jesus' ministry.

The most striking "turn around" in establishing a Jewish setting for the development of the Johannine gospel has been associated with the publication of the Dead Sea Scrolls and the subsequent interest in the study of Jewish apocalypticism and pseudepigrapha generally. In the Qumran writings, especially the *Manual of Discipline*, we find evidence for a sect which employs the dualistic symbols of "light" and "children of light" over against "darkness" and "children of darkness" to designate members of the sect who have true knowledge of God and non-members (also Jews) who do not (Jn 3:19–21). We also find language of divine predestination associated with belonging to the elect group, which recalls Johannine affirmations about the Father bringing people to believe in Jesus (Jn 10:29; 17:6). The statements about "truth" which form a large part of the gospel of John in contrast to the synoptics had been seen as evidence of a link to Gnosticism where the elect are awakened by the heavenly revealer from sleep, ignorance, darkness to knowledge of the truth, and the heavenly realm which the gnostic will share. "Truth" emerges in the Qumran writings in ways that parallel the gospel. The community seeks to know and to do God's truth. The spirit of God is connected with truth (cf. Jn 4:23). It remains active in the believing community, purifying that community. As in the fourth gospel, truth, and those who walk in truth, stand opposed to the realm of lies, deceit and error.

Other parallels between the Fourth Gospel and Judaism are found in the form of Jesus' "farewell discourses," (Jn 13:31–17:26). As in the *Testaments of the Twelve Patriarchs* and other such testaments, the departing hero instructs his gathered children by reminding them of his example, predicting their future, and exhorting them to a life of piety. Wisdom speculation, especially the identification of God's Wisdom with the Word, provides a plausible background for the opening verses of the gospel in which Jesus is acclaimed as the creative word of God.

The link between the religious language of Qumran and that of Johannine writings is often traced to circles around John the Baptist. John contains a number of traditions about the Baptist that diverge from what we find in the synoptics. They suggest that followers of the Baptist had become followers of Jesus (Jn 1:35–40) and that there had been on-going contacts between the followers of the two leaders (3:22–4:3). Though some scholars remain skeptical of an extensive group of disciples surrounding the Baptist and continuing after his execution, the plausibility of such a sect has been strengthened by the publication of a third century life of Mani, which shows that he had been a member of a baptist sect of Jewish Christians, the Elkasites, founded by a legendary prophet in Syria in A.D. 100.

The historically established connection between Mani and a Jewish Christian baptismal sect of Syrian origins confirms an emerging picture of Gnostic origins which establishes the place of the study of gnosticism in understanding the setting of the Johannine writings. Since the publication of the gnostic writings from the Nag Hammadi collection, scholars have firsthand examples of second century gnostic cosmologies, revealer myths, revelation discourses and I Am sayings with which to compare the Johannine writings. The importance of heterodox Jewish apocalyptic and mystical traditions, in the shaping of gnostic materials has become increasingly evident in the study of Gnosticism. Jewish wisdom speculation has also found its way into the portrayal of the Sophia figure in gnostic mythology. One of the tractates, *Tri. Trac.*, even substitutes a male, Logos figure, for the gnostic Sophia. Another, *Trim. Prot.*, contains first person affirmations by the divine revealer which parallel the prologue to the Fourth Gospel. A third, *Thund.*, exploits the revelatory I Am style of proclamation familiar in the Fourth Gospel.

Such parallels do not demonstrate the claim that John is either a "gnostic" or "anti-gnostic" writing. In their present form, the Nag Hammadi texts post-date the gospel, though they seem independent of it in many of these developments. Considerable textual, form-critical and "history of tradition" work remains to be done on the Nag Hammadi material before one can say with any confidence that particular examples represent tradition from the first century. However, there is sufficient evidence to suggest that the links between the Johannine literature and gnosticism both in literary forms and in some patterns of symbolic articulation can be found in the common milieu of late first century Judaism within which both traditions are taking shape.

2. Tradition-history Reflects Community Development. (See Bibliography number 4).

Possibly the most influential development in Johannine studies in the past twenty-five years has been the attempt to move from a study of the traditions in Johannine writings to a history of the Johannine community. J. Louis Martyn called attention to the conflict with the synagogue that structures so much of the discourse material. He noted the explicit references to expulsion of Christians from the synagogue as something to be feared (Jn 9:22; 16:2-3), and proposed that such an expulsion had been associated with the promulgation of a benediction against heretics, *birkath ha-minim*, at the time of Gamaliel II (ca. A.D. 90). Martyn proposes that many of the dialogues in the gospel move on "two levels," that of a story set in the time of Jesus, and that of the concrete experiences of Johannine Christians. Drawing on anthropological and sociological studies of community and religious symbolism, Wayne Meeks challenged scholars to describe the type of community whose experience would be illuminated and confirmed by the Johannine symbols of Jesus as "Man from heaven." Such a community, he concludes, would be sectarian in a way analogous to the Qumran sect. Its separation from Judaism is reflected in separation of Jesus and the believers from "the world." The community's identity is largely defined in negative terms making it a fertile ground for further sectarian and gnosticising tendencies.

The most extensive effort to move Johannine scholarship from tradition-history to the history of community development has been Raymond E. Brown's reconstruction of the history of the Johannine community from it's Palestinian origins (ca. A.D. 50) to the dissolution of the distinctive Johannine communities into churches of Petrine origins, on the one side, and the individualist, gnosticising sects, on the other, that seems to have occurred sometime in the first quarter of the second century. Assimilation of Johannine traditions in Petrine communities provided the combination of Johannine Logos Christology and a Christology focused on the incarnation and birth of Jesus that would be the cornerstone of "orthodox" Christology and which is represented in our Christmas liturgies to this day. Amalgamation of the dissident Johannine Christians rejected in 1 and 2 John into the emerging gnostics sects is responsible for its use as "gospel" in gnostic circles, especially in the commentaries of Valentinian teachers. Heracleon's commentary survives in part in the John commentary of Origen which sets out to refute its gnostic claims.

The basic method of moving from text to community story in Brown's work views the Johannine writings as reflections of their past development. New insights and interpretations are "added onto" but do not entirely replace the older expressions of the tradition. Brown rejects the view that the Johannine community was essentially sectarian, since he detects both an evangelistic and an apologetic thrust at each stage in the development of its tradition.

Two developments are characteristic of the originating period of the community (ca. A.D. 50–80). At first the community was one of many Jewish Christian groups of Palestine. Some of the members of the community had been followers of John the Baptist, whom the Johannine community continued to hold in high regard as one "sent by God" to witness to Jesus. Jesus was preached as the fulfilment of all Jewish messianic hopes (e.g. Jn 1:45). The miracles of Jesus may also have been used in the missionary efforts of the community. (They are said to distinguish Jesus from John in Jn 10:41.) Apologetic traditions from this period may have included the explanation of baptism and the midrash comparing the crucifixion to Moses' staff in Numbers from Jn 3:1–15. Incorporation of non-Jewish Christians begins with an influx of Samaritan converts (cf. Jn 4). Theological developments included presentation of Jesus as one "greater than Moses." Jesus has "come down from heaven," "seen God" and is the only one who can make God known. Polemic against the temple cult and the "Moses" of both Samaritan and Jewish tradition may have been part of these developments. Jesus is defended as the only one who can bring life and salvation to the world.

In the mid-eighties to nineties, Johannine Christians were expelled from Jewish synagogues. Some preferred to remain within the Jewish community (Jn 12:42), and provide the background for those "crypto-Christians," which the gospel finds among the Jews. The gospel portrays the grounds for the Jewish action against Christians to have been Christological. Christian claims about Jesus' special origin and relationship to God were rejected as blasphemous. Response to this crisis forced a choice. Johannine Christians came to argue that Jesus in fact replaced the Jewish cult, its feasts and temple. The identification of Jesus with God was intensified as Christians came to perceive that Jesus had already made eternal life, knowledge of God and salvation available to those who believed in him. At the same time, the bitter polemic led to the negative description of "Jews" as "children of the devil" and the symbolic links between Judaism and a world hostile to God's revelation that form such a prominent part of the gospel.

Cut off from Judaism, the Johannine Christians turned to a more extensive effort to evangelize the Gentiles. [Jn 12:20–23 has "Greeks" come seeking Jesus at the very hour when the Jews, blinded by God (Jn 12:37–40), will reject him.] The Jewish heritage of Johannine symbolism comes to be universalized so that it might speak to the pagan religious experience. At the same time, the Johannine tradition reflects a tension between universalism and the dualism of its symbolism (3:16–17/3:18–21). The dualistic symbols continue to "explain" experiences of hostility and rejection experienced in the Johannine mission (Jn 16:2–3).

Brown also suggests that the Johannine community may have moved from Palestine as a result of Jewish hostility (reflected in Jn 7:35?). Perhaps, the Johannine church relocated in the vicinity of Ephesus, the location traditionally ascribed to it. If so, that might have brought Johannine Christians into the developments of tradition that were taking place in other Christian communities. Sometime in the nineties the various elements both oral and written of the Johannine tradition were put down in "gospel" form, a narrative of Jesus' deeds, words, passion and resurrection. Some of the puzzles in continuity within the gospel, require commentators to suppose that the gospel that we have had been through more than one stage of compilation. Such activity might have been carried on by a "school" or circle of disciples linked with the beloved Disciple, who were the "tradition bearers" of the Johannine community and whose voice emerges in the collective "we" of 1 Jn 1:1–2.

The Johannine epistles bear witness to the final stage of Johannine Christianity. 1–2 John and 3 John address internal crisis within a network of Johannine churches which appear to be located around an urban center. Both the author(s) of the epistles and their opponents claim to stand within the Johannine tradition. In 1–2 John, the Johannine community has been split by dissident christians and their teachers who have separated from the group represented by the author. The lines of dispute are not always clear. It appears that the opponents held a view of Jesus which rejected the tradition of his death as atonement for sin. They may have based their case on the gospel images of the crucifixion as Jesus' exaltation to glory. They also held some view of Christian perfectionism, which negated the necessity for Christian repentance and the mediation of forgiveness by the exalted Jesus/paraclete. Since these Christians had separated from those addressed in the epistles, they must have made their own claims to "inspired" teaching in the Johannine tradition.

3 John presents a somewhat different crisis. Travelling missionaries associated with the author have been denied hospitality by the leader of a local Johannine community. Perhaps his refusal to receive such missionaries was motivated by a desire to keep out dissident preachers. The author of 3 John writes to another Christian in the area seeking his support and hospitality for travelling missionaries. The action by Diotrephes in excluding the missionaries may represent the beginning of a consolidation of local authority in the face of crises like that in 1–2 John. Brown suggests that the real solution for "orthodox" Johannine Christians came in accepting the Petrine traditions of other Christians in the area. The final editing of the gospel to include the affirmation of Peter's role as shepherd (Jn 21:15–19), may have taken place at this time.

3. The Complexity of "Sources" and Authorship.

Our understanding of the tradition history of Johannine materials and the development of the Johannine Christianity makes the conventional way of asking the question of "Who wrote John?" or "What sources did the author have?" impossibly simplistic. No one "wrote" the gospel in the sense in which one might sit at the computer to "write" this article and in the process pull in information about scholarly views of John from commentaries, library bibliography and assorted notes and text files. Even when the author of 1 John wishes to argue that his opponents are misrepresenting the truth of the Johannine tradition, he does not begin by quoting passages from the gospel and arguing against their interpretation. He appeals to what he, the other Johannine teachers associated with him, and the community being addressed "have heard from the beginning." They are to discern the truth of 1 John's presentation on the basis of their membership in the Johannine community (1 Jn 4:1–6).

The Fourth Gospel does look back to a special "disciple" of Jesus, whose name is never recorded, the Beloved Disciple (Jn 13:23; 19:26f.; 20:2–10; 21:7; 21:20–23; 21:24). This person is explicitly identified as the source of the community's tradition (21:24). By the end of the second century, when "apostolic" authorship of the canonical gospels was an important element in supporting their claims against other "gospels" from gnostic circles, we find claims that John was written by "John, the son of Zebedee" (Irenaeus, *Adv. Haer.* iii 1.1; probably also Papias, Eusebius, *H.E.* iii 39.3–6, if he intends to identify "John, the elder," with the disciple, John), at Ephesus when he was an old man. This identification appears to contradict the tradition preserved in Mk 10:39 that both James and John were martyred. Some scholars continue to hold that John, the son of Zebedee, was responsible for the founding of the community and for its early Palestinian tradition. However, the final author of Jn 21, which reports the death of the Beloved Disciple (vv. 20–23), appears to distinguish the Beloved Disciple from the apostle John by including two unnamed disciples in the list of those fishing (v. 2).

The fact that the Johannine community traces its tradition back to the witness and writing of an unnamed disciple of Jesus (21:24), does not require that this person be the author of the Johannine writings which we now possess. The Johannine epistles are linked to a person (or possibly two persons) who belonged to a circle of teachers in the Johannine community. A developmental approach to the Johannine tradition suggests that what we know as Johannine theology resulted from the assimilation of the diversity of traditions in different circumstances.

This process also makes it more difficult to employ the models of source and redaction criticism that were derived from synoptic criticism. Bultmann had proposed that the evangelist drew upon a "signs source," which encompassed the miracle signs attributed to Jesus; a "revelation discourse" source, which reflected the speech of the gnostic heavenly revealer, and a passion narrative. Each of these hypothetical sources has been subject to extensive analysis and reformulation. While many scholars would agree that the Johannine shaping of miracles and interpretative discourse, some forms of revelatory speech developed out of sayings of Jesus and some form of passion narrative independent of synoptics, were all part of the material with which the evangelist worked, there is no agreement that such sources can be isolated as independent literary units. Most scholars also agree that the Johannine parallels to synoptic traditions, especially in Mk and Lk, reflect an independent transmission of Jesus material.

Attempts to derive Johannine traditions directly from the synoptics continue to be made, but they flounder on the extensive differences in wording, order and narrative style between John and the synoptic parallels. Nevertheless, Brown's reconstruction of community history, for example, allows the possibility that the Johannine tradition might have been formed in its unique characteristics but then have encountered one or more gospels in other Christian communities. Such a casual acquaintance with the gospels emerging elsewhere would explain why the Johannine community gave written expression to its tradition in a form which parallels that of the synoptics and may even show some familiarity with them without exhibiting the direct relationships that can be found between Matthew, Mark, and Luke.

In addition, studies of the transmission of Jesus sayings in the early second century, which have been reawakened by the sayings embodied in some gnostic revelation discourses, opens up the possibility of extensive, somewhat diverging, lines of oral Jesus tradition. The incorporation of such materials into the Johannine tradition may not have occurred all at once or even in the same place. Such possibilities make it clear that we are not indebted to a single individual but to the Johannine community for the distinctive expression of Christian faith which has come down to us.

The Fourth Gospel as Literature and Theology

Fascination with the setting, the varied traditions and the development of the Johannine community should not obscure the considerable achievements of the Fourth Gospel as it was finally formulated. Although there are breaks in narrative sequence and shifts out of the time of the story into the timeless speech of the Johannine narrator that have even led to suggestions that the gospel be rearranged, individual sections of the gospel are finely crafted dramatic pieces, often consisting of a series of parallel scenes. Theologically, the Johannine presentation of Jesus' unity with the Father, of the presence of salvation to the believer, and of the centrality of the love command to the life of a Christian community is unique in it's single-minded intensity.

1. Dramatic Action in the Fourth Gospel. (See Bibliography number 5).

Literary studies of the Fourth Gospel have indicated the deliberate artistry evident in its composition. The major themes of Johannine theology are incorporated in dialogues which exploit symbolism, irony and misunderstanding. From the opening words of the prologue, the reader is

"in on" the secret necessary to understand what the protagonists in the narrative miss. All of Jesus' words and deeds
are grounded in the fact that he is "from the Father," the
source of "life, light and divine begetting for the believer,"
and that he returns again to the Father. In each of the
misunderstandings (Jn 2:19–21; 3:3–5; 4:10–15; 4:31–34;
6:32–35; 6:51–53; 7:33–36; 8:21–22; 8:31–35; 8:51–53;
8:56–68; 11:11–15; 11:23–25; 12:32–34; 13:36–38; 14:4–6;
14:7–9; 16:16–19), Jesus' divine origin, Jesus' saving revelation of God or gift of life, or Jesus' glorification in being
lifted up to return to the Father is at stake.

The reader is also clued in by the narrator who speaks
retrospectively (2:22; 12:16; 13:7; 20:9) and functions as an
authoritative interpreter of Jesus' words (2:21; 6:6; 7:1;
7:39; 8:27; 12:33; 13:11; 18:32; 21:19, 23). The narrator also
introduces into the story of Jesus' ministry themes which
will then be taken up in the Farewell Discourses ("hour,"
7:30; 8:20; 13:1; 16:32; 17:1; "glorify," 12:16; 13:31f.; 14:13;
15:8; 16:14; 17:1, 4f., 10; "Spirit," 7:39; 11:33; 13:12; 14:17,
26; 15:26; 16:13; "put out of the synagogue," 9:22; 12:42;
16:2). The Johannine community must have seen its own
experience of coming to understand Jesus reflected in the
words of the narrator. In addition, the discourses establish
the on-going connection between the Johannine community and the Father/Jesus. The love command (13:34f.), is
the condition of the manifestation of Son/Father to the
community (14:21), which establishes a new relationship so
that the disciples are no longer "servants" but "friends"
(15:12–17). Jesus' continuing presence (14:23; 15:10f), is
represented in the activity of the Paraclete which both
ensures memory of what Jesus has taught and its continued
interpretation in the future (14:26; 15:26; 16:7–8, 13–14).
The community can also pray to God, confident that such
prayer is heard (14:13; 15:16; 16:26).

We are also told from the beginning that the "plot" of
the gospel will involve rejection of the one who has come as
light and life from God by those who ought to have
received him (1:11–12). We know that Jesus' ministry provides salvation and a revelation of God that transcends the

Mosaic covenant that came before it (1:14–17). This theme is borne out in the narrative as Jesus either identifies with the great symbols of salvation in the Old Testament or replaces major Jewish feasts and customs.

The gospel as a whole can be described in terms of the inevitable movement toward the "hour" of Jesus' death, glorification and return to the Father. Chapters 1–4 establish patterns of belief and true discipleship culminating in the affirmation that Jesus is Savior of the world (4:42). Chapters 5–9 narrate a series of increasingly hostile encounters with Jewish authorities. In the process, we learn that Jesus lays claim to the divine "I Am" (8:58). The "light of the world" is worshipped by a grateful Christian community willing to suffer exclusion from the synagogue for its faith (ch. 9). We also learn that the Jewish plot to arrest and kill Jesus may play into his own mission and return to the Father 7:33–36). Chapters 10–12 make the transition to the death of Jesus, from Jesus' perspective as the one who must accomplish a mission from the Father. The good shepherd gives his life for the sheep (ch. 10). Paradoxically, the gift of life to the dead provokes Jesus' own death (ch. 11). Jesus is anointed for burial and is sought out by "the Greeks" even as he prepares for the death which will draw all to himself (ch. 12).

The public ministry ends on a note of division between the unbelieving Jews whose hearts have been hardened or who have preferred human glory and those who believe and keep Jesus' word. Chapters 13–17 prepare the community for its life and mission after Jesus' return to the Father. The disciples are cleansed; commissioned as those who must now represent Jesus to the world, and established as the community of "friends," characterized by mutual love and the indwelling presence of the Paraclete or the Father/Son. Chapters 18–21 show us that the "plot" as set by Jesus from the beginning is accomplished in Jesus' trial, death and exaltation (e.g. 18:37). Whatever the details of its tradition and process of composition, the Fourth Gospel presents a unified movement and point of view as a whole. This point of view shapes the readers' perception of Jesus, the World and the Christian experience in it. The reader comes to share the "stereoscopic vision" of the narrator; the heavenly truth about Jesus as opposed to the ironies and misunderstandings of the narrative level.

2. Christology, Revelation and Salvation. (See Bibliography no. 6).

The Johannine perception of Jesus' identity with the Father is presented as the critical issue in the separation of Johannine Christianity from its synagogue roots. This dispute with Judaism is focused on two issues: (1) Jesus' heavenly origin; and (2) the closeness of the relationship between the Father and Son. By the time the gospel is written, Johannine understanding of these points has gone well beyond any debate that could be conducted with Jewish objections. Instead, each discourse seems to take the original objection and push it forward to a level that is even more controversial. The Son of Man saying in Jn 1:51 moves beyond the collection of Jewish Christian messianic titles to speak symbolically of Jesus as the link between heaven and earth, the only revelation of God available to humans. Nicodemus' objections to the baptismal "rebirth" of the believer is pushed forward to the affirmation of the eternal life granted everyone who believes in the crucified/exalted Son of Man (Jn 3:12–15). Dispute about Jesus' relationship to the Father and his claim to speak the word of God is pushed to the affirmation that Jesus is greater than Abraham or the prophets; he voices the divine I Am (Jn 8:48–58).

John does not articulate the relationship between Jesus and the Father in the terms that would later be established in the classical creeds. But the gospel does presume that the closeness between Jesus and the Father is greater than a simple identity of will or function. The Johannine use of Jesus as the one "sent" from God, that is, the one who has come down from and returns to heaven goes well beyond any parallels in the Moses tradition. Johannine expressions of unity also go beyond any of the established Jewish traditions of the divine messenger, *šaliah.*

Scholars have come to emphasize the important role of Jewish wisdom themes in the shaping of Johannine Christiology. Wisdom descends from heaven and returns there again (Wisd 9:16–17; Bar 3:29; 1 Enoch 42). Crucial Johannine symbols for Jesus, light (Wisd 7:26, 29), food and drink, (Sir 24:19–22), and shepherd (Philo *Agr* 51; *Mut* 16), are identified with Wisdom. Wisdom's pre-existence and closeness to God are constantly emphasized (e.g. Prov 8:27–30; Sir 24:9; Wisd 9:9). Other Jewish traditions identified Wisdom and the Torah. Some scholars have found hints of this identification in the Jewish references to the Torah of Jn 7:49; 9:27f; 12:34; 19:7. The irony from the point of view of the evangelist is that they are confronted with God's Wisdom in Jesus but fail to recognize and believe in him.

This perception leads John to insist that there is no revelation of God apart from Jesus. The Law is not the final revelation of God. Only Jesus can make the Father known. The Law bears witness to Jesus (1:45; 5:39–46). But the Law is also revealed as defective when compared with Jesus (1:17; 3:9–15; 5:37–47; 6:35–58; 7:14–24; 10:34–36). The positive counterpart of John's insistence that God is only revealed through Jesus appears in the close association between revelation of the Father in Jesus and salvation.

"Eternal life" (or simply "life") is the most common expression for salvation in the Johannine writings. In the synoptic gospels, "life" refers to the future (e.g. Mk 9:43, 45; 10:17, 31). But in John "life" is deliberately anchored in the present. Whoever believes in the Son has eternal life, (Jn 3:15, 16, 36), or has passed from death to life (5:24). John does retain expressions which reflect the expectation of eternal life as future (e.g. 4:14, 36; 6:27; 5:39; 12:25; and the promise of life in 1 Jn 2:25). But the overriding use of such expressions is to speak of "life" as something which the believer can already be said to have entered. This shift is consciously expressed in the exchange between Jesus and

Martha prior to the raising of Lazarus, (Jn 11:23–27). The connection between this "realized eschatology" and Johannine Christology is made explicit in Martha's confession of faith in v. 27. Christ the life-giver has been sent by God from heaven for this purpose, (e.g. 6:33, 35, 48; 8:12; 11:25; 14:6). Faced with a schism in the Johannine community, 1 John emphasizes the fact that the possession of life creates a communion with the Father and Son (1 Jn 1:3; 2:23–24; 5:12), which is only open to those who remain in the community that has its roots in authentic Johannine tradition (1 Jn 1:2).

The danger of such expressions of "realized eschatology," the immediate presence of salvation to those who believe, may have been expressed in the perfectionism that 1 John opposes. Persons who believe and have eternal life cannot, they may have argued, be part of the world of sin or require atonement. 1 John responds by drawing upon the Johannine formulation of the "love command" as the obligation laid upon the community and the expression of the divine presence (Jn 13:34–35; 15:12–17). Love among Christians is the "proof" that they possess the divine life which they claim (1 Jn 3:14f.; 4:7–12, 16–21). One also finds in 1 John renewed use of the expectation of a future judgment, which those who remain in love need not fear (1 Jn 4:17). Similarly, 1 Jn 3:1–3 appears to modify the gospel's perception of the revelation of the Father in Jesus (e.g. Jn 14:8–11). The disciple does not have a clear vision of God or the heavenly destiny of the Christian until Christ returns and we become like him. Some exegetes continue to take this treatment of salvation as an indication that 1 John was written earlier than the gospel. However, most exegetes would agree that the setting presupposed by the epistles is that of a community in a later stage of development, internally divided rather than facing the persecution of a hostile world. 1 John can draw on expressions which are more common in early Christian eschatology generally because they too are part of the heritage of faith preserved in Johannine circles.

3. The Spirit-Paraclete and Johannine Ecclesiology.
(See Bibliography number 6).

Exegetes continue to be divided over how one should describe the Johannine understanding of church. The dualistic language about a "world" which is hostile and stands over against the believing community (e.g. Jn 15:18-26; 1 Jn 2:12-17), suggests to some a highly sectarian experience. 1 John may go even further than the gospel in this regard. The opponents are described as "antichrist" (1 Jn 2:18, 22; 4:3; 2 Jn 7). Christians are not to have anything to do with such persons (2 Jn 8-11; possibly 1 Jn 5:16-17, 21). The believer is "of God," the world is in the power of the Evil One (1 Jn 5:19). Others insist that despite these tendencies, the Johannine community remained "involved with" the world, since Jesus had commissioned the disciples to take his place as witness to that world. The concern over hospitality for travelling Johannine Christians in 3 John may also be understood as evidence of a continuing missionary effort directed toward the world.

The Johannine community also appears to have relied upon "spirit-inspired" application of the tradition (e.g. Jn 14:25-26; 16:12-15), to guide its life to a much greater degree than is apparent in the other gospels or even in the Pauline churches. The activity of the Paraclete may have been particularly evident to the community in the interpretation of the tradition that had developed under the guidance of the Beloved Disciple, the Evangelist and their disciples. Jn 21:23 corrects a rumor that had taken one of Jesus' sayings to mean that Beloved disciple would not die. But this same type of "spirit-inspired" leadership probably contributed to the crisis reflected in the Johannine epistles. There was no clear line of continuity to distinguish between the author of 1-2 John and his opponents. Both claim to represent authentic Johannine tradition. All the author can do is to appeal to the community's ability to "discern the spirit" and to acknowledge that his teaching represents the teaching as it had been from the beginning. Consequently, R. Brown has argued that the Johannine churches would have had to adopt models of ecclesial structure from churches in the Petrine tradition in order to meet this new crisis.

John in Today's Church

It has been said that there is no bigger gap between the scholarly understanding of a New Testament work and how that gospel is preached in the church than in the case of the Fourth Gospel. The narrative skill with which the evangelist has recounted individual stories about Jesus often leads to the gospel being preached as though it represented events in the life of Jesus "as they happened." Yet, we know that the gospel itself says that the disciples did not understand the significance of much of Jesus' ministry until they looked back on it from the perspective of Jesus' resurrection and exaltation to the Father (e.g. Jn 2:22). The gospel has come to understand Jesus through a process in which the community interpreted and developed its faith.

1. Symbolism and the Perception of Truth.

The Fourth Gospel stands as a challenge to the literalist fundamentalism that many people take to be the truth of biblical revelation. It shows us that those persons most opposed to accepting the truth that Jesus is "from God" are those who take the affirmations of the Jewish religious tradition that they have inherited from Moses literally. The only way to perceive the truth that Jesus reveals the Father is through the great religious symbols of the gospel.

A mature Christian faith, then, is not fixated at the stage of literal fundamentalism. It is possible to use Johannine stories like that of Nicodemus in Jn 3:1–15, 7:51 and 19:39 to illustrate the movement toward faith in Jesus. The story of the blind man in Jn 9 begins with the affirmation that Jesus is "light of the world." Challenges to the blind man's "faith" lead him to further affirmations of Jesus' relationship with God until he finally comes to worship Jesus. Testing, conflict and the move toward the symbolic level of affirming belief in Jesus is also evident in the story of the Samaritan woman (Jn 4:4–44), and in the raising of Lazarus in Jn 11.

2. Universalism and the Mission to the World.

Johannine use of symbolism does not isolate the believer from the larger world. Adaptation of the great religious symbols of humanity enables the gospel to move outward from its Jewish roots into the religious experience of the larger hellenistic world. Almost all the discipleship stories in John move from an individual encountering Jesus in faith to an episode in which that person bears witness about Jesus to someone else.

A mature Christian faith, then, is one which must be expressed in testimony about Jesus. The gospel shows that it is possible for Christianity to appropriate important symbols from its cultural surroundings in order to express its conviction that Jesus is the saving revelation of God. But the gospel also knows that continuing Jesus' testimony to the world is not "cheap." Christians may expect rejection and suffering because their message is not simply a reflection of the latest religious or "self-help" fads.

3. The Challenge of Johannine Ecclesiology.

John's understanding of the believing community as a place in which the tradition is constantly renewed by the activity of the Spirit may not be a comfortable one for churches which have sedimented the Spirit in fixed patterns of expression and authority. The story of the Johannine community shows us the need for established "offices" of teaching authority within the church. But that fact should not be allowed to eradicate the Johannine perception that the church's faith is continually growing.

A mature Christian faith, then, welcomes the new activity of the Spirit in expressing and reapplying the tradition which we have "inherited from the beginning." One of the most striking sets of images for our time has been the active role of woman witnesses in the Fourth Gospel. The Samaritan woman in Jn 4 becomes a missionary of the gospel and leads many to perceive that Jesus is indeed "savior of the world." Martha in Jn 11 is the first to gain true faith that Jesus is, "the resurrection and the life." Mary Magdalene in Jn 20 is the first witness to the resurrection, itself. And, though briefly, the mother of Jesus frames the ministry of her Son. Her request provokes the miracle of Cana, the first manifestation of Jesus "glory." She reappears at the cross, when Jesus has finished his mission, and, symbolic of the new Israel, she is entrusted to the care of the Beloved Disciple.

Just as the Johannine tradition challenged those in the first century to come to a new awareness of Jesus, so it challenges us today. We are not allowed to claim that all is finished as though the gospel were wrapped up in some package ready to be consumed. Instead, we are told to continue Jesus' witness to the world under the guidance of the Paraclete. If we do that, our faith is continually pushed to find Jesus anew.

BIBLIOGRAPHY

1. *Commentaries.*

Barrett, C.K.   *The Gospel According to St. John. An Introduction with Commentary and Notes on the Greek Text.* 2nd ed. Philadelphia: Westminster, 1978.

Brown, R.E.   *The Gospel according to John I-XII.* AB 29. Garden City: Doubleday, 1966; *The Gospel according to John XIII-XXI.* AB 29A. Garden City: Doubleday, 1970.

Lindars, B.   *The Gospel of John.* London: Oliphants, 1972.

Schnackenburg, R.   *The Gospel according to St. John. Vol. 1. Chapters 1-4.* Trans. K. Smyth. New York: Seabury,

1980; *The Gospel according to St. John. Vol. 2. Chapters 5-12.* New York: Seabury, 1980; *The Gospel according to St. John. Vol. 3. Chapters 13-21.* New York: Crossroad, 1982.

Brown, R.E. *The Epistles of John.* AB 30. Garden City: Doubleday, 1982.

Grayston, K. *The Johannine Epistles.* Grand Rapids, MI: Eerdmans, 1984.

Smalley, S.S. *1,2,3 John.* Word Biblical Commentary 51. Waco, TX: Word, 1984.

Schnackenburg, R. *Die Johannesbriefe.* HTKNT 13/3. Freiburg: Herder, 1965.

2. *General Surveys of Johannine Studies*

Dunn, J.D.G. "Let John Be John. A Gospel for Its Time." *Das Evangelium und die Evangelien.* Ed. P. Stuhlmacher. Tübingen: J.C.B. Mohr, 1983. 309–339.

Kysar, R. "The Gospel of John in Current Research," *RelStudRev* 9 (1983) 314-23.

Smalley, S.S. *John Evangelist and Interpreter.* Nashville, TN: Nelson, 1978.

Smith, D.M. *Johannine Christianity: Essays on Its Setting, Sources and Theology.* Columbia: University of South Carolina, 1984.

3. *Background to the Johannine Tradition:*

Charlesworth, J.H. "A Critical Comparison of the Dualism in 1 QS 3:13–4:26 and the Dualism Contained in the Fourth Gospel." *NTS* 15 (1968/69) 389–418.

Janssens, Y. "The Trimorphic Protennoia and the Fourth Gospel." *The New Testament and Gnosis. Essays in Honour of R. McL. Wilson.* Eds. A.H.B. Logan and A.J.M. Wedder-burn. Edinburgh: T & T Clark, 1983. 229–44.

MacRae, G.W. "The Ego-Proclamation in Gnostic Sources." *The Trial of Jesus.* Ed. E. Bammel. SBT 2/13. London: SCM, 1970. 122–24.

MacRae, G.W. "The Fourth Gospel and Religionsgeschi-chte." *CBQ* 32 (1970) 13–24.

MacRae, G.W. "Nag Hammadi and the New Testament." *Gnosis. Festschrift für Hans Jonas.* Ed. B. Aland; Göttingen: Vandenhoeck & Ruprecht, 1978. 144–57.

Meeks, W.A. "Am I A Jew? — Johannine Christianity and Judaism." *Christianity, Judaism and Other Greco-Roman Cults: Studies for Morton Smith.* Part One. Ed. J. Neusner. Leiden: Brill, 1975. 163–86.

Meeks, W.A. *The Prophet King: Moses Traditions and Johannine Christology.* Nov T Suppl. T 14. Leiden: Brill, 1967.

Neyrey, J.H. "The Jacob Allusions in Jn 1:51." *CBQ* 44 (1982) 586–605.

Pamment, M. "Is There Convincing Evidence of Samaritan Influence on the Fourth Gospel." *ZNW* 73 (1982)   221–30.

Pancaro, S. *The Law in the Fourth Gospel. The Torah and the Gospel, Moses and Jesus, Judaism and Christianity according to John.* Suppl. NovT 42. Leiden: Brill, 1975.

Purvis, J.D. "The Fourth Gospel and the Samaritans." *NovT* 17 (1975) 161–98.

Reim, G. "Targum und Johannesevangelium." *BibZeit* 27 (1983) 1–13.

Talbert, C.H. "The Myth of a Descending-Ascending Re-deemer in Mediterranean Antiquity." *NTS* 22 (1975/76) 418–39.

4. *The Johannine Community*

Brown, R.E. *The Community of the Beloved Disciple.* New York: Paulist, 1979.

Lindars, B. "The Persecution of Christians in Jn 15:18-16:4a." *Suffering and Martyrdom in the New Testament. Studies Presented to G. M. Styler.* Eds. W. Horbury & B. McNeil. Cambridge, UK: Cambridge University Press, 1981. 48-69.

Martyn, J.L. *History and Theology in the Fourth Gospel.* 2nd ed. Nashville: Abingdon, 1979.

Meeks, W.A. "The Man from Heaven in Johannine Sectarianism." *JBL* 91 (1972) 44-72.

Painter, J. "Christology and History of the Johannine Community in the Prologue of the Fourth Gospel." *NTS* 30 (1984) 460-74.

Segovia, F.F. "The Love and Hatred of Jesus and Johannine Sectarianism." *CBQ* 43 (1981) 258-72.

Wahlde, Urban C. von "The Johannine 'Jews': A Critical Survey." *NTS* 28 (1982) 33-60.

5. *Literary Analyses of the Fourth Gospel*

Attridge, H. "Thematic Development and Source Elaboration in John 7:1-36." *CBQ* 42 (1980) 160-70.

Crossan, J.D. "It is Written: A Structuralist Analysis of John 6." *Semeia* 26 (1983) 3-21.

Culpepper, R.A. *Anatomy of the Fourth Gospel. A Study in Literary Design.* Philadelphia: Fortress, 1983.

MacRae, G.W. "Theology and Irony in the Fourth Gospel." *The Word in the World. Essays in Honor of Frederick L. Moriarty.* Eds. R. Clifford & G.W. MacRae. Cambridge, MA: Weston College Press, 1973. 83-96.

6. *Theological Topics: Faith and Salvation, Christology, the Spirit*

Bammel, E.   "Jesus und der Paraklet in Johannes 16." *Christ and Spirit in the New Testament. Studies in Honour of C. F.D. Moule.* Eds. B. Lindars & S.S. Smalley. Cambridge: Cambridge University Press, 1973. 199–217.

Barrett, C.K.   "The Father is Greater than I, (Jo 14, 28): Subordinationist Christology in the New Testament." *Neues Testament und Kirche. Für Rudolf Schnackenburg.* ed. J. Gnilka. Freiburg: Herder, 1974.

Boismard, M.-É.   "Rapports entre foi et miracles dans l 'évangile de Jean." *EphTheolLouv* 58 (1982) 357–64.

Forestell, J.T.   *The Word of the Cross. Salvation as Revelation in the Fourth Gospel.* Rome: Biblical Institute Press, 1974.

Fortna, R.T. "Christology in the Fourth Gospel: Redaction-Critical Perspectives." *NTS* 21 (1974/75) 489–504.

Jonge, M. de   *Jesus: Stranger from Heaven and Son of God.* Trans. J. Steely. SBLSBS 11. Missoula, MT: Scholars Press, 1977.

Kaefer, J.P.   "Les discours d' adieu en Jean 13:31–17:26: Rédaction et Théologie." *NovT* 26 (1984) 253Ç82.

Lona, H.E.   "Glaube und Sparche des Glaubens im Joh.-Ev." *BibZeit* nf. 28 (1984) 168Ç84.

Malatesta, E.   "The Spirit-Paraclete in the Fourth Gospel." *Biblica* 54 (1973) 539–50.

Moloney, F.J.   *The Johannine Son of Man.* 2nd ed. Biblioteca di Scienze Religiose 14. Rome: Libreria Ateneo Salesiano, 1978.

Pamment, M.   "The Son of Man in the Fourth Gospel." *JTS* ns. 36 (1985) 56–66.

Wahlde, U.C. von.   "The Witnesses to Jesus in John 5:31–40 and Belief in the Fourth Gospel." *CBQ* 43 (1981) 385–404.

AMERICAN CATHOLIC BIBLICAL SCHOLARSHIP 1955—1980

John L. McKenzie
Claremont, California

I have been asked to review biblical scholarship in the Catholic Church in North America for the twenty-five years 1955—1980. During all of these years the Rev. Bruce Vawter, C.M., in whose honor this essay is written, has been active in biblical scholarship. To say that he has been active is an understatement made by an author who is not known for understatement. The bibliography of Vawter's books, articles, reviews and contributions to dictionaries and encyclopedias will give some idea of how deeply he has been involved in biblical scholarship. One must also reckon his work as an editor of several journals and his offices in learned societies. The history of this period of scholarship has not been written; I learn that it is in preparation. In the finished volume the name of Bruce Vawter will be as prominent as any other.

I. The State of Affairs in 1955
(See Bibliography numbers 1, 2, 3).

I choose to begin my recital with an event which occurred in the ecclesiastical world shortly before the beginning of my period; this was the appearance of the encyclical *Humani Generis*, issued by Pius XII in 1950. In the minds of many this encyclical was intended to bring to an abrupt halt the renascence of biblical studies initiated by the encyclical *Divino Afflante Spiritu*, issued by the same Pius XII in 1943. I remember reading the encyclical when it was published and wondering whether my new and modest ambitions in biblical studies must be abandoned. That others thought so I was soon made aware. But the world of biblical scholarship did not fall into a state of frozen terror, as earlier experiences in the twentieth century might have led one to expect, because *Divino Afflante Spiritu* had struck a resounding chord of sympathy in Catholic scholars, who knew at once that *Humani Generis* did not mean what it seemed to say. It took a few more years to bring the rest of the theological world to share this knowledge, often reluctantly.

One may wonder whether any feeling of security on the part of the biblical scholars towards the Holy See can ever be justified in the light of the history of the past eighty years. At this juncture the feeling was fortified by the publication of a letter from the Secretary of the Pontifical Biblical Commission in 1955. Almost from the day of its establishment this office was the agency through which the Holy See repressed any attempt of biblical scholars to express any independence or novelty in thought. It was somewhat significant that the commission fell into silence after 1955 in the sense that its repressive tone was ended. The letter of that year effectively removed all restraints placed upon Catholic scholars by the previous utterances of the Commission. Scholars felt free (and this feeling is now taken for granted) to discuss such topics as the Synoptic Questions, the literary origins of the Pentateuch, the composition of the book of Isaiah, the nature and quality of biblical history in both Old and New Testaments—all previously forbidden topics with strictly enforced, even if vague and unspecified, penalties. In my day Loisy was still remembered. Now American scholars have come to occupy a prominent position in international and interconfessional discussions of these and similar questions. The writer of this sketch was able to write (I believe in the 40s or the early 50s) that Protestants did not trust the honesty of their Catholic colleagues; Catholics were believed to say what they were told to say, not what they thought. The late W.A. Irwin of the University of Chicago was good enough to recognize the allusion to his own writings. It was inconceivable to Dr. Irwin, as well as to others, that Catholics saw no contradiction between their scholarly integrity and their surrender to a non-scholarly agency in their work, in spite of the fact that the Presbyterian Church had condemned Charles A. Briggs of heresy because he taught the multiple authorship of the Pentateuch. It was only after some years and the discovery of how unscholarly, even anti-intellectual, were the agencies which attempted to control thought and its expression that I began to find my own attitudes a bit incomprehensible. The problem of how to maintain honesty in a church many of whose officers were and are candidly dishonest was not solved in this twenty-five year period; it is too large and too permanent a problem for a quick theoretical solution. I may add my conviction that it cannot be solved by giving to scholars that same uncritical surrender which one denies to prelates.

II. The Translation of the Bible.

This brief review of the situation at the beginning of our twenty-five year period seems advisable. We may first turn to the collective achievements of American Catholic biblical scholars and then return to some more recent struggles to vindicate academic freedom and responsibility, although I fear that my younger contemporaries may be bored by this recital of battles long ago. Not necessarily the first achievement in magnitude, but certainly the first undertaken and the one which has affected most people is the production of the New American Bible, the exclusive work of the Catholic Biblical Association of America. I may feel all the more pride in this achievement because my colleagues did it entirely without my help. I wonder how many are still living who remember that the Catholic Biblical Association was founded in 1936 under the episcopal direction of the Most Rev. Edwin O'Hara of Great Falls, chairman of the Confraternity of Christian Doctrine, as a section of the same Confraternity for the express purpose of revising the Rheims-Douay Challoner Bible, then the only version approved for English-speaking Catholics. Nothing was further from the minds of Bishop O'Hara and his colleagues than a forum for the discussion of the problems of exegesis and criticism; it is probably not unfair to say that these most reverend gentlemen were unaware of the existence of such problems, or if they knew of them thought they should be suppressed. In fairness to the memory of Bishop O'Hara, who remained our episcopal moderator until his death in 1956 and who attended the annual mettings, he never to my knowledge attempted to interfere with the discussions which went on at the meetings.

The New Testament revision was done rather quickly and appeared in 1941. Unfortunately for those who did the revision so expeditiously, their work was rendered nugatory almost at once by the appearance of *Divino Afflante Spiritu*, a document which encouraged translation from the original languages and destroyed the last excuse for Catholics to claim that they were irrevocably committed to the Latin Vulgate and versions made from it by the Council of Trent. I still remember the reaction of a teacher and an old friend, the late James E. Coleran, S.J., who had done most of the revision of Exodus, when he found that most of his work must go into the waste basket. One would think that those who directed the Confraternity should not have been taken so completely by surprise when they found that what they thought was their fidelity to the Holy See did not demand such devotion to the Vulgate. In any case, an episcopal mandate and the express encouragement of the Apostolic Delegate to the United States were enough to institute a brand new translation in 1944. One now wonders why all this effort was required to do something which had been done in European countries generations before.

The New American Bible, when it finally got under way, was not done hastily. The complete Bible appeared in 1970; the Old Testament books from Genesis to Ruth were revised from the text published in 1952. The delay in producing the New Testament involves a story not told in the preface to *The New American Bible*. Not long after the mandate of 1944 (I cannot be certain of the exact date and cannot check it; for this discussion it does not seem important) the late James A. Kleist, S. J., the late Joseph A. Lilly, C.M., and Charles A. Pickar. O.S.A., were appointed by the Episcopal Committee to translate the New Testament from the Greek. Their work was finished in 1952 and was rejected by the bishops. The rejected version was published by the Bruce Publishing Co. in 1954; strangely the name of Charles A. Pickar was omitted from the title. The Gospels were done by Kleist, the Pauline letters by Lilly, and the other books by Pickar. I never heard what the specific complaints were (and I talked with Kleist shortly after the rejection) except that the version was so radically different that the faithful might be scandalized by its novelty. I suppose others besides me wondered how familiar the bishops thought the faithful were with the New Testament. The version was a creditable job and the American Catholic Church could have lived with it. I remember the amusement with which I read a review in which a British critic found too many Americanisms in the version. Kleist, the major offender, was a native of Germany who began the study of English when he came to this country at the age of thirty. The version abandoned that style of speech known as "Bible English," and that may have been the point of the bishops' objection; the version did not sound like the Bible, which might have meant that it would catch attention. When the New Testament appeared in 1970, no episcopal voice was raised about its scandalous novelty, although the translators went beyond Kleist, Lilly and Pickar in the use of modern speech. It shows how much progress had been made in twenty years, as well as the price that is exacted from theologians who are in advance of their time even in language, and even by as little as twenty years. Theological thought in Catholicism is admired and esteemed when it shows the mobility of a glacier.

Now that *The New American Bible* has appeared, nearly thirty years after the original mandate (a term of years which the active careers of few scholars exceed), it can be seen as the major achievement of a generation of scholars. Jerome is reported to have done his work in fifteen years, and it is now safe to say that it was a sloppy job even for one man working at that speed with limited resources. Jerome boasted that the book of Judith was the work of one night, and it looks like it. Unlike the names of the translators of the Authorized Version of 1609, the names of the translators of *The New American Bible* will not be lost in obscurity (althought the list given in the NAB does not include Kleist, which seems a bit ungrateful). Most users of the NAB will hardly notice the 123 pages of textual notes to the Old Testament. The student is impressed by this display of the free critical judgment which is the obligation of the textual critic. In comparing my own Anchor Bible *Second Isaiah* with the NAB I was surprised to find that the translators had shown almost as much freedom towards the Masoretic text as I had shown in a series where slavish fidelity to the Masoretic text is not recommended.

More than once I have had to eat the words which I uttered in a meeting of the Catholic Biblical Association before the entire volume was published. It was reported by the late Monsignor Patrick Skehan that in deference to the expressed wishes of seven (I believe) members of the Episcopal Committee the word "maid" was replaced by the older version "virgin" in Isaiah 7:14. I pleaded that their Excellencies seemed to know as little English as they knew Hebrew, and that I could never in conscience recommend this version. I hope I have learned never (or at least rarely) to say "never." There is no English version which you could not throw out for one bad verse; one striking example repeated twice in *The New English Bible* (which delicacy forbids me to quote) has been corrected in subsequent printings, no doubt leaving others just as bad but not indelicate.

Line for line, the NAB is simply the best English Bible in print. The revisers of the Revised Standard, who had a chance to reestablish its preeminence in a new revision now in process, have with full knowledge and consent, as we used to say about mortal sin, rejected this opportunity. When I use the NAB for quick reference, it never lets me down with a careless translation or sloppy or archaic English. John Noonan does not like "the place where travelers lodge" instead of the traditional "inn"; I question whether the exact word, which would be "caravansary," would be intelligible to the modern American reader for whom the version was made, unless they are as literate as John Noonan. I am happy to pay this tribute to the monumental achievement of my colleagues and to make a belated apology to the late Patrick Skehan, a good friend who was more responsible than any one else for shepherding the Old Testament through the long process. The Rheims-Douay-Challoner Bible endured for 360 years (more or less) for the good reason that no one read it; the Old Testament was reprinted once between its publication in 1610 and Challoner's revision in 1750. The NAB will be read, and hence has less chance of lasting 360 years. But it will remain a substantially good job long after we are all dead, and the clamor for revision will therefore be less. The only threat which the NAB has presented to the Catholic Biblical Association has been the threat of affluence. This threat was foreseen by Bishop O'Hara as far back as 1947; I believe I am the only survivor of a meeting of the officers of the Association that year where the atmosphere became quite heated on just this problem. The bishop thought that most of the proceeds should go to the Confraternity of Christian Doctrine and not to the Catholic Biblical Association. The Association has dispensed this affluence through professorships and scholarships and other projects which it has judged worthy of assistance for promoting and diffusing the knowledge of the Bible. I can conclude this section of my sketch on a definite upbeat.

III. The Jerome Bible Commentary.

The second achievement to be reported, scarcely less in magnitude but reaching a smaller audience, was the production of the *Jerome Bible Commentary*. This is a verse by verse commentary on the entire Bible, with accompanying articles on various topics in the style of literary companion. It is an enormous work of 637 + 889 pages, two volumes bound in one. It appeared in 1968 under the general editorship of Raymond E. Brown, Joseph A. Fitzmyer, and Roland E. Murphy.

A writer—I think it was my fellow Hoosier Rex Stout—once wrote a novel under the title of *The League of Frightened Men*. This title could have designated the Catholic Biblical Association up to 1952, the year in which it amended its constitution to admit non-Catholics as active members. Frightened they may once have been; but the JBC is not, does not read like, does not show the thinking of frightened men. To a senior member of the Catholic Biblical Association, the serenity and assurance with which it treads on ground which would have seared the soles off the feet of Catholic scholars thirty years ago is the most impressive feature of the JBC, not the competence and depth of its scholarship nor the unquestioned brilliance and clarity of its exposition, which may have astonished others who did not think that Catholics could do so well. I always knew my colleagues were capable of excellent work if they would just shake off their pathological fear of ecclesiastical authorities and move off the dime on which, as they say in baseball, they had been playing so long.

Lest I might seem here to be indulging in some self-praise, let me hasten to add that neither I nor others regard the articles on the biblical theology of the Old Testament and the Gospel of Matthew as among the more brilliant of the contributions. I may say that the article on Matthew was written in response to a request that something be done quickly because the Rev. David M. Stanley, S.J., was unable to fulfill his commitment. My pleas that not only David Stanley but many others were far better equipped than I to do Matthew were unheard; the success of Joseph Fitzmyer as an editor is largely due to his capacity to refuse to accept the impossible. He simple asserted that others might do it better, but none of them could do it as quickly as I. If the editors should replace Matthew with a better job done by another, neither my personal feelings nor my reputation as a scholar nor the Commentary will suffer. If the commentary on Matthew did hasten the publication of the JBC or remove the danger of a delay, it was worth the trouble, and I am proud of it.

Is the JBC the best one-volume commentary in existence? To say that would cover an enormous territory. If I limit myself to the English language, I can say it without hesitation. Is it pound for pound the best buy for any student of the Bible? Something like that has been said about another book in which I have some interest (here I am indulging in self-praise), so I cannot be sure my opinion is impartial. But to be fair, I think I have to say that if we are simply discussing bargains, my Dictionary is a motorcycle and the JBC is a Rolls-Royce. Both are bargains; the only thing they have in common is that they both beat walking. The JBC, with the Authorized Version and the Encyclopedia Britannica, is one of those rare pieces of excellent work done by a committee.

IV. A Fellowship of Scholars: The Catholic Biblical Association

The next achievement in my enumeration is the Catholic Biblical Association itself. At the last meeting I attended (1983) I noticed a number of things, possibly because I have reached an age at which any meeting may be my last. The numbers in attendance were, I believe, three times greater than they were in 1955. I have mentioned that since 1952 the Association has admitted Protestants, and for the first time in 1983 it elected a Protestant as vice-president (with the right of succession). The Association was not long ago a priestly fraternity; I do not wish to fault this fraternity, in which I have enjoyed membership for over forty years, but a learned society grows in all dimensions by broadening its base of membership. When I joined the Association the Bible was studied in the Catholic Church only in seminaries, and the study of the Bible was almost inevitably a professional interest of a few priests in the Catholic Church. The same was largely true of the Protestant Churches as well, *mutatis mutandis*. The Society of Biblical Literature elected its first Catholic president in 1966, and has elected several Catholics since. The Society was founded in 1880, so we became ecumenical at a slightly more rapid pace. It takes more than this to show that Catholic biblical scholarship is no longer a ghetto; but it contributes to showing it.

I was impressed also by the quality of the papers and discussions. For interest and relevance, others besides me believe that the meetings of the Association generally reach a higher level than the meetings of the venerable Society of Biblical Literature. In my experience (and I have attended the meetings of both organizations since 1950 except for half a dozen) this has not always been true. I may risk the hypothesis, rash at best, that the Catholic Biblical Association as a body is still aware of its mission in a church where its members must share their learning with their fellow believers. I should add, still being venturesome, that I see signs that the Catholic Biblical Association may become a society of mandarins who speak only to other mandarins. This is not to say that there is no place for mandarins, nor that mandarins should never be able to come together and share interests. Mandarins, I suppose, do not feel that their society is enriched by broadening its base of membership. For some years I was a member of the American Oriental Society, which you would think was a group of mandarins if ever there was one. What I remember about that Society and what drew me to its meetings was that a society of mandarins is precisely what it is not. What it achieved for its members was never quite reached by either the Catholic Biblical Association or the Society of Biblical Literature. I am aware of the vagueness of my dissatisfaction with the procedures of both biblical organizations; and I am ready to be told that no one else who holds membership in all the societies mentioned has felt the same vague doubts.

While the production of books on the Bible is the work of individual scholars rather than of societies, except for such collective enterprises as the *Jerome Bible Commentary,* a learned society is expected to furnish some kind of assistance to those of its members who engage in such work. Such tangible assistance is rendered by series such as the Catholic Biblical Association Monograph Series, to which I shall return briefly below. These series are intended to assist younger scholars at the beginning of their career, when such assistance is most needed. Older and presumably self-sufficient scholars are more likely to receive no more than the intangible assistance found in a forum for the informal discussion of ideas, and in the encouragement and criticism of their colleagues. This assistance is intangible, but all who have experienced it recognize it as quite real, especially those who must perforce live without frequent contact with their colleagues in biblical studies. American Catholic scholars have produced a respectable shelf of books both scholarly and popular. For nearly a generation they have been invited to participate in collective works such as series of commentaries and encyclopedias written mostly by Protestants and Jews. At the beginning of my career such participation was not invited nor would its acceptance have been smiled on by ecclesiastical superiors. It may be hard for my younger colleagues to realize that such participation was cooperation in the production of books which were by definition on the Index. In 1943 I was one of several approached by John Courtney Murray to contribute some articles to a new edition of the *Encyclopedia Britannica.* That monumental work had been produced without the cooperation of Catholics since 1768. In a later edition I found a particular pleasure in writing an article which had been covered in the famous eleventh edition by Julius Wellhausen. The article "Pentateuch" was not the only reason why that particular edition—I have forgotten its number—did not acquire as lasting a reputation as the eleventh did. *The Interpreter's Bible* is probably the last major effort to be planned without Catholic collaboration. A number of Catholics are enumerated among the contributors to the *Anchor Bible*. When I was given the responsibility of editing the book reviews for the *Catholic Biblical Quarterly* in 1951, I could not get the volumes of *The Interpreters Bible*, then appearing, for review except by purchasing them. I hardly found it diplomatic when John McConnell described the first volume we reviewed as a massive tomb of the Bible. Now and for thirty years the *Quarterly* reviews books in all languages written by authors of all denominations. Perhaps it is worth remembering that when I was given the reviews in 1951, the *Quarterly* in the last issue before my appointment reviewed six books.

V. The Catholic Biblical Quarterly and other Publications

This leads me to the next achievement in my enumeration, the *Catholic Biblical Quarterly* and other publications produced by the Association. In 1952 the Catholic Biblical Association devoted its annual meeting to a revision of its constitution and by-laws. Actions included the aforementioned opening of membership to non-Catholics. It was moved and the motion was passed after some long and rather intense debate that the name of the *Catholic Biblical Quarterly* be changed and specifically that the word *Catholic* be deleted. The late Edward F. Siegman, C.PP.S., appointed editor the preceding year to replace the late Michael Gruenthaner, S.J., was among those who felt the *Quarterly* had become such an embarrassment that the determination to change its character and its policy would be best exhibited by a change of name. Father Gruenthaner, in one of the most embarrassing moments I have ever experienced in a public meeting, first heard of his discharge at the business meeting without any previous discussion or warning. Very few at the meeting in 1952 disputed the embarrassment; a minority disputed a change of name which seemed to suggest that we were ashamed of being Catholic. The mistake of those who advocated the change of name (we were called most politely "young Turks") was to move the change without having a concrete name to propose for adoption; so the defenders of the existing name argued for a postponement of the final decision to the following morning, and we went to bed happily secure that this millstone would be buried in the depths of the sea without being attached to our necks. We underestimated the power of corridor politics, a mistake of which I was to be reminded at another meeting nine years later. Next day Edward Siegman found that he was still editor of the *Catholic Biblical Quarterly* at the insistence of members who rarely read the *Quarterly* and never contributed articles or (I can attest) book reviews. That is the reason, if any one ever wondered, why I wrote so many book reviews to the end of 1954, when I was compelled by illness to turn the book reviews over to Bruce Vawter.

The millstone did not drown the *Quarterly*. A stubborn insistence on quality maintained by Edward Siegman and his successors, an insistence supported by the membership of the Association, has overcome the handicap of the name of the journal and its inglorious past. Protestants and Jews (not to mention Catholics) now feel no embarrassment at publication in the *Quarterly*. Many readers say that the *Quarterly* presents a better mix of material than the *Journal of Biblical Literature*. This, I think, can be attributed to the fact that the Rev. Joseph A. Fitzmyer, S.J., formerly the editor of the *Journal* (the first Catholic in the position), has since become editor of the *Quarterly*. Thus it may seem that all the blood, sweat and tears (I exaggerate) of the summer of 1952 were wasted; the desired results were achieved. And so they were—but not without unnecessary blood, sweat and tears. In what is generally regarded as the twilight of my years, I find myself more and more frequently wondering whether it is only Catholics who so often have to do things the hard way. I think I know the answer, but this is not the context in which to introduce it.

In spite of some self-defeating quality in our membership, the *Quarterly* has achieved international and interconfessional eminence and the respect due to the high level of scholarship which is admitted to its pages. Like the other achievements, this one appears to be enduring, safe from such threats as that which I shall mention shortly.

But before I turn to this topic, I should not pass over *The Bible Today*. This popular journal was conceived at the 1958 meeting of the Catholic Biblical Association, held at St. Bonaventure's College. I was fairly familiar with the genesis of the idea; I thought that the American Jesuits, of whom at that time I was one, formed a unified corps of some size and wide geographical distribution which furnished an almost natural editorial committee. I called a meeting of the Jesuits present, and they manifested more than sufficient interest. The Jesuit sponsorship never happened because the Rev. Walter Farrell, S.J., refused to entertain any discussion of the location of the editorial headquarters at his college. It passed into the capable and more receptive hands of the Benedictine monks of Collegville. In those hands the journal has prospered and become all that it was hoped to be when it was founded. It is not easy to produce a popular journal of biblical learning which succeeds in being popular without becoming shallow. This I believe the editors of *The Bible Today* have accomplished.

The Catholic Biblical Association, like the Society of Biblical Literature, sponsors a series of monographs; these I have kept up with because, in spite of the singular indolence into which I have fallen (it goes with the territory), I am still ranked as an associate editor and I receive free copies. These two series afford young scholars an opportunity to publish the results of research which has usually consumed several of the best years of their lives. Such publications are never intended for a large public, nor do they reach one. It is the nature of the scholarly beast that it demands these offerings; except for a few such establishments as the two monograph series, the beast renders no subsidies for publication. The monograph series of the

Association is a worthy expenditure of the affluence previously mentioned, and the contributors are not drawn exclusively from Catholics.

VI. Some Obstacles to Progress. (See Bibliography numbers 5, 6)

These recollections seem to contain nothing but material for a chronicle of success. It is a story which ends with the notice that they all lived happily ever after, or at least they were so living at the point where the narrative ends. There are other elements in the recollections which are not so drenched in sunshine: elements which I have tried to forget, or at least have moved towards oblivion by not retaining any personal records of these transactions. I have already been jawed enough by friends and colleagues for what is, to a historian, vandalism. I can plead only that it is not pleasant to remember, still less to preserve records of episodes in which everyone looked small, including me. But this vanity, I suppose, should not be a good reason for burying something which should not be forgotten. The forces which brought these minor events to pass are still active in the Church, as they have been since the first century, and the scenario should be and probably will be repeated. I hope to be out of the cast and out of the theater before the replay.

By 1961 it had become evident that many of our colleagues in theology and in the priesthood stoutly disapproved of the activities of biblical scholarship. This disapproval was not limited to America; the forms of expression which this disapproval took in Europe are not part of my recital. In America the major organ of this opposition was the *American Ecclesiastical Review*, and, only to a slightly smaller degree, the *Homiletic and Pastoral Review*. These had long been and still are the major professional clerical journals published in the United States. The *Review* was edited by the late Monsignor Joseph Clifford Fenton, the *Homiletic* by Aidan M. Carr, O.F.M.

Conv. In that year, June 5, 1961, the Apostolic Delegate to the United States, the late Most Rev. Egidio Vagnozzi, delivered the commencement address at Marquette University. This address, to put it mildly, was a vile and slanderous attack on biblical scholars, in no way founded on scholarly arguments, which his Excellency was incapable of handling. I found out in the following few years where his capacities lay.

The Catholic Biblical Association met at Mt. St. Mary's Seminary in Cincinnati in August, 1961, under the presidency of the late Monsignor Eugene Maly; at the time the Association still awarded its presidency to the host of its annual meeting. I mention this because Gene was handed an unexpected hot potato which he fielded with grace, no small courage and some cost to his standing with his own ordinary, the late Most Rev. Karl Alter. At the meeting I was accosted by the late Monsignor Patrick Skehan, of the Archdiocese of New York and the Catholic University. Pat, a long time friend (we were nearly of the same age), expressed great concern with what he thought were libelous articles about biblical scholars in the two clerical journals. He suggested a meeting of a few colleagues to draw up a resolution to be presented to the Association for its approval, expressing our vigorous disagreement with such articles; we all thought that such a massive response was due, since the attacks had gone beyond the point where any single respondent could deal with them. It was agreed that the Rev. Bruce Vawter, C.M., (not yet late, thank God, as all the other agents seem to be) and I would collaborate in drawing up the text of the resolution. This we did almost at once. It occurred to some one, either in the small group or in the general meeting—I forget which—that such a severe resolution would not look good unless we cited by name the author, the title of the article, the name of the publication, the pages and the date of issue of just what we were objecting to. This task I undertook, and I spent a couple of hours in the seminary library that evening. Naturally the first name on my list was Egidio Vagnozzi, whose commencement address had been published with much less delay than was usual for *Amerian Ecclesiastical Review*.

Monsignor Skehan, who had conceived the whole idea of the resolution, begged off from presenting it on the floor of the meeting. He pleaded that his own personal feelings were so wrought up that he feared he could not make the motion without an undue loss of self-restraint. He was right; he took an active part in the angry debate which followed the motion, and he did lose some of his usually admirable self-restraint. In that debate self-restraint vanished from the room. At the suggestion of someone, I forget who it was, I agreed to make the motion myself. And thus calmly and deliberately I threw trouble into the fan and then stood in front of the fan.

All hell broke lose. Once the resolution was made, the ensuing uproar took the thing completely out of my hands, and all I could do was watch without further participation. It soon became clear that the objectors were a noisy and fearful minority, but a very small minority. The business meeting, at which the resolution was proposed in the late afternoon, dragged on to the dinner hour, was carried on after dinner, and was finally wound up the next morning. The objectors were not so much opposed to the resolution itself—a few of them were touched by it—as they were afraid of offending the hierarchy. I, at least, did not know that Vagnozzi had offended most of the hierarchy as much as he had offended us, and that he could not have got the bishops to support him on a vote for the Apostles' Creed. But the general vague fear was compounded when I came up with my list with Vagnozzi's name at its head, and the fear surfaced very palpably. The members of the Association have never been and are not tigers. But the mass mind of the Association came out as I had never seen it before at the opportunity to talk back as a body to what they deemed unfair and untruthful criticism. More and more frequently those who wished to speak out against the resolution were drowned out by calls for the question. I had the satisfied feeling politicians have when they know where the votes are; as I have remarked, no one really looked great. The minority succeeded that evening in getting a postponement of the final vote to the following morning, an action more significant than it appeared to be. I was told by some one, I think by Eugene Maly, that the telephone lines from the seminary to Washington were kept hot that night. This is gossip. I remember better, because it is my own memory, a colleague who came to the door of my room when the hour of retiring finally arrived. He stood in the doorway with tears in his eyes and asked to be struck from the list, and I said brusquely, "No way." Had I known what the consultors of the Association were deliberating at that very moment, I would have said "Yes" and retired from the whole business; but it was too late to put the genie back in the bottle.

The next morning the resolution was passed by an overwhelming majority. I voted for it with doubts; the consultors of the Association (a permanent standing committee, a kind of Supreme Soviet) had voted the preceding night after the general meeting to omit the name of Egidio Vagnozzi from the resolution, and the Association approved their decision. I thought this was cowardice, and I still think so; I forget whether I said so at the meeting. Even in its emasculated form the resolution did its work very well. It shut the public mouths of the Apostolic Delegate, Joseph Clifford Fenton and others. This it accomplished in spite of the fact that it was almost completely suppressed in the Catholic press, including those great liberal beacons *America* and *Commonweal*; the *Catholic Universe Bulletin* of Cleveland alone carried it. I suppose this was due to the Rev. John J. Whealon, then a young professor at the seminary in Cleveland, now Archbishop of Hartford. The late Archbishop O'Boyle of Washington would not permit its publication even in the report of the annual proceedings published in the *Catholic Biblical Quarterly*. In spite of these obstacles (and possibly others unknown to me) the message reached those for whom it was intended, and the results suggest that it was worth the effort.

How much did the effort cost? If I am to record this at all, I think this should be stated, at least as a warning to future young Turks. There were some costs, but as far as I know they were minimal weighed against the accomplishments. Again as far as I know, Monsignor Skehan escaped unscathed; Cardinal Spellman literally hated Vagnozzi, and among his virtues was an admirable loyalty to his diocesan clergy. The umbrella of the Archdiocese of New York was proof against the Apostolic Delegate. The Society of Jesus, I am sorry to say, did not furnish as effective an umbrella, of which more shortly. Bruce Vawter, as far as I know, suffered no permanent damage. No one else involved, again as far as I know, suffered more than a trip to the red carpet. But in those telephone calls to Washington (in which I obviously believe) and certainly in later conversations, Vagnozzi heard that the resolution was proposed by me and that I had listed his name. For the first time I became aware of a world something like the fictional world of *The Godfather*. I do not wish to exaggerate; I never feared that I would be gunned down or garrotted or assaulted. I did wonder whether my reputation as a priest and a theologian and my standing in the Catholic community would be shredded beyond repair. It was only a few years later that I learned that the publishing house of Sheed & Ward had been requested by some Roman congregation—I never learned which one—to withdraw from circulation all copies of *Authority In The Church*. To their honor Sheed & Ward refused. I have never been so happy that I had a clean nose. I have sometimes thought that my greatest sin was to have destroyed—rather to be thought to have destroyed—the illusion of the power of the Apostolic Delegate. It was not quite like the case of the Wizard of Oz, who told Dorothy that he was a good man, but a very bad wizard. Vagnozzi was a good Delegate, but a very bad man. But his power was not all illusory; his patron, I have been told, was the late Cardinal Ottaviani, who, like the late Alfonso Capone, included small children in his charities—but not adults, unless they met his standards of orthodoxy.

Nothing that is said here reflects any blame upon any one except myself for what happened. I accepted the suggestion of others with enthusiasm, I did quite willing all I was asked to do in the enterprise, which I made my own, and I felt that the concern was as much mine as it was of any other. That I did not foresee all the consequences was an ignorance I shared with my colleagues; that I did not have as large an umbrella as others could have been met by staying out of the rain; that others kept a lower profile is hardly an excuse for any one who has spent as much of his life looking for a high profile as I have. In the last analysis, I am rather proud of the part I played in the resolution, and I think I could afford the costs, as I shall explain shortly.

These can be totted up rather briefly, and in spite of all the sounds and alarums, they did not amount to much. I have already mentioned the ineffective attempt to suppress *Authority In The Church* through Sheed & Ward. One of the most revealing features of the whole experience was the consistent refusal of hierarchical figures to deal with me personally; I suppose they must have thought it beneath their dignity. I was excluded from appearance in an unknown number of dioceses, as many as the personal influence of the Delegate could reach. I simply do not know how many sponsoring institutions and organizations yielded to the Delegate's request to send him a tape recording of lectures I delivered; when I learned of this, it gave me the only opportunities I ever had to deliver to him a personal message. At some time in 1962 or 1963 the Rev. John R. Connery, S.J., provincial superior of the Chicago Province of the Society of Jesus (and a former student) informed me that he had been requested by the Delegate to do something—I forget what it was—which would have effectively suppressed me, as I remember it. John refused to do this without some reason for doing it, and the Delegate responded that the Provincial left him with no choice. What he felt compelled to do was to use his Roman friends to get all my writings submitted to Rome for special censorship. Since the late John B. Janssens, General of the Society, had a well established reputation as no tiger, this censorship was imposed, and it endured during the few years I had left as a Jesuit. This was something of a nuisance, most of it more to others than to me; otherwise I rather enjoyed sharing an undeserved honor with John Courtney Murray and Karl Rahner, and probably with others whom I do not know. Perhaps I should add that the Roman censorship (actually executed mostly in the United States and Canada) neither stopped nor modified anything I submitted after it was imposed; certainly it caused some annoyance to the eight men (instead of the usual three) who had to handle the censorship of the *Dictionary Of The Bible,* submitted in 1962 (900,000 words). I cannot lay claim to the type of original theological thinking which invited the attention of the Holy Office to men like Henri de Lubac, John Courtney Murray, Karl Rahner and, more recently, Hans Küng and Edward Schillebeeckx. It seems a bit ridiculous to invoke this vast ecclesiastical machinery to silence a man whose most unorthodox statement ("Come off it, your Holiness") was not published until 1969 (I think).

I do not mean what was intended to be some record of biblical studies in America to degenerate into a psalm of personal lamentation. My justification for this recital is, as I said above, that the forces which brought about this encounter are still active in the Church. It seems worth repeating at this late date because, to quote from one of my non-favorite authors, eternal vigilance is the price of liberty. I have an uneasy feeling that the complacency of my colleagues will, in the near future, be as rudely shattered as ours was. Among lessons to be learned is the lesson that theologians and exegetes are foolish to count on the support of others, even their own kind. Another lesson is that it is equally foolish to count on any restraint which might be exercised upon the wielders of power by such factors as charity, justice or truth. I do not like the politics of confrontation, which worked in this instance; but I like the politics of bullying and mendacity, which the Holy See often uses, even less. I think there is some biblical precedent for confrontation—Jesus and the Pharisees, for example; I find no precedent for bullying and mendacity. The model of Christian resolution of differences should be tolerance and rational discourse; but this is sometimes hard to set up. John Courtney Murray once said that when you think you are invited to a theological discussion, you are led into the confessional. I suppose my only doubt arises from the fear that Murray would not approve of my response to the situation. He chose another way, and it is impossible to give anything but respect to his integrity.

The theological implications of my experience have not escaped me; but this is not the place to elaborate upon them. To sum them up, it is and for some years has been impossible for me to give the Holy See (defined in the old Canon Law as the complex of bureaus and offices through which the Sovereign Pontiff is accustomed to transact the business of the universal Church) the kind of allegiance which I believe, perhaps erroneously, that it demands. What allegiance do I give it? That is a point of theology which I have not yet worked out. At my age it is a matter of finding a way of life which will carry me a few more years rather than elaborating a doctrinal system; I do not have much use any more for theology which is concerned with doctrine rather than with how to live. But as long as there is doctrine, the unresolved question is going to come up for others besides myself; I see it now in the contemporary Church, but it is evaded, as usual, and as I have so long evaded it. This means that everyone who is forced to face it must learn to answer it or to find a way to live with it, alone and unaided. There is a feeling abroad that the simple faithful should not be troubled by such questions. Pastorally (I do have such inclinations) I agree that little good is served by telling people about problems which they do not have, but which I have decided they ought to have. But how much balderdash does my pastoral duty compel me to manufacture for the simple faithful to explain why the Holy Father is so exercised about girls who serve at the altar?

NOTES—BIBLIOGRAPHY

1. *Humani Generis.* Text and Translation. *American Ecclesiastical Review* 123 (1950) 383–98.

2. By an inexplicable coincidence all the bound volumes of periodicals which could contain the text of *Divino Afflante Spiritu* were absent from the shelves of the only library available to me at the time of writing.

3. *Catholic Biblical Quarterly* 18 (1956) 23–9. The letter of the Secretary of the Biblical Commission is quoted and discussed by Edward F. Siegman.

4. The letter of the Apostolic Delegate, Archbishop Cicognani, recommending translation from the original languages, appears in the prefatory material of *The New American Bible.*

5. *American Ecclesiastical Review* 145 (1961) 71–9. The address of Archbishop Vagnozzi appeared here.

6. *Catholic Biblical Quarterly* 23 (1961) 470ff. The proceedings of the meeting of 1961 (without the resolution) appear here.

A PROTESTANT LOOKS AT CATHOLIC BIBLICAL SCHOLARSHIP

Walter Harrelson

The Divinity School — Vanderbilt University

Rome (See Bibliography numbers 1,2,3,9,11,27, and 28)

The look begins in Rome, where I spent a year of study on a Fulbright grant in 1962–63, working at home and also at the Pontifical Biblical Institute. As I was made welcome by the Rector and by friends on the faculty (especially by Fr. William L. Moran S.J.), repercussions were still awaited from the attacks being leveled at the Biblicum by near-fundamentalist clergy of Italy and (especially) Sicily. But the Institute was counting on and receiving the continual backing of the late Cardinal Bea, and it also benefited from the start of the Second Vatican Council.

In 1962–63 the Biblical Institute was still doing most of its instruction in Latin, was working industriously on a number of technical projects, but was not too heavily engaged in the wide-ranging exegetical forays that were soon to come. But already the institute was an ecumenical and international center, its library crowded with scholars from around the world, often pursuing their own private studies (as I was doing), but benefiting from the collection and from the many informal conversations with colleagues and friends of the faculty and the student body.

There were of course many other centers of biblical scholarship and theological instruction in the city, but the Biblicum was in a class by itself. Even with the sniping attacks upon it, it carried on with special studies of the Dead Dea Scrolls, the Ugaritic corpus, work in Ethiopic language and literature, Coptic studies, and especially (in those days) the combing of the newer finds in Akkadian. The import and impact of the encyclical *Divinio Afflante Spiritu* (1943) were very much in evidence, and it was this charter of freedom that prevented the Institute's critics from having their way. Moreover, by the end of Vatican II, a strong implicit affirmation of the work of the Biblicum and a heartening fresh impetus to sharing the results of biblical scholarship among the laity were unmistakable and unstoppable. Small wonder, then, that during 1983–84, when as it happened I was again in Rome for a year's sabbatical research, the spirit and engagements of the faculty and student body of the Pontifical Biblical Institute everywhere showed the fruit of the 1943 encyclical and of the Second Vatican Council.

The publications of the Institute during the last twenty-five years are mostly of a very technical and scientific sort, concentrating heavily in languages and exegetical studies. But the Institute has also done much to make the fruits of biblical scholarship accessible to church and society, to the scholarly community but also to the laity. The periodical *Biblica* and its companion guide to the scholarly literature on the Bible, the *Elenchus Bibliographicus Biblicus*, are heavily read and used resources for biblical scholars. The grammars, lexicons, and specialized studies of non-biblical literature of the ancient Near East have also been widely used. For example, the researches on Ugaritic literature by the late and beloved Mitchell Dahood, S.J., will stimulate generations of researchers in coming years.

The variety of approaches to the study of the Bible which are present in curriculum, library, and faculty study at the Biblicum today is extraordinarily impressive. During my earlier stay, the bulk of the work was of literary-critical and historical sort. Today all approaches to the critical study of Scripture are to be found on the faculty and represented within the international and ecumenical student body. Professor Luis Alonzo-Shökel, for example, gave his Presidential address at the 1983 International Organization for the Study of the Old Testament meeting in Salamanca, Spain, on the new literary approaches to the study of the Hebrew Bible, arguing that the treating of the text in this literary way offered the best protection against subjectivism and the imposition of one's own canons of interpretation upon the text. Such an address to the IOSOT by a Spanish Jesuit serving as President of the IOSOT would hardly have been thinkable twenty-five years earlier.

Biblical scholarship in Rome today is of course carried on in many centers, including the University of Rome, where Protestant and Roman Catholic biblical scholars of note are at work (for example, Professor J. Alberto Soggin of the Waldensian theological faculty in Rome, who also has faculty standing at the Biblicum). The Gregorian University continues its graduate programs in Scripture, in close collaboration with the Pontifical Biblical Institute, and the many overseas institutes and universities with their Rome branches carry on their programs. But it is the work of the Pontifical Biblical Institute that could perhaps be said to set the standard. The death of Dennis J. McCarthy, S.J. at the end of August 1983, and the earlier death of Mitchell Dahood, S.J., have been severe blows to the Biblicum and to biblical scholarship worldwide.

Jerusalem (See Bibliography numbers 15,21,25)

My exposure to Roman Catholic biblical scholarship in Israel is of fairly recent date and is not comprehensive. I have somewhat mixed impressions of the quality of biblical scholarship in Israel, and in particular in Jerusalem, though the dominant impression is extremely positive.

During my eighteen months at the Ecumenical Institute at Tantur, Jerusalem, I was able to come to know the work of the École Biblique, the program of the Studium Biblicum Franciscanum, of the Dormition Abbey, of the Ratisbonne convent, and of the Pontifical Biblical Institute in Jerusalem, as well as the marvelous special studies and publications of the White Fathers located at St. Anne's. In Jerusalem, the École Biblique is the standard-setter, in my judgment. Its programs cover many aspects of biblical literature, history, archaeology, and exegetical interpretation generally. Of special importance has been the contribution of the École Biblique to the study of the publication of the Dead Sea Scrolls, to the production of the magnificient French-language *Bible de Jerusalem*, to which the Doubleday *Jerusalem Bible* owes its virtues, and to a sane and critical approach to the interpretation of the sacred sites for tourists and scholars alike. I know of no work as sensible and lucid as Jerome Murphy-O'Connor's *The Holy Land* (1980). And a trip through Jerusalem conducted by Pierre Benoit, O.P., enables one to share the wisdom of that longtime resident of Jerusalem and also to sample his ironic handling of the sentimental piety that so abounds throughout the city. The École Biblique has a magnificent library, now renovated and enlarged through the gifts of scholars and friends of many lands, Protestants, Jews, Roman Catholics, and not least the Catholic Biblical Association of America. That library is a worthy companion to the holdings in biblical and archaeological studies of the Hebrew University and its related institutions.

The École Biblique has scholars in residence from many lands and ecclesiastical confessions, and provides an excellent base for their studies. The degree-granting privileges recently conferred on the École will make its contributions all the more impressive. This ecumenical center has done much to change the very face of Roman Catholic biblical scholarship in the world, and especially the scholarship that is concentrated upon history, geography, and archaeology.

What characterizes Catholic biblical scholarship in the

Holy Land? A few observations may be hazarded.

1) It is open, critical, ecumenical scholarship, although some of the institutions represented do not work as closely with scholars of the Hebrew University or of other Israeli institutions as they might. The close working relations with Christian Arab families and church bodies helps to account for this reservation with regard to Israeli and Jewish institutions. It is gratifying that such reservations do not extend to work with individual scholars of Israeli institutions. Moreover, as noted above, some of the Catholic institutions are indeed very closely identified with the Hebrew University and with other Israeli institutions and see it as their mission to work especially diligently to overcome the longtime Christian ignorance of Judaism or outright Christian prejudice.

2) Some of the work on Scripture by Catholic institutions does concentrate heavily on archaeology, history, and geography and on the import of these for the life of faith today. This Christian piety that finds stimulus in the sacred sites, in pilgrimages and retreats to them, and in identification with the biblical terrain can be a quite wholesome thing, especially as it is tempered by the gentle Gallic irony practiced with such finesse by the Dominicans of the École Biblique. But it can also breed a sense of proprietary connection with sacred sites, a temptation hard to resist by some of the Franciscan institutions, it seems, and by representatives of the Holy See in the Holy Land. Here too, the excellent work accomplished, especially in the period since the Second World War, helps to balance the picture. The difficulty is to keep in check any sense of Christian prerogatives that might feed upon hostility to the state of Israel. One very important new development that is sure to prove salutary is the renewed archaeological work on Byzantine sites in Israel and Jordan, and especially in the Negeb, as withdrawal from the Sinai requires relocation of military installations on Byzantine sites, or near them, thus making urgent archaeological surveys and excavations. The sheer volume of work has drawn more Christian scholars and institutions into the field, and this collaboration is proving

valuable in and of itself, and also contributes to mutual respect and a deepening of comradeship across religious and ethnic lines.

3) The renewed interest in the total sweep of the history of the Holy Land is sure to assist biblical scholarship, in my judgment. Two of the projects undertaken by the Ecumenical Institute in Jerusalem offer considerable potentiality in this regard, and the work being carried on by Christian and Jewish scholars, with some promise of collaboration from the side of Muslim scholars, looks very hopeful. The issue is basically the history of the transmission and interpretation of the Bible. The Jerusalem textcritical project directed by Professor Goshen-Gottstein of the Hebrew University is most important, as is the fertile development of fresh text-critical understandings as a result of the work of Professors Shemaryahu Talmon and Emmanuel Tov, among many others. Catholic scholars in Jerusalem and in other lands are close partners with these Israeli scholars. The project at Tantur dealing with Christianity in the Holy Land is seeking to enlist scholars from the Arab Christian world, from Islam, and from Judaism. This undertaking, now directed by an Arab, a Maronite trained in Rome, can do much to contribute incidentally to collaborative research in the field of biblical studies as such, even though it concentrates on historical questions of post-biblical times. The same is the case with a second project of the Ecumenical Institute, a study of Prayer in Eastern Christianity, which seeks to explore texts and practices and understandings with regard to prayer in several non-Chalcedonian churches that are present and active in Jerusalem (in particular, the Armenian, Coptic, Ethiopic, and Syrian churches).

Even more fascinating is the question of whether Catholic biblical scholarship might take the lead in bringing together the many Christian traditions in the Holy Land, deliberately working on biblical hermeneutics intensively, with an eye to seeing if principles of biblical understanding and interpretation might not be forged there, in the heat of conflict, surrounded by the biblical sites, that would enable biblical religion to contribute more to peace and reconciliation than to hostility and misunderstanding. The persons committed to such an effort, and able to carry it through, are on the scene. What is needed is a fresh commitment across religious, political, and ethnic lines that might bring about such a long-running seminar. Perhaps it could become a project of the new Peace Academy of the Ecumenical Institute.

North America (See Bibliography numbers 4,5,6,7,8,9,10,12,13,14,15,16,18,19,20,22,23,24,26)

More striking have been Roman Catholic biblical research and teaching in North America. Nothing less than a revolution has occurred in the field of Catholic biblical scholarship and courses on the Bible in Catholic colleges and universities in the last quarter century. Every field of biblical scholarship is represented, every trend in biblical interpretation has its Catholic counterpart, and the educational and social movements that have altered our approaches to the Bible in higher education have had a very heavy influence on the campuses of Catholic institutions.

But the most important matter to address in this review is the extraordinary achievements of Roman Catholic biblical scholars during the past twenty-five years. Every area of biblical research has been markedly advanced through the work of Catholic scholarship, worldwide. While I shall concentrate on the work of North American Catholic scholars in what follows, the story would not change with the inclusion of Catholic scholars from other lands. Some references to these, in fact, will be included along the way.

I want now to enumerate some of these areas of biblical scholarship and mention a representative number of important publications or research undertakings, along with a number of the leading persons involved. No doubt, I shall overlook several works and areas of great importance, and shall fail to mention persons who should be mentioned. I hope that I will be forgiven such oversights as occur; my acquaintance with the field and with the leaders in it is limited.

a) Textual studies. (See Bibliography numbers 9,14)

The study of ancient texts of importance for biblical research has been carried through with the help of a number of the world's leading scholars who are Roman Catholic. William Moran has been one of the world leaders in the relating of Akkadian texts and ideas to those of the Bible. The late Dennis J. McCarthy carried on this work at the Pontifical Biblical Institute when Moran took up his post at Harvard University. In the area of Ugaritic literature and the Hebrew Bible no name stands out like that of the late Mitchell Dahood, S.J., also a longtime member of the Biblical Institute in Rome. Many of the students of these three carry on this work, while Moran continues the research program for which he is justly renowned.

The Dead Sea Scrolls have been published, interpreted, and used for scholarly reconstructions by Catholic scholars the world over. The scholars of the École Biblique, especially the late Roland de Vaux and Fr. Pierre Benoit, along with other scholars now located elsewhere (Fr. Barthelemy and Josef Milik, in particular) have contributed massively to textual, archaeological, and interpretive work on the Scrolls. But the list of Catholic scholars who have been of decisive importance for an interpretation of the Scrolls is longer still. The late Patrick W. Skehan of Catholic University and Jospeh A. Fitzmyer, S.J., have contributed massively to the interpretation of the Scrolls and to textual studies in general. A younger scholar who has been greatly influential in recent years is Eugene C. Ulrich of the University of Notre Dame. Contemporary textual studies of the Hebrew Bible, of the Septuagint, of the Vetus Latina, and of other biblical translations include among the world leaders of the effort such scholars as those mentioned, along with many collaborators.

b) Historical and Archaeological Studies. (See Bibliography number 21)

The studies of Roland de Vaux on historical and archaeological subjects, plus his writings on Israelite institutions and cultic rites are among the best such investigations in the field. How regrettable it is that Fr. de Vaux did not live to complete his new history of Israel. His colleague Jerome Murphy-O'Connor, O.P., who has written many exegetical studies as well, and his senior colleague Pierre Benoit, have likewise contributed greatly to this field. Murphy-O'Connor's new guide book, *The Holy Land*, is a magnificent book—brief, lucid, witty, and utterly candid. He carries the study up to 1700, thus avoiding the need to talk about many aspects of a Christian presence in the Holy Land that require critical comment. And the work of the American scholar Philip J. King, one of the most outstanding Presidents of the American Schools of Oriental Research in recent times, is an excellent blend of sound historical scholarship and equally sound archaeological procedure.

Another of the outstanding historians who also has been engaged in fine archaeological work is Joseph Blenkinsopp of the University of Notre Dame. Blenkinsopp has also contributed to exegetical and theological interpretation of the Hebrew Bible, to the history of prophecy, and to many other aspects of biblical research. In his work too one finds an excellent blend of the work of the empirical historian and of the careful philosophical/theological thinker.

c) Reference works. (See Bibliography numbers 14,27,28)

Some of the same scholars mentioned above have been actively at work on the major reference works and tools completed during the past twenty-five years. The publication of the *Jerome Biblical Commentary*, edited by Raymond E. Brown, S.S., Joseph A. Fitzmyer, S.J., and Roland E. Murphy, O.Carm. (Prentice-Hall, 1968), was a major event, offering a fine work of reference covering the entire Bible (with most of the Apocrypha), and including immensely important articles on topics related to biblical interpretation. All scholars and students of the Bible continue to benefit from this compact, encyclopedic work. The contributors provide an incidental Who's Who of Roman Catholic biblical scholarship, with the editors' names appearing very prominently in the Table of Contents, along with the honoree of the present volume.

Joseph A. Fitzmyer's *The Dead Sea Scrolls: Major Publications and Tools for Study* (Scholars Press, 1975, 1977) is a most important reference work, as are the Hebrew and Aramaic lexicons published by the Pontifical Biblical Institute and authored, respectively, by Francis Zorell, S.J. and Ernest Vogt, S.J. (in Latin). The list could continue.

d) Commentaries, Special Exegetical Studies. (See Bibliography numbers 4,5,6,12,19,26)

The major commentary series on the Bible commenced during the past quarter century include a number of Roman Catholic authors of note: John L. McKenzie's Anchor Bible commentary and translation of Second Isaiah was the first of the Catholic contributions to the Anchor Bible to appear. But others were to follow, in particular the massive work on the John literature by Raymond E. Brown, S.S., the commentary on Luke by Joseph A. Fitzmyer, S.J., and the ingenious work of Mitchell Dahood, S.J., on the Psalms. Roland Murphy has led off with the first volume (on the Wisdom materials) of the Eerdmans' *The Forms of the Old Testament Literature*, a multi-volumed work that will cover the entire Hebrew Bible. Less Catholic participation appears in the *Old Testament Library* of Westminster and the *New Century Bible Commentary* (Oliphants and Eerdmans).

Special exegetical studies deserving mention are Raymond E. Brown's *The Birth of the Messiah*, Joseph Blenkinsopp's study of the prophetic movement entitled *A History of Prophecy in Israel*, (Westminster, 1983), Bruce Vawter's *On Genesis, A New Reading*, Roland Murphy's

many works on the Wisdom traditions and their import for
an Old Testament theology, and John J. Collins' fine
studies of Daniel and apocalyptic literature. New Testament apocalypses and other subjects have received splendid interpretation by Elizabeth Schüssler Fiorenza and
Adela Yarbro Collins. Alexander Di Lella also has done
outstanding work on the Wisdom materials and continues
to do so, as has Joseph Jensen, O.S.B., on the prophet
Isaiah. This list could go on for pages.

*e) The Pseudepigrapha and other literature outside the
canon.* (See Bibliography number 8)

I consider the Catholic contributions to the study of
Apocrypha and Pseudepigrapha to be among the best in
that field. Daniel J. Harrington, S.J., John J. Collins,
Alexander Di Lella, George MacRae, S.J., Pheme Perkins,
and dozens of other scholars have worked on the apocryphal literature of Old and New Testaments, on the Gnostic
texts, and (as pointed out above) on the Dead Sea Scrolls.
In Volume One of the *Old Testament Pseudepigrapha*,
edited by James H. Charlesworth, one of the longest and
finest parts is the translation of the Sibylline Oracles, with
introduction, done by John J. Collins (a total of 156
pages!). Other Catholic contributions follow in Volume
Two, soon to appear. The Foreword to Volume One is
written by George MacRae.

MacRae's work on the Nag Hammadi texts is well
known, though some may not know how important were
his contributions to the initial work of preparing the
manuscripts for photographing, or his assistance in the
negotiations that led to James M. Robinson's being able to
publish the entire corpus and to provide English translations of all.

f) Bible Translation. (See Bibliography numbers 15 and
22)

Roman Catholic scholars have given us the English
Jerusalem Bible, and the French introductions, notes, and

translations that lay behind it; the *New American Bible* (with some help from Protestant scholars), and have collaborated on other modern translations, notably the work toward the New Revised Standard Version (not necessarily to be the title of the new edition). The importance of the production of two outstanding English translations of the entire Bible by and for Roman Catholics — the *Jerusalem Bible* and the *New American Bible* — is difficult to overestimate. The *Jerusalem Bible* has the merits of its French original, and those are very great indeed. The *New American Bible*, done by the Catholic Biblical Association of America, following the decision to work not any longer from the Vulgate but from the original languages, is the most accurate of the available translations of the Bible, though its style may not, at all points, be as good as it should be (and no doubt will be on revision). It is a marvelous achievement in translation, tied not to any English translation that precedes it and unencumbered by any decision to apply the principle of "dynamic equivalence." Again, the scholars involved in the production of this Bible translation were the leading figures in biblical studies in North America. The late Louis F. Hartman chaired the editorial board, and the late Patrick W. Skehan served as the vice-chair. Those working on the revision of the RSV today make very good use of the *New American Bible*, and of the *Jerusalem Bible* as well.

Catholic membership on the committee responsible for the RSV has increased markedly during the past two decades. At the present time, six members of an active committee membership of thirty-three are Roman Catholic. If the RSV appears in a revised edition by 1990, as is the hope, the work of these six scholars, and of those Catholics who have preceded them, will have helped greatly to make possible the event.

g) Production of biblical interpretations for the laity.

Among the most striking biblical scholarship during the past two decades (and the last decade in particular) has been the publication of commentaries, biblical handbooks, and popular guides to biblical study for the church communities. Recently, the series entitled *New Testament Message* and *Old Testament Message* (Wilmington: Glazier) have produced excellent, up to date, brief, and always thoughtful commentaries on all the biblical books, plus some introductory studies, providing a popular analysis of biblical and apocryphal literature and thought as a whole.

The Paulist Press has also been active in making available popular interpretative literature dealing with biblical themes that are central for preaching, for church education, and for the organizing of congregations for significant political representations. Orbis Books have dealt with feminism, with the theology of liberation, with other fundamental issues of public justice, as well as with some other much discussed and debated issues, such as biblical hermeneutics.

h) Roman Catholic leadership in the biblical societies.

Noteworthy is the fact that the Catholic biblical scholars have been at the center of the revitalization of the Society of Biblical Literature and of biblical research efforts throughout all of North America. There was no Roman Catholic President of the Society of Biblical Literature, I believe, until John L. McKenzie's election in 1966. Since then, three other Roman Catholic Presidents have been elected. They are: Raymond E. Brown, Joseph A. Fitzmyer, and Roland E. Murphy. We have had outstanding executive officers of the SBL who were Roman Catholic: George MacRae as Executive Secretary for two terms; and dozens of Roman Catholics as Chairs of Committees, Seminars, Groups and Sections. This leadership continues, and it grows annually. The untimely death of George MacRae on September 6, 1985 brought a great loss to biblical scholarship as such, not only to its Catholic side.

The Catholic Biblical Association of America has become one of the leading international associations of biblical scholars. Its periodical, the *Catholic Biblical Quar-*

terly, has been edited for several years by Joseph A. Fitzmyer, with his familiar aggressive leadership, industry, and accuracy. Many non-Catholics hold membership in the CBA today and one, Paul J. Achtemeier, has held the position of President. Many non-Catholics contribute to the *Quarterly*.

Catholic contributions to periodical publication also include the production of *New Testament Abstracts* and *Old Testament Abstracts*, two magnificent aids to scholars, libraries, and the public. In these two publications, to which persons subscribe, but at very modest cost, periodical literature as well as books published in a dozen or more languages, are reviewed regularly, briefly, but thoroughly and critically. Currently, *New Testament Abstracts* is edited by Daniel J. Harrington. The founding editor of *Old Testament Abstracts* is Bruce Vawter; it is difficult to imagine how these publications could be better edited.

i) Doctoral programs in biblical studies.

One notable change in Catholic biblical scholarship during the past two decades has been the increased enrollment of Catholic Scripture scholars in Ph.D. programs at the major universities of North America. Once, Catholic scholars intending to specialize in Scripture would almost certainly have studied at one of the Pontifical universities, and most likely would hold degrees from such an institution located in Rome. Many still follow this path, and it has been noted above that this path is itself quite different from what it once was. But today, Catholic scholars teaching in Catholic theological schools, colleges, and universities, as well as Catholic scholars teaching in non-Catholic institutions include an increasing number whose Scripture studies have been done, at least in part, at the scholarly centers of private institutions such as Harvard, Yale, Chicago, the Graduate Theological Union, Duke, Emory, Toronto, Vanderbilt, or others.

Moreover, these programs just enumerated have Roman Catholic scholars on their faculties, persons who have (many of them) been trained largely at non-Catholic theological institutions or universities. This pluralism of advanced study and teaching has had an extraordinary influence upon all forms of work in biblical research in North America today. Young biblical scholars who take up posts in very conservative Protestant theological schools and colleges, for example, will likely have studied with Catholic teachers and alongside of Catholic scholars. And Catholic teachers and scholars have thus necessarily confronted the religious and confessional pluralism of contemporary North America.

Catholic leadership in the whole field of religious studies, and in the theological societies as well, has made significant advances, which is important for biblical studies, as noted above. In many of the religious studies programs today, non-Catholics work alongside of Catholics, offering a program of religious studies, with theological subjects included, that aims at being ecumenical and open to religious understandings over a wide, interfaith spectrum. It is not simple, under such circumstances, to give as much attention to the standard interpretations of Scripture that have become a part of the Catholic tradition as was once the case. In a day of increasing political and religious conservatism, such a development often provokes criticism and protest.

Issues and Problems.

In this context lie some of the thorny questions facing the field of biblical scholarship, especially in North America. Some problems are more acute among Catholics; others are apparently as weighty among non-Catholics as among Catholics. I wish to single out three areas where I believe that Roman Catholics, like many of the rest of us, have further and important work to do.

a) Confronting the tradition head-on. (See
Bibliography numbers 4,14,17,26)

Catholic biblical interpreters have frequently done what
their Protestant counterparts have done; they have done
their scientific work, treated their theological outlook and
position as their private affair, and left to other colleagues
the problem of helping to relate the findings of scientific,
scholarly biblical research to Catholic theological thought.
That is, studies of biblical issues such as prophetic eschatology, messianism in the Psalms, the relations of the
Hebrew Scriptures to the New Testament generally, the
miracles, the birth narratives, the uses of Old Testament
text in the New Testament, often have stopped when the
"facts" or the best alternative ways of understanding were
laid out, from the side of biblical scholarship in the narrow
sense. No effort was made to show how these findings
could be best related to notions of Christian messianism, to
doctrines such as the Virgin Birth, to questions of the inspiration of Scripture, and the like.

Happily, a number of the recent works on the Bible by
Catholic scholars have taken up such difficult issues and
have struggled with them. For example, the articles in the
Jerome Biblical Commentary dealing with inspiration and
inerrancy (Section 66), canonicity (Section 67), modern
Old Testament criticism (Section 70), hermeneutics (Section 71), and church pronouncements (Section 72) are all
designed to relate critical biblical scholarship to aspects of
church tradition and classical Christian belief. The closing
articles in the *Jerome Biblical Commentary* dealing with
Old and New Testament theology are also of great importance for this purpose. The biblical scholar should not,
many of us believe, leave entirely to theologian-colleagues
the task of sorting out the results of our work for the life of
faith, and for those who must deal directly with how the
life of faith is claimed and deepened.

Two works that are fine examples, in my judgment, of
this direct confrontation of the tradition with the fruits of

critical biblical scholarship are Raymond E. Brown's *The Birth of the Messiah* (Doubleday, 1977) and John McHugh's *The Mother of Jesus in the New Testament* (Doubleday, 1975). These two works, quite different in approach and method, are at one in seeking to determine what can be known of the two subjects (the infancy narratives in Matthew and Luke and the biblical evidence dealing with the mother of Jesus), and how that which can be known can be brought into best and most satisfying association with the Church's theological understandings. Such difficult undertakings can be avoided, and perhaps some scholars should avoid them, if they lack the skill and the commitment to work at them productively. But some biblical scholars surely need to deal with the theological questions straightforwardly, do what they can to illuminate these, and do so in closest possible connection with the philological, historical, literary, structuralist, redactionalist talents and findings available. This means that the historian, the linguist, the literary and formal critics have to do some of this theological/interpretive work, otherwise some of the best available talent for relating the two areas will not have been applied.

The notes to the *New American Bible* and to the *Jerusalem Bible* are helpful in this regard, but they do not go far enough. Perhaps some fresh efforts might be made to include brief essays on how critical biblical scholarship and church tradition interrelate. But it might also be the case that new working groups in the Society of Biblical Literature, in the Catholic Biblical Association, and in evangelical and charismatic biblical groups could be formed and supported.

One interesting sign of the separation of biblical scholarship from church tradition and authority is the use or lack of use of the imprimatur on scholarly works. Some have the imprimatur; others simple assume that there is no need for such. I do not know the whole situation well enough to have an opinion on whether seeking the imprimatur would be a way of furthering the interrelating of biblical scholarship and church tradition. But with or without the imprimatur, there must be works that further that interpenetration.

b) Relating our work to Jewish life, tradition, and thought.

It is deeply gratifying to see that Roman Catholic biblical scholarship proceeds in close collaboration with Jewish biblical scholarship worldwide. The associations are particularly close in Israel, as noted above, and in North America. But there still remains, in Protestant and in Catholic circles, too much claiming of the Hebrew Bible as the Christian Old Testament in such a way as to arrogate the Bible of the Jewish people to the Christian community alone. Such a view is of course wrong and wrong-headed, but it remains too much in evidence. When the contemporary issues between Jews and Arabs (Christian and Muslim) in Israel and elsewhere in the eastern Mediterranean come into view, then the exponents of some forms of the theology of liberation tend to let their sympathy with oppressed Arabs carry over into their attitude to the people of ancient Israel. The result can be a presentation of the Hebrew Scriptures in a form that feeds and nourishes anti-Semitism, even if this happens inadvertently.

Catholic biblical scholarship has, on the whole, done better than Protestant biblical scholarship, I believe, to contain such a development. But it does seem to be the case that more Catholic theologians and ethicists, more historians and philosophers of religion, rather than biblical scholars, have been working on improving relations and mutual understanding of Jews and Christians. We biblical scholars need to give larger place to this specific issue: how are our researches being shared in such a way as to demonstrate the legitimacy of a Jewish understanding of the Hebrew Scriptures, while also helping to show that the Christian community has its right to claim those writings as its Old Testament?

c) The import of biblical religion for contemporary ethics.

Much good work is beginning to be done on biblical ethics, by scholars from Catholic, Protestant, Jewish and other backgrounds. More needs to be done. Here too, a next step beyond those we normally take may be required: the deliberate placing of the question how does the message of Amos or Isaiah or Jeremiah illuminate the common life? How does the demand laid upon the people of Israel apply to the community of faith in all times? How can we present this ancient message, in its central affirmations, in such a way as to display its power and truth for any time and for all times? Once more, it is not good enough for all biblical scholars to leave this kind of issue to other colleagues; the ones who know the text best, know its context best, know what sorts of applications would be distorted ones, must be working at this undertaking.

Among the most vexing failures in this regard is the lack of any adequate treatment of the ethical import of the prophetic eschatological messages. We continue to hear of the "failure" of the prophetic movement as though that failure consisted in its having made promises that, in time, came to be incredible and were therefore succeeded by other messages. Along that line of understanding lies an almost inescapable mis-hearing of the prophets. An interfaith team of biblical scholars, ethicists, and theologians, in my view, needs urgently to examine this question afresh.

Conclusion

Catholic biblical scholars today continue to have the advantage of working together in their own religious communities while also sharing a community of scholarship, life, and thought with persons from other religious traditions or from no specific religious body. They have the opportunity to work as individual scholars, pursuing their research, seeking to discover what can be known of the subject areas in which their greatest competence lies. They have the opportunity also to determine whether they might not be a part of that group of Catholic scholars determined to confront the theological and dogmatic traditions of the Church directly, with an eye to helping clarify, illuminate, and (where necessary) reformulate those traditions. They have the opportunity to watch diligently for any misapplications of Christian theology to the detriment of the Bible of the Jewish people. And they have the opportunity to contribute to the never-ending task of reclaiming, restating, and perhaps reconceiving the moral power of the biblical message for a world that badly needs the Bible's eschatological vision, its confident hope, its demand for peace and right.

The one we seek to honor with this volume has seized the opportunity to work on all three of these fronts, and for that we thank and honor him the more.

BIBLIOGRAPHY

1. *Analecta Biblica.* Series published by the Pontifical Biblical Institute (PBI) in Rome.

2. *Biblica.* Published three times annually by the PBI in Rome.

3. *Biblica et Orientalia.* Series published by the PBI in Rome.

4. Brown, Raymond E., S.S. *The Birth of the Messiah.* Garden City, NY: Doubleday, 1977.

5. _____. *The Epistles of John.* Anchor Bible 30. Garden City, NY: Doubleday, 1982.

6. _____. *The Gospel of John*, Vols. I, II. Anchor Bible, 29, 29a. Garden City, NY: Doubleday, 1966, 1970.

7. Challis, William. "Biblical Studies and Roman Catholicism." *The Churchman* 94 (1980) 320–334.

8. Charlesworth, James H., ed.   *The Old Testament Pseudepigrapha.* Vol. I. Garden City, NY: Doubleday, 1983.

9. Dahood, Mitchell, S.J.   *Psalms.* Vols I, II, III. Anchor Bible 16, 17, 17a. Garden City, NY: Doubleday, 1965, 1968, 1970.

10. Dulles, Avery, S.J.   "Scripture: Recent Protestant and Catholic Views." *Theology Today* 37 (1980) 7–26.

11. *Elenchus Bibliographicus Biblicus.*   Series published by the Pontifical Biblical Institute (PBI), Rome.

12. Fitzmyer, Joseph A., S.J.   *The Gospel of Luke.* Vol. I. Anchor Bible 28. Garden City, NY: Doubleday, 1981.

13. Ford, J. Massyngbaerde.   *Revelation.* Anchor Bible 38. Garden City, NY: Doubleday, 1975.

14. *The Jerome Biblical Commentary.*   Vols. I, II. Raymond E. Brown, S.S., Joseph A. Fitzmyer, S.J. and Roland E. Murphy, O. Carm. Englewood Cliffs, NJ: Prentice-Hall, 1968.

15. *The Jerusalem Bible.*   Garden City, NY: Doubleday, 1966.

16. Legrand, L.   "Issues in the Roman Catholic Approach to Biblical Hermeneutics Today." *Canadian Journal of Theology* 31 (1982) 192–202.

17. McHugh, John.   *The Mother of Jesus in the New Testament.* Garden City, NY: Doubleday, 1975.

18. McKenzie, John L.   "Biblical Studies Since 1950." *Cross Currents* 31 (1981–82) 400–406.

19. _____.*Second Isaiah.* Anchor Bible 20. Garden City, NY: Doubleday, 1968.

20. Megivern, James J.   "Current Trends in Roman Catholic Biblical Studies." *Moravian Theological Seminary Bulletin* (1963) 30–58.

21. Murphy-O'Connor, Jerome, O.P. *The Holy Land: An Archaeological Guide from Earliest Times to 1700.* Oxford, U.K: Oxford University Press, 1980.

22. *The New American Bible.* New York: Catholic Publishers, 1971.

23. *New Testament Abstracts.* Ed. Daniel J. Harrington, S.J. Washington: Catholic Biblical Association. Begun in 1956.

24. *Old Testament Abstracts.* Ed. Bruce Vawter, C.M. Washington: Catholic Biblical Association. Begun in 1978.

25. *Proche Orient Chrétien.* Ed. the White Fathers of Saint Anne, Jerusalem.

26. Vawter, Bruce, C.M. *On Genesis: A New Reading.* Garden City, NY: Doubleday, 1977.

27. Vogt, Ernestus, S.J. *Lexicon Linguae Aramaicae Veteris Testamenti.* Roma: Pontificum Institutum Biblicum, 1971.

28. Zorell, Franciscus, S.J. *Lexicon Hebraicum et Aramaicum Veteris Testamenti.* Roma: Pontificum Institutum Biblicum, 1954, 1968.

Contributors

John J. Collins is Professor of Theology at the University of Notre Dame. His books include *Daniel, First Maccabees, Second Maccabees with an Excursus on the Apocalyptic Genre,* Old Testament Message, vol. 16 (Michael Glazier, 1981), *The Apocalyptic Imagination* (Crossroad, 1984), and *Daniel, with an Introduction to Apocalyptic Literature* (Eerdmans, 1984).

John Dominic Crossan is Professor of Religious Studies at DePaul University. His books include *In Parables* (Harper, 1973), *The Dark Interval* (Argus, 1975), *In Fragments* (Harper, 1983), and *Four Other Gospels* (Winston-/Seabury, 1984). He is editor of *Semeia*, an experimental journal for biblical criticism.

Walter Harrelson is Professor of Hebrew Bible in the Divinity School of Vanderbilt University, and former president of the Society of Biblical Literature. His books include *Interpreting the Old Testament* (Holt, Rinehart & Winston, 1964), *From Fertility Cult to Worship* (Doubleday, 1969, 1970; Scholars Press ed. 1980) and *The Ten Commandments and Human Rights* (Fortress, 1980).

Daniel J. Harrington, SJ is Professor of New Testament at Weston School of Theology in Cambridge, MA. He has been general editor of *New Testament Abstracts* since 1972. His most recent books are *The New Testament: A Bibliography* and *Targum Jonathan of the Former*

257

Prophets (Glazier, 1985, 1986). He has also served as President of the Catholic Biblical Association.

Robert J. Karris, OFM is Professor of the New Testament Studies at Catholic Theological Union. His books include *Invitation to Luke* (Doubleday, 1977), *The Pastoral Epistles* (Michael Glazier, 1979), and *Luke: Artist and Theologian* (Paulist, 1985). He is also editor of the CBQ monograph series.

Dennis J. McCarthy (†) was Professor of Old Testament at the Pontifical Biblical Institute until his death in 1983. His books include *Treaty and Covenant* (Analecta Biblica 21; Pontifical Biblical Institute, 1963) and *Old Testament Covenant* (John Knox, 1972).

John L. McKenzie, retired Professor of Religious Studies at DePaul University, now resides in Claremont, CA. A former President of both SBL and CBA, his books include *Dictionary of the Bible* (Macmillan, 1965), *Second Isaiah* (Anchor Bible 20; Doubleday, 1968), *Source* (Thomas More, 1984), and *The Civilization of Christianity* (Thomas More, 1986).

Roland E. Murphy, O.Carm. is George Washington Ivey Professor of Biblical Studies at Duke University. A former President of both SBL and CBA, his works include *Wisdom Literature* (Eerdmans, 1981), and co-editorship of *The Jerome Biblical Commentary* (Prentice-Hall, 1968).

Pheme Perkins is Professor of Theology (New Testament) at Boston College. She is Vice-President of the CBA, serves on several editorial boards, including CBQ and JBL, and has written numerous books, including *The Gospel According to John* (Franciscan Herald Press, 1978), *The Johannine Epistles* (2nd ed., Michael Glazier, 1984), *The Gnostic Dialogue* (Paulist, 1980), *Love Commands in the New Testament* (Paulist, 1982), and *Resurrection* (Doubleday, 1984).

Carroll Stuhlmueller, CP is Professor of Old Testament Studies at Catholic Theological Union in Chicago. A past

President of CBA, his books include *The Psalms*. 2 vols. (Glazier, 1983), with Donald Senior, *Biblical Foundations for Mission* (Orbis, 1983), *Biblical Meditations*. 6 vols. (Paulist, 1978–85), and *Thirsting for the Lord* (Alba House, 1977; Doubleday Image Books, 1979).

F. Bruce Vawter, C.P. is Professor of Religious Studies at DePaul University. He is editor of *Old Testament Abstracts* and former President of CBA. His books include *This Man Jesus* (Doubleday, 1973), *On Genesis: A New Reading* (Doubleday, 1977), *Job and Jonah* (Paulist, 1983), and *The Path of Wisdom: Biblical Investigations* (Michael Glazier, 1986).

Name Index